SOME CONTRIBUTIONS OF SOUTH INDIA TO INDIAN CULTURE

SOME CONTRIBUTIONS OF SOUTH INDIA TO INDIAN CULTURE

S. KRISHNASWAMI AIYANGAR

GYAN

Published by

GYAN

Gyan Publishing House
5, Ansari Road
Daryaganj, New Delhi-110002
Phone: 011-47034999, 9811692060
E-mail: books@gyanbooks.com

Distribution Network
gyanbooks.com
India, USA, Canada, UK, Australia, France

ISBN : 978-81-212-4037-6 (PB)
First Published, 1923

2nd Impression 2020

Printed at: Gyan Press, Delhi.

Some Contributions of South India to Indian Culture
Author: S. Krishnaswami Aiyangar

Calcutta University Readership Lectures

SOME CONTRIBUTIONS OF SOUTH INDIA TO INDIAN CULTURE

BY

S. KRISHNASWAMI AIYANGAR, M.A. Ph.D.,

READER, CALCUTTA UNIVERSITY, 1919

PROFESSOR OF INDIAN HISTORY AND ARCHAEOLOGY, UNIVERSITY OF MADRAS, HONORARY CORRESPONDENT OF THE ARCHAEOLOGICAL DEPARTMENT OF THE GOVERNMENT OF INDIA, FELLOW OF THE ROYAL ASIATIC SOCIETY OF GREAT BRITAIN AND IRELAND, FELLOW OF THE ROYAL HISTORICAL SOCIETY, FELLOW OF THE UNIVERSITY OF MADRAS, FELLOW OF THE MYSORE UNIVERSITY

Author of

'ANCIENT INDIA', 'BEGINNINGS OF SOUTH INDIAN HISTORY', 'SOUTH INDIA AND HER MUHAMMADAN INVADERS' ETC.

PUBLISHED BY

THE UNIVERSITY OF CALCUTTA

1923

INSCRIBED

As a mark of personal regard and esteem to

The Hon'ble Justice

Sir ASUTOSH MOOKERJEE, Kt., C.S.I.,

Sarasvati, Sastra-Vachaspati, Sambuddhagama-

Chakravarti,

Vice-Chancellor, Calcutta University,

President of the

Council of Post-Graduate Teaching,

Calcutta University.

PREFACE

The following pages contain the substance of the Readership Lectures that I originally intended to deliver at the Calcutta University early in 1920. The honour of a Readership at the University was bestowed upon me, in distinguished company, at the instance of the ever watchful President of the Council of Post-Graduate Teaching at the time, the Hon'ble Justice Sir Asutosh Mukherjee, whose exertions in the cause of Indian History and Culture are too well-known and too well-founded to require any commendation from me. Owing to official exigencies and ill-health it was impossible that I could carry out my engagement as originally intended, although I was able later to discharge the responsibilities involved in the honour by delivering a shorter course of lectures on the same subject. Among a certain number of subjects 'Some Contributions of South India to Indian Culture' was selected as likely to be more attractive to the Calcutta University, and hence the effort in the following pages to lay before the public some of the main contributions to Indian culture which South India could be credited with having made in the course of her history.

Any estimate of the contributions made by South India to Indian culture involves, as a necessary preliminary, an elaborate study of the history of India as a whole, in all its cultural aspects. An attempt at such a study in a systematic way has but recently been inaugurated in the University of Calcutta by the institution of a Master's Degree in "Indian Culture" with provision for teaching the subject as a part of the scheme for post-graduate teaching at the University. It is a happy sign of the times that the need has been recognised in Calcutta, but Calcutta will need the co-operation of the other Indian Universities to study the subject in all its vast and varied ramifications. South Indian history and culture has a character of its own notwithstanding the fact that the interaction of cultural forces between the north and the south is very much more full and frequent than has hitherto been recognised. Despite this constant and almost continuous influence, it is possible to distinguish the special features in the course of cultural development which are ascribable to South Indian influence. An attempt is made here to describe a few of the main contributions, and for obvious reasons the treatment has to be historical in character.

The first question, therefore, that attracts attention, is the peculiar position the Brahman has occupied in the South, so much so that, to an outside observer, South India presents to-day Brahmanical orthodoxy almost in its *Vaidic* form though not unmodified in essential particulars. The position of the Brahman in South Indian society has been very much to the fore latterly, and a historical investigation of his position may not be uninteresting. His position in the Indian society of the age of the *Brāhmaṇas* is clearly indicated in the *Satapatha Brāhmaṇa* passage, an extract from which is quoted, and that seems to be the identical position that he occupied in South India to which he emigrated from the north. That position involved the double responsibility of performing the elaborate ritualistic sacrifices for the benefit of society, and the conservation and cultivation of learning that is involved as a necessary corollary. This conservation and cultivation of learning implied its propagation as well. From a careful investigation of the subject, as far as the material accessible to us enables us to do so, the Brahman has striven to discharge these responsibilities to the best of his ability and opportunities, setting up such a high example in actual life as to invariably exert influence in the direction of uplift which has been felt throughout. The tendency has always been for those below him in the social organisation to imitate him and come up to his level. It was a characteristic feature of the Brahmanical organisation that the least developed communities in the vast and varied population of India had a recognised place in society moving upwards slowly, it may be too slowly for enthusiastic social reformers, but none the less surely in the direction of rise. In the sphere of conservation of learning through ages when the material agencies for its preservation were so ill-developed and so easily capable of destruction, the success he achieved is nothing short of marvellous. It was not exactly that he enjoyed the monopoly, but it was undoubtedly his influence that gave it the form, and cast it in a mould, to enable its preservation notwithstanding the destructive hand of time itself, and other historical agencies which contributed towards that end. In the sphere of propagation of learning he may have fallen short of the modern compulsory universal education, but his achievements in the sphere both in Sanskrit, and the Sanskritic and other vernaculars of the country, were magnificent. One has only to examine the names of eminent contributors to the literature of Tamil to confirm this statement. The manuscript imperfections of to-day are largely capable of rectification by the traditional handing down of this learning; but this traditional handing down is primarily responsible for the preservation of much that must otherwise have been irrecoverably lost. It may be said with truth that the Brahmanical organisation of society was mainly responsible for this.

The transformation of the ritualistic Brahmanism into the much more widely acceptable Hinduism of modern times is due to the increasing infusion of the theistic element into the religious system of the day. In this new development South India played an important part. It probably borrowed the elements of *bhakti* from the rising schools of *Vaishṇavism* and *Śaivism* in the north, and gave it a special realistic development by infusing into it features characteristic perhaps of the Tamil land and its literary development, making thereby religious experience fall in line with life itself. This development worked itself to its full in the age of the Pallavas so that about the end of the first millennium after Christ the religion of *bhakti* got to be so associated with South India that the reputation as a land of *bhakti*, stuck to it ever afterwards. Along with this notion of *bhakti*, or devotion to a personal God, runs another stream which is perhaps best described as *Tantrism*, worship offered by means of mystic signs and formulæ of various character. The same influences seem responsible for the transformation of Hīnayānist Buddhism into the Mahāyāna.

Even in this latter transformation India south of the Vindhyas bore an important part, but it does not appear to be the Tamil country, or South India proper, that really played the most important part. The honour of it perhaps must be ascribed to a region farther north than the Tamil country—the country of the Āndhras. Bhakti that transformed Brahmanism into Hinduism may therefore be regarded as an important contribution of South India to Indian culture, not in reference to its origin but in regard to the important features of its further development.

Another important contribution of South India consists in the spread of Indian culture and the expansion of Indian Commerce. In both of these important departments South India played a prominent part. South India is primarily responsible for the spread of Hindu culture to the islands of the East and the Indo-Chinese peninsula, reaching even as far east as China. The outspread of Southern Buddhistic culture into the islands belongs to a later period of South Indian history. In commercial enterprise, articles of trade from South India were carried in great quantity to the west. In this commerce the commodities of the Eastern Archipelago formed a considerable part of the exports. The import of the eastern commodities into India seems to have been managed as a thoroughly

Indian business though their transportation across to the west might have been in part, or even as a whole, in the hands of others. The expansion towards the east seems to have been in full and self-contained colonies of Hindus, including Brahmans, as the Koetei epigraphs and the statement of Fa-hien together will indicate. In overseas enterprise therefore, South India comes in for comparatively, perhaps the most important share.

In administration, particularly in local administration, which is a characteristic feature of Indian administration generally, South India has its own characteristics which appear to have developed early and been carried to the fullest fruition under the great Cholas A.D. 850-1350. The local part of it seems to have been developed on the indigenous system such as it was, and even in respect to central administration South India shows characteristics which may justify giving it a distinct character though the prevalent general notions and admitted general principles were the same both in the north and in the south. This has been carried to such perfection that it continued undisturbed down to the end of the period of Vijayanagar Empire. Even after, much of it has been carried down intact so that the revenue and fiscal organisation of a considerable part of the Madras Presidency under the East India Company is derived from the system that obtained at the commencement of the nineteenth century, as a lineal descendant of the ancient Chola administration. It was this continuity that gave South India its distinct character, and made a separate treatment necessary even in the now famous "Fifth Report" which was submitted to Parliament on the eve of the renewal of the charter of the East India Company in 1813.

These are some of the main features of the contributions that South India made to Indian civilisation and culture generally, and much more could be said by way of details both in the preservation of Indian religions and Indian learning when they were subject to great pressure and unavoidable modifications by the impact of Islam which came with the Muhammadan invasions. The conservation of both was due, as was pointed out, to the Empire of Vijayanagar, the supersession of which empire by the Muhammadans being a short parenthesis in the history of the general development of religion and culture in South India.

The whole of this investigation rests upon the Chronology of Tamil literature and history which I have adopted as the result of a long series of researches by a band of South Indian scholars, and my own. The main features of this, setting aside details which are not of much moment, are that that portion of Tamil literature, generally called Śangam literature, is of a pre-Pallava character and as such referable to the early centuries of the Christian Era; that the literature, the typical representatives of which are the Tēvāram and Tiruvoymoḷi of the saints of the Śaivas and Vaishṇavas, belongs to the age of the Pallavas and, as a whole, is assignable to the period AD. 300 to 900. Then follow the works of the later writers who gave form and shape to the teachings of these saints, and those marked the third age beginning from very near the end of the first millennium and going on to about the end of the seventeenth century. There is not much difference of opinion among scholars in regard to the third of these periods. The main lines of the second are also more or less agreed upon though there is a certain amount of difference of opinion in regard to details which however do not affect the general position. In regard to the first however there continues to be an acute difference of opinion yet. Even in regard to this the chronological difference will not affect the general position except in the case of one school of scholars who base their conclusions upon astronomical considerations and thus claim for their investigations a finality which an exact science like mathematical astronomy would give them a title to. It therefore becomes a matter of some necessity that the position should be examined, however imperfectly, so as not to lay one-self open to the charge of neglect of an important line of investigation bearing vitally upon this question. This astronomical position so called, falls into two divisions; one of these concerns itself with the collection of such details as are found in literature of an astronomical character and their investigation from the point of view of astronomy with a view to arrive at a chronological conclusion. The second is of a more general character and has reference more or less to a knowledge of the zodiac that the Hindus had generally, and the use of the week days in Indian literature. The two are connected more or less closely, but can for the purpose of this investigation be treated separately.

The first of these questions has assumed great prominence, as it naturally should, in the data provided in a poem included in one of the ancient collections, called Paripāḍal, generally regarded as a *Śangam* collection. This has reference to an eclipse of the moon of which the author gives some details. These partake of the character of fixing the position of the planets leading to the casting of a horoscope of the occurrence of this eclipse, thus making it possible for calculations to be made as to the particular eclipse of the moon to which this has reference. My esteemed friend, Dewan Bahadur L. D. Swamikkannu Pillai, in his valuable work on the Indian Ephemeris, published by the

Government of Madras, has investigated this question with sufficient elaboration and has offered his conclusion that the actual date of the eclipse is June 17, A.D. 634. If this conclusion should be acceptable without question, it will make a fundamental change in the angle of vision in regard to the literary and cultural development of South India, and therefore has to be examined with care. In this examination I do not propose to go into the mathematical part of his work for which I have none of the qualifications that my friend has. But the data upon which he bases his conclusions seem capable of re-examination with a view to considering whether the avaliable data would justify his inference.

Poem 11 of the collection, generally described as a *Śangam* collection, Paripāḍal, is a work by the author Nallanduvanār, a *Śangam* celebrity, by all known literary tradition. The object of the poem is to celebrate the river Vaigai which flows by Madura, and the poet chooses two annual features of the river for special description. The one is a description of the river when the monsoon bursts on the Western Ghats and the river is in full freshes when people go to it in large numbers to take a bath in the fresh water. The other has reference to the river in low water in the cold weather when people, particularly unmarried women folk, go to bathe in it in the month of Mārgaḷi (Mārgaśiras), December-January, in celebration of a bathing festival generally described as *Tai-Nīr*, the bath of *Tai* (the month of Pushya). The second does not concern us at present. The first part of it is what actually does describe the eclipse. In the first three lines the poet describes that the starry heaven has a road falling into three divisions beginning with *Kṛttika*, *Ārdra*, and *Bharaṇi*, standing respectively as the commentator explains, for *Rishabha*, *Mithuna*, and *Mēsha*. This kind of division is described also in the Tamil Nighanṭu *Pingalandai*. Then follows the position of the planets. Śukra was in Rishabha, Angāraka was in Mēsha, Budha was in Mithuna, Guru was in Mīna, Śanaiśchara was in Makara, when Rāhu appeared and shut off the moon from view. So far the statements of the poet are direct and may be taken not to admit of any doubt. The position of the Sun and the Moon, and of Rāhu and Kētu are so far not indicated; but there is an expression after fixing the position of Budha which merely states that at dawn or break of day "Kṛttika was on high." This statement, the commentator takes to mean that Kṛttika was at the zenith at daybreak, and explains it as having been put in there to indicate that the sun was in the house of the zodiac, Simha or Leo, at daybreak. The fixing of the position of the Sun in Leo would naturally give us the position of the Moon, and since Rāhu is described as being with the Moon, Kētu will naturally occupy the house opposite. Thus the poet would have supplied the position of all the planets in the zodiac. Objection is taken to this interpretation of the commentator, and the expression equivalent to 'on high' is rendered somewhat more loosely so as to indicate that the commentator was responsible for giving it the interpretation to fix the position of the Sun, thus releasing the author from that responsibility. If the expression could be interpreted as the Kṛttika being merely high up in the heavens, not necessarily at or near the zenith, the position of the Sun could be fixed elsewhere and the position of the Moon, Rāhu, and Kētu would therefore be altered also.

Proceeding on these data and rejecting such of the lunar eclipses as are necessarily to be rejected as not satisfying these, there seem to be two possible dates which satisfy the conditions more or less. The first, according to Mr. Swamikkannu Pillai, is the lunar eclipse on the 27th July, A.D. 17, and the other is that on the 17th June, A.D. 634. As against the first date there are two objections: it necessitates, first of all, the complete abandonment of the position of

Mercury (Budha) as given by the poet, and the position of Venus (Śukra) is only approximate. The second and perhaps a still more valid objection is that the eclipse took place an hour after sunset, whereas the poem requires an eclipse in the early morning of the day. Rejecting this on these grounds the other alternative is considered, and that alternative falls short of the data in the poem in that it makes the position of Saturn fall 130 short of Makara, the position ostensibly given to the planet in the poem, and the eclipse is in the month of Āshāḍa instead of Śravaṇa as the commentator takes it. To explain the first inaccuracy, Mr. Swamikkannu Pillai has recourse to finding the commentator wrong in his explanation of the phrase describing the position of Saturn, and giving a new explanation suggested to him by another Tamil scholar Mr. Mānikka Nāyagar. The text has in regard to Saturn, '*villirkaḍai Makaram mēva*,' reaching Makaram adjacent to the house of the bow (*vil*). The first term '*villirku*' breaks into, *vil il ku* The last of these is the dative affix, the second means house, the first means a bow, to the house of the bow. That would make the commentator quite correct; while the interpretation actually given by my friend takes the whole of the first part of the term to mean "from the end of the bow passing on to Makara," taking the second part *il* meaning house and the third *kadai* meaning end. It seems unusual to express in this fashion the transit of Saturn from Dhanus to Makara. It would make no difference in meaning if *il*, the middle word be omitted. The inaccuracy of statement in regard to Saturn according to calculation will still remain. The second point of defect in this date is that it rejects the commentator's position of the Sun in Leo. This would make the poet give a horoscope without indicating the position of the Sun, Moon, Rahu and Ketu. This is hardly satisfactory if the data are to be gives a chronological interpretation. It may be that the commentator is wrong as the poem leaves the matter open to differences of interpretation. What we feel bound to consider is that each of the two dates, the two most satisfactory ones, according to my friend, falls short of being satisfactory from the point of view of the poem itself. It seems open therefore to question whether the author had astronomy enough in him either of the practical observational kind, or of the more scientific, to give us astronomical data for chronological purposes. Since an elaborate investigation does not yield correct results, it would be quite justifiable if we consider that the horoscopic details in the poem had other objects in view than the chronological. The point that the author wishes to indicate seems to be the commencement of the rains.

He seems merely to be projecting in the poem such a position for the planets, etc., as would be propitious for a copious rainfall. The month of Simha seems therefore necessary to be postulated in that connection.

Then there is one statement in the poem itself, that the star Agastya (Canopus) abandons his position on high (in the zenith) and enters Mithuna when "scorching summer gives place to the rains."[1] According to Hindu Astrology, the heliacal setting of Agastya begins at the commencement of the rainy season and his heliacal rising is a general indication of the cessation of the rains. In some parts of the country there are ceremonies performed in propitiation of Agastya for rains at the commencement of the rainy season. The authorities for this are fully described by Mr. R. Ganapati Ayyar, B.A., B.L., in the Tamil Journal, Sen-Tamil, in Vol. XIX, No. 11, October 1921. Hence it is open to us to make the inference that the poet had no other object in view in giving these astronomical details in the poem than to describe the coming of the rainy season with the planets in such position as to produce an abundant rainfall. Strict astronomy perhaps is not to be expected here, and perhaps, false astronomy from the scientific point of view, may even be possible.

[1] Vide Proceedings of the First Oriental Conference at Poona, pp. 118-9 for another movement of Canopus.

That I am not alone in this view will become clear from the following extracts from the letters of Professor Jacobi (to whom I acknowledge my obligations with gratitude) who was so good as to put himself to the trouble of investigating the matter on my account and giving me the results of his investigations.

Letter dated 4th May 1922.

* * * * *

"After having looked at the matter from all points of view imaginable, I have arrived at the persuasion that the horoscope has been invented by the author, because it is astronomically *impossible*."

* * * * *

"Now, it is not difficult to guess what prompted the author to assign to the planets and the Sun the positions stated in the horoscope under discussion. For he places the Sun and the five planets in those Rāśis of which they are the *Adiphas* (*cf.* Laghu Jātaka I. 8) where they are the most powerful (*Ib.* II. 4). Only the Moon is not in his dominion, because in an eclipse, which is a *very auspicious* moment, he stands opposite the Sun. The author had the dominions of the planets before his mind; for describing the place of Jupiter he mentions that he was next to the two signs belonging to Saturn; and the latter was in the sign next to that belonging to the former. So I think we can account for the places which the author assigned to the several planets. Now, if the horoscope is, as I believe to have proved, altogether fictive, it may not be used for chronological purposes, and the Age of Early Tamil Literature must be proved by literary and historical arguments as you have tried to do."

Letter dated 15th October 1922.

"I beg to thank on for your kind letter of 20th September about the horoscope in the Paripāḍal and the date to be assigned to it. You refer to Mr. L. D. Swamikkannu Pillai who kindly visited and discussed the whole question with me. The divergence of our results was caused by the difference of interpretation of the passage in the Paripāḍal. Mr. Swamikkannu has given his interpretation in Indian Ephemeris, I, Part I, p. 109; I went on your interpretation which is also that of the commentator Parimēla̤agar. The points of difference are: (1) The commentator understands the passage, 'at first dawn, when Kṛttika stood high up' to mean that Kṛttika was *culminating* just before sunrise, thus indicating the place of the Sun and implicitly that of the Moon and Rāhu; but Mr. Swamikkannu denies to the statement any astronomical signification assigning it only this meaning that the Kṛttikas were high up in the sky, *i.e.*, at a good altitude above the horizon. (2) The commentator places Saturn in Makara, Mr. Swamikkannu at the end of Dhanus. The point is of less importance.

Now, if the commentator is right regarding (1), then as I told you in my last letter and has also been pointed out by Mr. Swamikkannu l. c. p. 101, the positions of Mercury and Venus are *impossible*. Nor can we avoid this difficulty by assuming that not the *true* planets, but *mean* planets are intended; because the place of mean Mercury and mean Venus always coincides with that of the Sun (*cf.* Surya Siddhanta, I, 29). My conclusion, therefore, was that the horoscope in question is not a real one, but has been freely invented by the author as in the horoscopes of Rama, Yudhishtira, Buddha, etc., the idea of the poet being that the planets should have been in the signs which are their own houses as the commentator puts it. Such a horoscope is, of course, without any value for chronological purposes. If, on the other hand, Mr. Swamikkannu's interpretation, is admitted, then his chronological conclusions must also be accepted; for it goes without saying that his calculations can be relied on without reserve. The whole question, therefore, depends on the right interpretation of the original passage, and as I am ignorant of Tamil, I must leave the decision of the question to those who know it and are well versed in its old literature. I may, however, call attention to one point. The statement that "Kṛttika stood high up" occurs in the midst of entirely astrological items; hence it was very likely also intended to convey an astrological information, *viz.*, that suggested by the commentator. Besides, as the whole passage no doubt states a horoscope, it would be strange indeed, if it contained no explicit hint about the place of the Sun, the Moon, and Rāhu. But whether this course of reasoning is borne out by the mental habits of ancient Tamil writers, is beyond my ken. I have stated the case and my way of looking at it; now it is for you to decide the matter."

In the light of these remarks of the veteran scholar, and Mr. Swamikkannu Pillai's own, "Horoscopes are liable to all the failings to which human compositions are subject and unless one was certain of all the elements in a horoscope having been recorded, the time inference drawn therefrom may turn out to be widely discrepant from the truth," I may be excused if I hesitate to accept the conclusion of my friend in regard to the date indicated by the horoscopic details such as they are in Paripāḍal 11. The acceptance of this date would make the Paripāḍal, at least Nallanduvanār, the author of the particular poem, an author who lived in the middle of the seventh century A.D. Nallanduvanār would then be contemporary with the great Pallava king Narasimhavarman Mahāmalla of Kanchi and of the two most prominent of the Tēvāram hymners, *viz.*, Sambandar and Appar. If this conclusion regarding poem 11 of Paripāḍal should be made to apply to the Paripāḍal itself as a whole and to the whole of the so-called Śangam Literature as a consequence, the position becomes far less acceptable from considerations, literary, historical, and linguistic.

One influencing consideration that led to the preference of this date by my friend is the general position that he has taken in regard to the borrowing of the week days by the Hindus from the Roman week after Constantine had changed the Sabbath from the seventh day of the Jews to the first day of the week. In regard to the naming of the week days the following quotation may be appropriate. "The Semitic peoples gave no names to the days of the week, and Babylonians had apparently no week, their sabbath being the 15th of the month, the Arabs named it Yom el Jumah or day of congregation and the Yom es Sebt or sabbath. The Aryans, on the other hand, dedicated one week-day to a God, apparently under Roman influence in the West, while the Hindus and Tamils alike have such names in India. * * * * All alike, place the Sun first and the Moon second. Tuesday is sacred to Mars and Śiva, Wednesday to Mercury or Budha, Thursday to Jove or (Bṛhaspati), Friday to Venus or Śukra, being also the sacred day of the Arabs who worshipped the Venus of Makka. Saturday belonged to Saturn, originally the God of Agriculture." * * * The Greek week days are those of Christian times. The Tibetan planets are connected respectively with light, water, flame, copper, wood, gold, and earth. The Semitic names only mean first, second, etc., excepting those above stated—Friday and Saturday.[1]

It will be seen from a comparison of the names that there is no connection between the one set of names and the other except that they indicate the same object. The Hindu notion of Budha is perhaps something quite different from Mercury as also Jove or Jupiter and Bṛhaspati. It would be very difficult to trace any connection between the names Venus and Sukra except that they stand as the names of the same day. Unless it be that the Hindus borrowed the week days from the Greeks and invented their own names for the presiding deities, these differences can hardly be accounted for.

[1] J. G. R. Forlong, Faiths of Man, I, pp. 514-15.

Apart from these considerations it is open to doubt whether the week originated from the astronomical considerations that are held to have brought the week day into existence. It is generally taken that, for the constitution of the week, the division of the day into the nychthemeron or of twenty-four hours is absolutely necessary. As another consideration, the planets are supposed to be taken in the order of diminishing distances beginning with Saturn, appointing each of these planets to be the presiding deity of a particular hour of the day in rotation. At any particular date when the week got to be originated, reversing of the order with a view to bringing it in line with the twenty-four hours division would perhaps imply very much more knowledge of scientific astronomy than could have been possessed by the originators. Hence it would bear the conclusion that this probably is a later astronomical adjustment of an already existing week system. It would seem more reasonable to ascribe the origin of the week to causes other than astronomical, for which there is a considerable volume of evidence in Hindu literature. The week seems actually to have originated in a division of the month into quarters, and each quarter is taken roughly to be seven days, necessary adjustments following when the error got to be discovered. There were several such divisions known from Vedic times, as Dr. Shamasastri demonstrates[1] clearly. That the week arises naturally from a division of the day into sixty periods as the Hindus have, comes out clearly from the following remarks of Professor Rawlinson.[2] 'There is further no evidence to show that the Medes, or even the Babylonians were acquainted with the order of the planets which regulated the nomenclature of the days of the week. The series in question, indeed, must have originated with a people who divided the day and night into sixty hours instead of twenty-four ; and so far as we know at present, this system of horary division was peculiar in ancient times to the Hindu calendar ; the method by which the order is eliminated is simply as follows :—The planets in due succession from Moon to Saturn were supposed to rule the hours of the day in a recurring series of sevens, and the day was named after the planet which happened to be the regent of the first hour. If we assign then the first hour of the first day to the Moon we find that the 61st hour which commences the second day belongs to the fifth planet or Mars ; the 121st hour to the second or Mercury, 181st to the sixth or Jupiter, the 241st to the third or Venus, 301st to the seventh or Saturn, 361st to the fourth or the Sun. The popular

[1] Annals of the Bhandarkar Institute, for July, 1922, pp. 1-31.

[2] Herodotus, I. 226.

belief (which first appears in Dion Cassius) that the series in question refers to a horary division of twenty-four is incorrect; for in that case, although the order is the same, *the succession is inverted.* One thing indeed seems to be certain, that if the Chaldeans were the inventors of the hebdomadal nomenclature, they must have borrowed their earliest astronomical science from the same source which supplied the Hindus; for it could not have been by an accident that a horary division of sixty was adopted by both races.' Dr. Shama Śastri has attempted to prove that this division originated with the Hindus, while a school of Assyriologists would give the credit to the Babylonians.

Without labouring the point further we might proceed to the consideration whether we have any evidence of the Hindus having had any knowledge of the planets either generally, or in the week day order. It is now generally admitted that the division of the ecliptic into 27 constellations was known to the Hindus from Vedic times. It is not quite clear that they knew its division into the twelve houses of the zodiac. It seems inferable from the mention of the term Sauramāsa of thirty [1] days and a half, and a few other details like Uttarāyaṇam and Dakshiṇāyanam, that some kind of division answering to the division of the zodiac existed among the Hindus

[1] Chapter XX of the Artha Śastra, Shama Śastri's translation.

in the fourth century B.C. The mention of the planets in the week day order in the Baudhayana Dharma Sūtra is equally significant in this direction. This happens to occur in the first two books (actually in II. 5.9) of the Sūtra which are regarded by the late Dr. Bühler as not having been tampered with to the extent that the later books are, and these Sūtras, at least the genuine parts of them, are referable to the fourth century B. C. according to the same authority.[1] The Śārdūla Karṇāvadāna, which was translated into Chinese in the third century A.D. and 'the framework of (which) *avadāna* itself must be of great antiquity' according to its learned editors Cowell and Neil, not merely contains reference to the planets including Rāhu and Ketu, but even a division headed Dvādaśa-rāśika, the twelve signs of the zodiac. This *avadāna* contains a volume of astrological information which would warrant great astrological knowledge among the Hindus. In *avadāna* 19 of the same work, called Jyotishka-avadāna, there is a reference to an astrologer named Bhūrika as having made a calculation and verified a prediction of the Buddha.[2] It is hardly necessary to multiply references. In the face of these, it would be too much to postulate that the Hindus had no knowledge of astrology, or of the signs of the

[1] Sacred Books of the East, II, pp. xxiv and xliii.

[2] *Ib.*, p. 263.

zodiac, or that they borrowed the week day from the Christian week in the age of the Guptas. It would be safer to hold with Bühler, 'I do not think it has been proved that every work that enumerates the rāśis must be later than the period when Ptolemy's astronomy and astrology were introduced into India.'[1] From the point of view of mere historical considerations, parts of India were very much more in contact with the Greek world of Asia from the time when Selucus I became king of Asia down to the end of the Kushans, and cultural elements like astrology or the week days, if they came from the West of India, had ample opportunities of coming into the country before the days of Paulus Alexandrinus, or even before the days of Ptolemy. In the present state of our knowledge of the cultural histories of India and of Western Asia respectively, it is too much to build on the available evidence to state categorically that any reference to a week day in any work of literature *ipso facto* condemns it to a period posterior to the age Aryabhaṭṭa. Aryabhaṭṭa was born, according to his own statement, in A.D. 472-73 and composed his principal work in his 23rd year, *i.e.*, A.D. 496-97. But the inscription of Budhagupta mentions the week day, Thursday, more than ten years before this. In the light of the evidence cited above, and

[1] Bühler's Manu, p. cxvii.

having regard to the uncertain character of the evidence offered I may be excused if I show myself to be somewhat sceptical, however regretfully, in regard to the conclusions of my esteemed friends Messrs. Swamikkannu Pillai and Kameswara Ayyar, who have committed themselves, each in his own particular way, to the view that the Hindu knowledge of astronomy is post-Alexandrian in all its details. I do not exclude the possibility that Hindu astronomy, such as it was, was wrong in details and adopted corrections from the Greeks when Greek astronomy came to be fully known to them in the age of Āryabhaṭṭa, or somewhat later in that of Varāhamihira. If I still persist in relying more upon historical considerations in my classification of Tamil literature, I hope I have demonstrated above, that I have good reason to support me in my position.

In concluding this introduction I must acknowledge my gratitude to the Council of Post-Graduate Teaching at the Calcutta University, and, to the University as a whole, for the honour they have done me in nominating me Reader. My acknowledgments are also due to my friend Professor D. R. Bhandarkar and several other members of the Calcutta University. My debt of obligation to Sir Asutosh Mookerjee is so great that I could hardly dream of acknowledging it adequately. I have dedicated the following lectures to him as in some measure expressive of my great esteem, without his permission. I trust that he will accept this token of my personal regard for him and the high esteem in which I hold his services to the cause of University Education in general and to Indian History and Culture in particular. I have great pleasure in acknowledging the assistance that Mr. R. Gopalan, B.A. Hons., the University Research Student working with me, rendered in the compiling of the index. I acknowledge with equal pleasure the ready courtesy of Mr. A. C. Ghatak, the Superintendent of the University Press, Calcutta, and the excellent manner in which he saw the work through the Press, which under his expert guidance proves to be very efficient.

MADRAS UNIVERSITY: } S. K. AIYANGAR.
26th March, 1923.

CONTENTS

CHAPTER I.

THE BEGINNINGS OF SOUTH INDIAN HISTORY.

History begins for India with the coming of the Āryans into the country. It may be said with almost equal truth that the history of South India, of India south of the Krishna-Tungabhadra frontier, begins with the coming of the Āryans into the South. In this particular context the term "Āryan" seems to stand for the Brahman. The coming of the Āryan therefore would be the coming of the Brahman as a settler in this remote and sequestered region of India from the point of view of the northern Āryan. As far as we could trace the term Āryan in early Tamil literature, it is used in a broad and narrower sense. In the broader sense, it means the *northerner*, with the northern culture; the typical representative of the latter was, so far as the southerners were concerned, the Brahman. But there is a sense in which the term is used synonymously with the Tamil "Vaḍavar" (northerner). There is specific reference to a class known by this name, whose profession seems to have been elephant-training. They are referred to as men who were expert in capturing wild elephants by trained female ones.[1] In the general sense there are references to Āryans, who were defeated in the battle-field of Vallam by the Cholas.[2] These Āryas are also said to have been defeated in a northern invasion by a Chera king who is said to have imprinted his bow emblem on the face of the Himalayas and brought some of the Āryan kings captive to his capital Vanji. These are associated with the Himalayas.[3] They come in for another reference as laying siege to the hill fortress of Muḷḷūr, the citadel of the Malayamān chieftain Tirumuḍik-Kāri.[4] A people therefore other than Brahmans were known under the name "Ārya" in the south. That this is synonymous with the northern Āryans is in evidence in the title assumed by the Pāndyan Neḍuṁ-Śeḻiyan "who overthrew the forces of the Āryas."[5] Among the synonyms given to the term in the Divākaram, the oldest Tamil Lexicon, occurs the term Mlēchcha. This term seems to be used in the sense in which it is explained in the Satapatha Brahmaṇa,[6] and not meaning a foreign barbarian as in later times.

---

[1] Paraṇar in Aham 296, ll. 9 and 10, and Mullaippāṭṭu, ll. 35-36.

[2] Pāvaik-Koṭṭilār in Aham 336, ll. 20-22.

[3] Padiṟṟuppattu. Poem I, ll. 23-26, and II, Padigam.

[4] Naṟṟiṇai, 170 of an unknown author.

[5] Śilappadhikāram, canto XXIII. Epilogue, ll. 14 to 18.

[6] III. 2. 1. 23 and 24, Manu X. 45. Sacred Books of the East, XXVI, pp. 31 and 32. *Cf.* Mṛchchakaṭika, p. 255, speech of Chandanaka: (Bo: Nirṇ: Edn. of 1916).

These Āryas are known to the Tamils by the general name Vaḍavar, literally northerners. They seem also to carefully distinguish those that were immediately to the north of their frontier as Vaḍukar. This word seems to be formed on the analogy of perhaps the later Kanarese word Baḍaga, which, in its origin, had the sense northerner also. But the use of the word seems confined to those immediately to the north of the regular Tamil frontier. This frontier was marked by Pulikat, the northern extremity of the Tamil country proper, on the east coast, and possibly Karwar point on the west coast. These people the Vaḍukar, are described as robbers by profession habitually engaged in cattle-lifting. The chieftain Erumai of Kuḍanāḍu is referred to as a Vaḍuka.[1] The corresponding chieftain on the eastern side with his capital at Tirupati[2] was also possibly a Vaḍuka by name Pulli who is described as the chieftain of robbers, Kaḷvarkōmān. Entering this region from the Tamil country, the language changed.[3] They are described by one poet as *Vaḍukas* who kept cruel dogs and the words of whose language were " long and unlearned," as much as to say " barbarous," in the original sense of the term.[4]

---

[1] Narkirar in Aham 253, ll. 16-19.

[2] Māmūlanār in Aham, ll. 15-17.

[3] Māmūlar in Aham, 31, 127, 211 and 295.

[4] Kārik-Kaṇṇan of Kāveripaṭṭaṇam in Aham 107, l. 11.

Another poet of this group refers to the sacrifices that these people offered in thanksgiving for the capture of herds of cattle. In this connection the hill Vēngaḍam (Tirupati) is described as belonging to Toṇḍaiyar on the borders of the country of the Vaḍukas. These are some of the references to the Āryas or the northern people in the earliest extant literature of the Tamils.

KNOWLEDGE OF SOUTH INDIA IN SANSKRIT AND PĀLI LITERATURE.

Looking from the other side it is a well known fact that the grammarian Pāṇini has[1] little or nothing to say about South India. We have to come to the time of Kātyāyana for some knowledge of places in South India. Kātyāyana had heard of the Pāṇḍya and the Chola Kingdoms. Contemporary Buddhist literature does not mention anything beyond Danḍaká lying south of Aśmaka on the Godaveri, so that down to the middle of the 4th century, comparatively little was known of the South, as far, at any rate, as our knowledge of it goes at present. This is in a way confirmed by the dramatist Bhāsa whose political vision seems to be bounded by the Vindhyas and the Himalayas for the south and north, and the seas for the west

[1] Śarabhanga Jātaka (522) and *cf.* Arthaśāstra, p. 11, ed. 1911.

and east.[1] Megasthenes had however heard of the Pāṇḍya country. It was under the rule of a woman and her territory extended from sea to sea in the south. It was, according to him, composed of 365 villages. He gives a queer story that one village or township brought in its revenue every day. This arrangement, according to him, was intended to give the queen the assistance of the escort carrying the tribute to compel others who may not be so readily inclined to pay. He gives the precise information that the Pāṇḍyan army was composed of 500 elephants, 4,000 cavalry and 130,000 infantry. He also refers to the possession of the rich fishery for pearls which the later Greek writer Arrian says were sought for by the Greeks and the Romans. Coming to the Arthaśāstra of Chanakya, referable almost to the same time as Megasthenes himself, we gain a few details which exhibit a certain amount of definite knowledge. He speaks of two classes of pearls which must be referred to this country. One is called Tamraparṇika, apparently pearls fished for near the mouth of the Tamraparṇi, namely, the Gulf of Mannar; and then Pāṇḍya *Kavāṭaka* that which is obtained in Pāṇḍya *Kavāṭa*, which would mean literally the door of the Pāṇḍya. The commentator, however, renders this expression by "Malayakoṭi." That could

---

[1] Imām sāgaraparyantām Himavad-Vindhyakuṇḍalām mahīm ēkātapatrānkām Rājasimha praśāstu naḥ.

only mean the pearls fished for in the Pāṇḍya country where the promontory of Malaya, the southern portion of the Western Ghats, dips into the sea; in other words, the sea very near Cape Comorin. Speaking of cotton cloth he refers to the fabrics of Madhura noted then as now, for the fine textures produced in the town or district. When we come down to the age of Patanjali a little more knowledge of South India is exhibited. He knew Māhishmati and Vidarbha[1] both of which might be referred to the Dakhan, and Kānchipuram and Keraḷa in the south. One point of some importance in his references is where he says that the word "*Sarasi*" is used in the South to denote large lakes, giving us a hint that he knew not only the geography of the country, but had noted even some of the peculiarities of the language of the south. That is so far only from literature.

Evidence of Epigraphy.

Coming to inscriptions there are no South Indian inscriptions, as far as is known at present, anterior to the Christian era excepting copies of the Asoka edicts that have been found in two localities, one in the North-Eastern corner of Mysore and the other in the South-Western

[1] Already known to Brahmaṇa literature: Ait. Br. vii, 14 and Jaimini Up. Br. ii, 640.

corner of Hyderabad. There are a few cave-inscriptions in Brahmi character which may be referable to the first century B. C. or even somewhat earlier, but they await interpretation. Lastly there is just one Śātavāhana inscription in Talgunḍa in the state of Mysore. Beyond these, inscriptions that throw light upon the history of South India are to our knowledge up to the present, non-existent. We are therefore driven necessarily to a body of literature referable to the century on either side of the Christian era most of them, and which contain embedded in them glimpses of an earlier time. But turning to the northern inscriptions, the inscriptions of Asoka give us some definite knowledge of the political condition even of the remote south, and provide the earliest reliable information on the political condition of South India. Such of Asoka's edicts as do mention these Southern kingdoms mention them as outside the pale of the empire of the great Buddhist ruler liable only to be influenced by the emperor regarding the teaching of "the law of piety." The Chola, the Pānḍya, Kēraḷaputra and Satiyaputra are mentioned as among "those nations and princes that are his neighbours," and therefore outside of his empire. Coming down to the next century the Hathigumpha inscription of the Kalinga King, Kharavela refers to the arrival of a tribute of jewels and elephants from the Pāṇḍya King to the Kalinga ruler thereby confirming, what is inferable from the word *kalingam* used in Tamil for cloth of a particular kind, that there was trade connection with the country of Kalinga. Even these inscriptional sources do not advance our knowledge of South India very much; but they do give us to understand that there was a certain degree of communication and a certain amount of knowledge of each other between the two parts of the country. Asoka's edicts themselves make it clear that his empire stopped short of South India, and such communication as did exist was of the peaceful neighbourly kind without giving us any hint of any warlike effort either on his own part or on that of his predecessors. What is wanted in detail in these edicts is supplied to us in Tamil Literature to which we shall now turn.

The Mauryan Period.

From what has been said above it is clear that any definite knowledge of South India does not reach back beyond the Mauryan period. What we do learn from the scanty sources of information accessible to us gives us but a glimpse into the political condition of India in the age of the Mauryas. Such glimpses as we get warrant the presumption that the states of the south must have had an anterior history of some length. Our knowledge of that history however does not carry us back beyond the period of the Mauryas. Thus the Buddhist chronicles of Ceylon which pretend to carry us back to the age of the Buddha himself are so meagre in point of that history before the age of Asoka that the conclusion seems inevitable that there was in Ceylon itself no real knowledge of its history anterior to the age of the great Buddhist emperor. We shall presently see that such information as we get from Tamil Literature does not take us any further back than this, and we are driven round again to the same conclusion that our knowledge of the history of the south dates back to the age of the Mauryas and no farther, although absence of information available to us does not inevitably mean absence of history in the region concerned.

The Main Source of Information, Tamil Literature.

The main source of information for the period previous to the rise of the Pallavas into importance is Tamil Literature, of which we have a body with a character all its own. This body of works is known among Tamil Scholars by the collective designation, "Śangam works." This designation assumes the existence of a body or an academy of scholars and critics, whose imprimatur was necessary for the publication of any work of literature in Tamil. The Tamil word "*Śangam*" is the Sanskrit "*Sangha*" and means ordinarily no more than an assembly. In this particular application, however it means a body of scholars, of recognised worth and standing in the world of letters, who were maintained by the contemporary kings and constituted themselves a board before whom every work seeking recognition had to be read. It is only when this body as a whole signified its approval that the work could go forth into the world as a Śangam work. It does not, however, mean that other works were not written and published. There are some which have come down to us, which do not appear to have gone before the Śaṅgam. The function of this body seems therefore to be merely to set up a standard of excellence for works which aspire to the dignity of Śangam works. Tamil Scholars recognise a body of works that are acknowledged to have passed this gauntlet of criticism among the Śangam works. Some others also are included in this group apparently as belonging to the same age and partaking of the same character. This is not done by scholars of today, nor is it a matter purely of present-day opinion. The commentators who lived five or six centuries before us, and more, also make this classification and treat the works accordingly. It is the tradition of the commentators that has come down to us and the whole position in respect of this classification rests upon the authority generally of these commentators.

Of these Śangams, tradition knows of three. The numbers of scholars in the first and the second, and the numbers of Pāṇḍya kings that took an active part in the work of these bodies, were according to this tradition very large. Although some of the works referred to as belonging to these Śangams, and mentioned as such, have come down to us in isolated quotations the actual existence of these bodies as stated in tradition would be difficult to postulate with the evidence accessible to us. It rather seems to be that this body of scholars was a permanently existing body, and did exist for a certain number of centuries continuously. In the work of these bodies there were periods of great output and periods of comparative barrenness. We have no means of ascertaining what exactly might have been the cause of this alternation. But such brilliant periods seem marked as the period of the first Śangam and of the second Śangam, not very far behind their historical successor, the third Śangam. What actually does make the tradition look very suspicious, is the extraordinary length of time that is given to each one of these periods. It is this impossible longevity in the traditional account that stamps the whole tradition connected with these two bodies as entirely false in the estimation of modern scholarship. The third Śangam counts among its scholar members 49, and 3 Pāṇḍya rulers, who bore an honourable part in the work of the academy. The bulk of the works that have come down to us may be ascribed actually to this body, in our present state of knowledge of these three academies, as a whole. It would perhaps be better to assume that they refer to three brilliant epochs in the active work of a single academy which might have existed for a number of centuries. This body of *antique* literature contains embedded in it various details reminiscent of what to them must have been contemporary or other history, as also a considerable amount of information very interesting to us in regard to their own times.

Its Character and Chronology.

The bulk of this body of works in Tamil partakes of the character of heroic pieces celebrating incidents in the lives of particular patrons, or illustrative of various modes of composition according to the canons of Tamil rhetoric. Several of these fugitive pieces are like the heroic tales from out of which sprang

Homer's Iliad, and, according to modern criticism, the Rāmāyaṇa and the Mahābhārata of our own country. As such therefore they are of great value historically. Most of these are short poems relating to some particular kind of emotion, or to the exploits of an individual hero, and fall into two classes which might be labelled for convenience "erotic" and "heroic." As a rule these are short poems in various styles of composition, and should have been collected and thrown into the form in which they have come down to us, at a particular period. In collecting them, this classification into two is the main principle of division. There are various cross divisions which are of minor importance for our purposes. The feature that makes them all common to a particular period of activity of this body of learned men, is that a very large number of these collections receives poems in invocation from one poet Peruṁ-Devanār who is distinguished from others of the name by the qualifying designation "who rendered the Bhārata in Tamil." There are 4 celebrities of this name Peruṁ-Dēvanār, in Tamil literature and the attribute is absolutely necessary to mark out the particular individual. The Bhāratam that he composed in Tamil has not come down to us, and is quite different from the portion of the Tamil Bhārata that is available as the work of another Peruṁ-Dēvan. The rendering of the Bhāratam in Tamil, the establishment of the Śangam in Madura and the winning of a victory over the forces of the other Tamil kings and chiefs at a place called Talai-Ālangānam are described as the achievements of an ancient Pāndyan in the Śinnamanur-grant of the 10th century.[1] This ancient Pāndya is treated as distinct from and as having preceded by a stretch of time, the dynasty to which the donor of the Veḷvikuḍi-grant, who is the seventh in succession from the first member of this particular dynasty, belonged according to the genealogy of the Pāndyas accepted by the Epigraphists.

One of the most important of these collections which is known to Tamil scholars under two names Ahanānūṟu, which means the 400 relating to "erotics," or Neḍum-togai, meaning collection of longer poems, was made by a Brahman Rudraśarman, the son of Uppūrikuḍi-Kiḻān of Madura at the instance of the Pāndyan Ugrapperuvaḻudi. This by itself would not lead us very far; but this Rudraśarman comes in contact with a well known poet and president of the Śangam by name Narkīrar who wrote the accepted commentary on an abridged work on the vast department of rhetoric relative to this particular section of Tamil poetry. This poet Narkīrar was the contemporary of the Pāndyan

---

[1] Madras Epigraphist's Report, 1907, pp. 62-67.

victor at Talai-Ālangānam. Hence this great Pāndyan, Narkīrar, Rudraśarman, and Perum-Dēvan all belonged apparently to the same generation, and that is the generation when the Śangam activity was at its height under this Pāndya, and Narkīrar, when the Bhārata was rendered into Tamil verse by Perum-Dēvanār and the Ahānānūru was collected into its present form by Rudraśarman. The works therefore which are thus collected relate to the generations preceding, several of them proximate, some of them, it might even be remote. It would be impossible in this context, to deal in sufficient fulness with all the arguments that would enable us to fix the age of this Śangam activity. But some of the more salient arguments that lead to the conclusion that the age of the Śangam is the first and the second century of the Christian era may be indicated :—

(1) The whole body of the Śangam works taken collectively give us a picture of the Tamil country in a period of great prosperity.

(2) There are a considerable number of references direct and indirect to active trade both internal and oversea.

(3) This commercial prosperity and the prevalence of comparative peace is reflected in the writings of the classical authors from whom we gain a considerable amount of knowledge of the commercial prosperity of the land.

(4) There is no indication in this vast body of literature of the existence of various dynasties of the Pallavas known to history. The rulers of Kānchī appear as viceroys of the Cholas, and oftentimes princes of the blood-royal of the Cholas. The only chieftain who is called in Tamil "Tonḍamān" is "Tonḍamān Iḷaṁ-Tirayan" said to be the son of a Chola ruler by a Nāga princess. His designation Iḷaṁ-Tirayan presumes another Tirayan, and there is one such not associated necessarily with Kānchī. The name Tonḍiayar is given to the people inhabiting the country round Kānchī; and the hill of Tirupati, the northern limit of the Tamil country, is said to have been in the country of Tonḍiayar or the Pallavas, thus establishing the equation that the people called Tonḍiayar in Tamil are the Pallavas of Sanskrit.[1]

The inference is clear that the age of the Śangam activity must be regarded pre-Pallava in character.

(5) An epic work composed of the twin *kārya* Śilappadhikāram and Maṇimēkhalai, not a Śangam work in the sense that it received the Śangam imprimatur, is the work of two authors. The first was written by a Chera prince, a younger brother of the great Chera ruler Śeṁ-Kuṭṭuvan, who adopted the life of an

[1] Old poem quoted by Nachchinārkiniyar in his comment on Sūtra 54 of Poruḷadhikāram.

ascetic; and the second by his friend Śīttalai-Śāttan of Madura, who was one among the 49 who composed the third Śangam and a friend both of the King Śeṁ-Kuṭṭuvan and his ascetic brother Iḷaṁkō-Aḍikaḷ. Śeṁ-Kuṭṭuvan undoubtedly was a Śangam celebrity having been celebrated in several poems by poets like Paraṇar, which poems are found in the collections known as the Śangam collection. Without going into fuller detail we might say at once that he was the exact contemporary of Gajabāhu of Ceylon, undoubtedly the earlier of the two Gajabāhus in the Ceylon list.

The name Gajabāhu occurs as among those who congratulated Śeṁ-Kuṭṭuvan on the successful celebration of the establishment of the temple to the goddess Pattini (chaste-lady) in his capital of Vanji. Attempts have been made to get round this by saying that this reference occurs outside the body of the work and by arguments based thereon. Except betraying the ignorance which often adds emphasis to an opinion, the objection is not worth consideration. It may be pointed out that this reference to Gajabāhu among those that were present, occurs in the body of the poem in line 160 of canto thirty, not in the epilogue that comes at the end of it; although the statement in regard to the establishment of a temple to this same goddess in Ceylon by this Gajabāhu occurs in the prologue which might be the composition of another author and possibly of a later time even. Without labouring the point further it is clear that this particular period of activity of the Śangam must be referred to the second century A.D. The works collected during this period have undoubtedly a range of a few generations which may amount at least to a century, possibly to a period much longer.

This body of literature relating to the two sections already indicated contain embedded in them many expressions by way of compliment or some otherwise to actual patrons. They give a number of ethnographical and geographical details of an important character relating to various parts of the country, and various other details from which important inferences could be drawn if they should be sorted and arranged with sufficient knowledge of the general background in which to set these small details. In dealing with the whole matter the classical grammarians recognise two modes which, for convenience, may be described as the conventional and the real. The first of these they call *nāḍaha vaḻakku* (the dramatic usage) in which it is open to them to introduce creations of pure imagination. It seems nevertheless to be an understanding that as the purpose of these works is the general impression that these produce upon the people for didactic purposes, they must still have a realistic colour. To achieve this they make use of even real historical material somewhat idealised to produce the correct impression according to their notions. This mode is applicable generally to subjects that come under the classification "erotics." In regard to the really dramatic part of the subjects treated, *viz.*, those which relate to action, the mode adopted is that of what actually obtained in the world around them, *ulak-iyal-vaḷakku* (the usage of actual life). This section having mainly to do with the doings of kings and chiefs, both principal and subsidiary, are admittedly of a historical character.[1] In the use, therefore, of the mass of material which, with labour, one could collect from this literature, a considerable degree of discrimination and judgment is required. Carefully studied and properly selected one could obtain a very considerable knowledge of the history of the times to which this body of literature relates.

For an examination of this literature the standard work of grammar and rhetoric is the Tolkāppiyam though its original, Agattiyam comes in for large application, though the work itself is not extant. The traditional belief among Pandits is that the text of the Tolkāppiyam,

[1] Tolkāppiyam Poruḷ 58 and comment thereon by Nachchināṛkkiniyar and Iḷaṁ Pūraṇar.

as we have it at present, is anterior to the great bulk of this class of literature now extant. Reading through the various commentators on this vast grammatical work one often comes across statements which would imply the existence of a body of this kind of literature before a systematic work like the Tolkāppiyam could have been written. That, however, is matter which it is hardly necessary to labour in this connection. What is to the point here is that the literature available contains a considerable mass of material which with judgment could be made to yield very good material for history. Such as it is, it does not take us back beyond Mauryan times.

Glimpses of Mauryan Invasion in it.

In this mass of literature we get some allusions to the Mauryas and Mauryan invasions of South India which throw a new light upon this particular period of history. Among the number of poets whose works are found collected in this volume of literature there are three authors that refer to the Mauryan invasions specifically. One of them is the Brahman poet, Māmūlanār, the much respected Brahman poet of the *Agastya gotra* belonging to the south country, the other is one Paraṁ-Koṟṟanār and the third is Kaḷḷil-Āttirayanār. Māmūlanār has got two references in respect of this particular matter, and the other two one each. The general character of these references is to a distant hill worn by the rolling cars of the Mauryas beyond which a young lover might have gone in quest of wealth. His love-lorn sweetheart at home, pining away in solitude for his return, is assured in various ways that even if he should have got past this hill he would keep his promise and return on the appointed day. That is the general purport of the passages[1] in the first two authors. This means that a particular hill marks the frontier limit of the Tamil land, going beyond which one gets into foreign land and unknown country, return from which in safety is problematical. The hill under reference marks therefore some well-known frontier hill a considerable distance from the Tamil land across which the war chariots of the Mauryas had to be taken at considerable labour. A tribe of people, foreigners apparently, specifically called Kośar, advanced southwards so far as the Podiyil Hill and defeated some enemy there when the chieftain of Mōhūr declined to submit. In consequence the Mauryas marched upon the territory. In regard to this the points to be noted are that the Kośar, of whom 4 divisions are known in this body of Tamil literature, were somehow connected with

---

[1] Aham 251.

the Mauryas. There is only one Mōhūr known to Tamil literature of which a chief of the name Paḻaiyan played an important part against various enemies, most conspicuous among them being Śeṅ-Kuṭṭuvan Śēra. It is to subjugate this Mōhūr which is a place about 7 miles north-east of the town of Madura with a fortified temple and some remnants of a comparatively old chieftaincy, that the Mauryas are said to have advanced after the failure of the Kośar. The other poem of this author refers to the southern invasion of the Mauryas. This time the Mauryas came led forward by the Vaḍukar, or pushing them in front. In this connection there is the same reference to the hill worn by the war chariots of the Mauryas.[1] The second author merely refers to the Mauryas and the cutting down of the hill to make a roadway for the war chariots of the Mauryas. The third author refers similarly to the cutting down of the hill side to make way for the rolling cars. But the word Mōriyar has a second reading Oriyar which the learned commentator on the work has adopted as the reading. On this point it must be noted that a dispassionate and close examination of the passage shows clearly that the reading Mōriyar would read very much better and would be very much more in

[1] Aham 281.

keeping with the general sense of the passage than the reading Oriyar. Having regard to the class of works concerned, the other passages under reference in connection almost with the same matter ought to be the best commentary on this doubtful passage. It therefore leaves no room for doubt that there is a Mauryan invasion or invasions under reference, and that in the course of this invasion they had to get across a difficult hill making a roadway for themselves. That this hill was at some considerable distance, from the point of view of the Tamilian, and to a love-lorn damsel of the Tamil land going across the hill is as much as Shakespeare's "her husband is to Aleppo gone." The author Māmūlanār refers in the first passage rather familiarly to the wealth of the Nandas. The same author in another[1] passage refers to this wealth of the Nandas as having accumulated in Pāṭali (Patna), but got hidden in the floods of the Ganges in times gone by. The point of the reference in these cases is, as is borne out by a corresponding passage[2] of the same author in connection with the accumulated wealth of the Śōras, that the Nandas had accumulated vast wealth and the accumulated wealth at one time came to be of no use to them having been hidden in the one case in the waters of the Ganges, in the other

---

[1] Aham 264. [2] Aham 127.

by being buried in the earth. We have then in Māmūlanār an author who had heard of the wealth of the Nandas and who speaks of the southern invasions of the Mauryas. By way of confirmation, the two other authors speak of the invasions of the south by the Mauryas also in equally clear terms excepting for a difference of reading in one of the two cases. We shall now proceed to consider who the Vaḍukar and the Kośar are, the two people that are brought into connection with these Mauryan invasions.

Vaḍukar.

Of these two sections of people referred to, the term Vaḍukar is used for those that lived across the Tamil frontier on the north for which Pulikat on the one side and the northern frontier of Nannan's territory, including in it both Tuḷu and Konkan, provide the limits. The Chief of Vēṅgaḍam (Tirupati), Pulli by name, comes often in contact with the people who are described in various ways in these poems. The general trend of all this description is to make of them a class of hunters. Their chief occupation was cattle-raiding and they are always said to be accompanied by cruel dogs.[1] Entering into their territory language changed.[2] This language is referred to by a poet Kāri-Kaṇṇan of Kaveripaṭṭaṇam[3]

[1] Aham 213 and 381. [2] Māmūlanār, Aham 295. [3] Aham 107.

as unlearned in character and long in sound. The latter characterisation would apply to Telugu even now, if it is the Telugu of the northern districts, from the point of view of the Tamilian. The former characteristic, whatever foundation there was for it in the days of our author, has long since worn off, and Telugu is regarded now-a-days as specially musical among Indian languages. The Vaḍukar were found on the frontier across the hill of Tirupati. Narkīrar speaks of Erumai of Kuḍanāḍu as the chief of the cattle-lifting tribe of Vaḍukar.[1] Another poet gives a Chola ruler a victory at Pāḻi against the Vaḍukar.[2] Thus we find the Vaḍukar all along the northern frontier from sea to sea. When therefore Māmūlanār [3] says that the Mauryas came to the south, sending in front of them the Vaḍukar, the natural interpretation is that they came practically into occupation of the territory which was the natural habitat of these Vaḍukar, and pushed the Vaḍukar in front of them in their further march southward.

Malavar.

Another tribe of people are described almost in the same terms as these Vaḍukar. They are called Maḻavar in Tamil, who suffered a defeat at

---

[1] Aham 253. See Aham. 115, l. 5, for Māmūlanār's reference to Erumai as the chieftain of Kuḍanāḍu.

[2] Iḍaiyan Śēndan Koṟṟan. in Aham 375. [3] Aham 281.

the hands of Neḍuvēḷ Āvi at Podini (Palnis).[1] They were habitually resident in forests and lived by way-laying travellers. They worshipped Naḍukal[2] (stones planted in honour of warriors that fell in battle), and offered sacrifices to them. These are again referred to as uneducated and with raised bows, and entering their country language changed.[3] The forest ways infested by these Maḻavar, says Māmūlanār, were safe as at the time they happened to be under the protection of Kuṭṭuvan[4] (Chera ruler). In another connection the same author refers to the subjugation of these Maḻavar by Pulli of Vēngaḍam.[5] This series of references to the Vaḍukar and Maḻavar, and their being described in almost identical terms would lead to the inference either that the Vaḍukar and the Maḻavar were the same tribe of people, or were at any rate of very similar habits and language. It was already pointed out that this term Vaḍukar, on the analogy of the Kanarese Baḍaga, might be interpreted as northerners. They were northerners to the Tamil in the purely geographical sense; but in the sense of northern Āryas, the term used is Vaḍavar, the grammatically correct form in Tamil.

---

[1] Māmūlanār in Aham. 1.

[2] Ammūvan in Aham 35; also Kuṟal verse 771.

[3] Māmūlanār, Aham 127.

[4] Aham 91. [5] Aham 61.

Kośar.

Passing on to the Kōśar they are referred to as entering the country of Tuḷu by defeating Nannan and killing his state elephant.[1] Nannan's territory included in it both Tuḷu[2] and Konkan (Koṇkānam).[3] These Kōśar are under reference in Aham 196 as having put out the eyes of the father of a lady Anni Gñimili, and to have been destroyed at her instance by two chieftains Kurumbian and Tidiyan.[4] They are found mentioned as Kongiḷam-Kōśar in the Śilappadhikāram, and get themselves associated with the Kongu country (Salem and Coimbatore districts). One clan of them get associated with Podiyal Hill and the tribe that settled there is known as Nallūr Kōśar.[5] In almost the same terms Māmūlanār describes the Kōśar winning a victory against their enemies at Podiyil hill, and as Mōhūr declined to submit to them the Mauryas advanced south.[6] The other poets such as Marudan-Iḷanāgan, Kallāḍanār, Narkīrar and Aiyūr Mūḍavanār make mention of these Kōśar also. Of these the first and the

---

[1] Paraṇar in Kuruṁtogai 73.

[2] Māmūlanār in Aham 15.

[3] Pālai-pāḍiya-Peruṁ-Kaḍungo in Naṟṟiṇai 491.

[4] Paraṇar in Aham 196-262.

[5] Kuruṁitogai ; Perum-Kaḍungo.

[6] Aham 251.

fourth associate the Kōśar with Śellūr. It seems to have been a place in the Chola country.[1] Narkīrar's reference is to a Chola having made an effort to conquer their territory. Kallāḍanār's reference is to their having protected on one occasion the chieftain Aḥdeai. They therefore seem to have been a well-known tribe of people, foreigners to the Tamil country, who settled in various localities ultimately and came to be known as Nālūr Kōśar, meaning the Kōśar that settled in four places, if the particular reading of the first word is correct. Who were these Kōśar and what was their connection with the Mauryas? The suggestion was made elsewhere[2] that these may be a tribe of people the same as the Kōśakāra of the Rāmāyaṇa, and possibly the Khaśas who led the advanced part of the army that marched upon Pāṭalīpura in favour of Chandragupta according to Mudrarākshasa. They were a people who have had a great reputation in the south as warriors and are described invariably as people who kept their word. Kāri-Kaṇṇan of Kaveripaṭṭaṇam refers to the practice of the younger members of this tribe learning the use of weapons by hurling them against a pillar made of the wood of the Murungai[3] (*Erythrina Indica*) tree. The four places of their establishment, if the reading Nālūr is not a

[1] Aham 90 and 220.

[2] Beginnings of South Indian History, pp. 92-95.

[3] Puram., 169.

corruption for Nallūr,[1] would be the Nallūr near Podiyil hill, Śellūr probably in the Chola Country on the east coast [2]; Pāḷi in the Chera country wherefrom they were dislodged by the Cholas; and Kongu south east from this territory. The incidental details brought together from various authors in regard to this particular race of people make a Mauryan effort at the conquest of the south clearly a historical fact.

Asoka's Southern Limit of Empire.

Turning to the inscriptions of Asoka the southernmost limit reached by them is in the north-east corner of the Chitaldroog district of Mysore where Brahmagiri, Siddhāpura and

---

[1] That the Kōśar were known in four divisions is clearly stated in ll. 508-9 of the Maduraik-Kānji. The author there institutes a comparison between the appearance of the four groups of councillors, at the Pāṇḍyan Court (other than the ministers) to the coming of the four sections of the Kōśar "*of unfailing word.*"

[2] There is a Śellūr between the Railway station Koraḍācheri on to Tanjore-Negapatam line, and Koḍaivāśal, a place of some importance now and of great repute in the age of the Śangam. The only objection to the identification is that it is not as near the sea as the texts would require. The local Aiyanār (Śāsta) temple seems identifiable with the "sacrificial abode" of Parasurāma. There is a Śellūr, on the West-Coast associated with Parasurāma, in the Kēraḷolpetti. This work calls the place Parum-Śellūr, great Sellūr. This must have been near Cannanore. The coast near Mont D'Ely is called Rāmandali=Tam. Raman and taḷi or Rāma's temple, and must be regarded as a later settlement or a colony. It may seem farfetched to connect the Kósar with the Cushites who were banished from their native land of Elam after the Assyrian conquest till we get more evidence of a definite character, or identify them with Satiyapatro of the Asoka edicts, taking the word as the Sanskrit Satyaputra.

Jaṭingarāmēśvara hill edicts were discovered. Rock edict II speaks of " his neighbours such as the Chodas, the Panḍiyas, the Satiyaputra, the Keralaputra ; "ambapanni, the Yona king Antiyoka as well as among those who are the vassal kings of that Antiyoka " in connection with the establishment of hospitals, etc. The Vth edict refers to the appointment of the overseers of the Law who were concerned with the " welfare and happiness of my loyal subjects, as also among the Yonas, Kamboyas, Gaṁdharas, Rishṭikas, Piṭinikas and *all other* nations who are my neighbours." In respect of these overseers of the Law a distinction is clearly made between Asoka's loyal subjects forming one class ; Yonas, Piṭinikas and others forming another class, and his neighbours forming the third class. The second of these have therefore to be regarded as not his subjects, nor exactly his neighbours. The geographical position of these would make them his feudatories, the first three being on the north-western frontier, the last two Rishṭikas and Piṭinikas in the coast region set over against the Dakhan plateau, being respectively Rāshṭrikas and Pratishṭhānakas. In Rock edict XIII referring to conquests through the sacred law he claims having effected that conquest over his subjects in his empire and over all his neighbours for a distance of 600 *yojanas* of the country of Aṁtiyoka and the four kings his neighbours. Coming down to the south he refers to the Cholas, the Pāṇḍyas and Tambapanni or Ceylon. Then he proceeds to the second class in edict V of whom specific mention is made of Viśas, Vajris, the Andhras, and Pulidas (Pulindas) apparently tributary communities in the neighbourhood of the emperor's regular territory, but politically tributary to him according to the notions of the Artha Śāstra. Then follows the important statement "even those to whom the messengers of the 'Beloved of the gods' do not go follow the sacred law, as soon as they have heard of the orders of the 'Beloved of the gods' issued in accordance with the sacred law, and his teaching of the sacred law, and they will follow it in future."[1] The corresponding portion of this last statement in Vincent Smith's version of rock edict XIII based on the Shabbasgarhi edicts, reads slightly differently, and the reading may be set down here for comparison "and here too, in the king's dominions, among Yonas, and Kambojas, among the Nābhapantis of Nābhaka, among the Bhojas and Piṭinikas, among the Andhras and Pulindas—everywhere men follow his sacred majesty's instruction in the law of piety. Even where the envoys of his sacred majesty do not penetrate, there all men hearing his sacred majesty's ordinance based on

[1] E. Ind., Vol. II. Bühler's edition of the edicts of Asoka.

the law of piety and his instruction in that law practise and will practise the law." This makes a considerable difference in respect of the recital of the tribes that are concerned. While Smith's version is certainly fuller and more correct than that of Bühler quoted above, the tribes Viśas and Vajris are clearly mentioned in the Shabbasgarhi and Mansera edicts as Visha, Vajri. In the Kalsi version however, the reading[1] is Viśa, Baji. Therefore the *Visha* of the one version is what exactly is *Viśa* in the other, and the Baji of the other version is *Vajra* of the former. The point I am particularly concerned with here is that the Viśas and Vajris are apparently tributary tribes of whom Tamil literature refers to the latter. One passage in the classical work Śilappadhikāram referring to the northern invasion of the great Chola Karikāla states that three kings made him presents which formed the ornaments of his capital Kaveripaṭṭaṇam. Of these three kings one was a friend, another an enemy recently compelled into treaty terms, and the third one was neither friend nor an ally, that is, a neutral. The king of Vajra is referred to as the neutral king who was neither his ally nor his enemy. His territory must have reached the sea-shore at any rate, and is explained by the

[1] *Vide* Rāmāvatāra Sarma's Piyadasi Inscriptions, Variant readings, p. 20.

commentator as territory on the banks of the river Sone. If we make an inference from the general description given, it would mean the territory of Bengal between the Sone and the Ganges reaching down to the sea as it is clearly stated to be bordered by "great waters on all sides." The next king is the king of Magadha who having been an enemy submitted and became his friend. The next one is the king of Avanti who was his ally. The first one presented a canopy of pearls. The king of Magadha gave him what is called a Vidyāmanṭapa,[1] apparently an ornamented platform pillared and roofed over. The king of Malva gave him a triumphal arch by way of a present.[2] The Vajras therefore as a people of considerable importance and holding the important territory of Bengal on this side of the Ganges, were known to the Tamils of the first century A.D.[3] It was apparently a princess of this kingdom, which seems to have been powerful at the time, that Kharavela of Kalinga married.[4] In such a case Simhapura would be the capital of the Gangetic Kalinga included

---

1 For a description of this see-Rājaśēkhara's Kāvyamīmāṁsa. Ch. X.

2 Silappadhikāram, Canto 5, ll. 95-105.

3 Vajra was one of the two divisions of Lāḍha or Rāḍha, the two divisions being Vajjabhūmi and Subbabhūmi. Āyāranga Sutta and other references quoted in "The Ājīvikas" by B. M. Barua, Pt. I, pp. 57-8. Calcutta University Publications.

4 J. B. O. R. S., Vol. IV, p. 378.

in the Kalinga[1] kingdom very often referred to as the capital of Kalinga as a whole.

Asoka's empire then may be regarded in three parts; the whole of Hindustan, the country between the Vindyas and the Himalayas, with an outstretch along the west coast to take in the Piṭinikas, Rishṭikas, and along the east coast to take in the whole of Kalinga, would have constituted his own kingdom. Then comes the borderland of the great forest of Daṇḍaka. On the frontiers of the forest were situated the territory of the several of the semi-civilised tribes till we come to about 14° of north latitude roughly. These had been reduced to some kind of allegiance which apparently involved the responsibility of paying tribute and being in the kind of tribal subordination recognised in the Artha Sāstra. Then follow naturally the territories of his southern neighbours. This disposition is what is actually reflected in Tamil literature which states in clear terms that Pulikat was the northern boundary in the east and that Tuḷu-Konkan the kingdom of Nannan was the western boundary, a whole belt of country across being occupied by tribes whom the Tamilians called Vaḍukar. These were border-tribes engaged in cattle-lifting and

[1] Referred along with Kapilapuram in the Silappadhikāram as the two capitals of Kalinga; Canto XXIII, ll. 140-41.

waylaying people as occasion offered. Referring to the achievements of a Chera ruler who is known to literature Āḍukoṭpāṭṭu-Śeral-Ādan, that is, the Chera who captured cattle, the poetess Kakkaipāḍiniyār Nachchel̤l̤aiyār states in clear terms that he captured cattle in *Danḍā-raṇyam*, distributed them in Tonḍi, among Brahmans, giving along with these one special kind of a cow classified as *kapilai* (a cow of a dark colour, the darkness spreading over even to the udder) and a village in Kuḍa-nāḍu (western hill country), and having defeated the other Mal̤avar, in battle turned back the kings, apparently their kings. The term Danḍāraṇya in this reference is explained by the old commentator as a nāḍu or division of country in Ārya-Nāḍu thus confirming the statement in the Śarabhanga Jātaka that Dandaka was a Bhoja-kingdom with capital Kumbhavatī. This means clearly that the forest of Danḍa or Danḍaka was, according to the political divisions of those days, included in the territory of the Āryas as distinct from the Tamils, the semi-civilised tribe or tribes being interposed between the two frontiers across the whole of the Peninsula.

Buddhist Propaganda stopped short of the Tamil Land.

This political southern limit of Asoka's empire marks also the limits of active Buddhist propaganda reflected in the last sentence quoted above from rock edict XIII. The meaning of this statement in the edict is that while people in the neighbouring kingdoms followed the teachings of the Buddha of their own motion the active propagation of the gospel that he actually organised stopped short of this limit. This inference is confirmed by what we find detailed in the Mahāvaṁśa of Ceylon. Referring to the missions for the propagation of the faith sent to various localities for the purpose of spreading the teachings of "the enlightened one" the Mahāvaṁśa has the following passage: "When the *thera* Moggaliputta, the illuminator of the religion of the conqueror had brought the (third) council to an end and when, looking into the future, he had beheld the founding of the religion in adjacent countries, (then) in the month of Kattika he sent forth *theras*, one here and one there. The *thera* Majjhantika he sent to Kasmira and Gandhara, the *thera* Mahadeva he sent to Mahiṣamaṇḍala. To Vanavāsa he sent the *thera* named Rakkhita, and to Aparāntaka the Yona named Dhammarakkhita, but the *thera* Mahārakkhita he sent into the country of the Yona. He sent the *thera* Majjhima to the Himalaya country, and to Suvaṇṇabhūmi he sent the two *theras* Sona and Uttara. The great *thera* Mahinda, the *theras* Itthiya, Uttiya, Sambala and Bhaddhasala his disciples, these five *theras* he sent forth with the charge: "Ye shall found in the lovely island of Lanka the lovely religion of the Conqueror."

In this recital the places referable to the country south of the Vindhyas stopped short at Vanavāsa, all the other places being obviously north of Vanavāsa with the doubtful exception of Māhiṣamanḍala. This was hitherto identified with what is now the state of Mysore, but from Tamil literature we find the present state of Mysore occupied altogether otherwise, though undoubtedly one frontier chieftain of Kuḍanāḍu (western hill country) was known by the name Erumai (Sans. Mahiṣa) and apparently gave the name to the country in the following generations. It could hardly be regarded as the country to which Asoka's mission was sent as it is doubtful if it was known by that name in the days of Asoka. Māhiṣmatī the capital city of the Māhiṣakas has satisfactorily been identified with Māndhāta on the Narbada round which there were a tribe of people called Māhiṁsakas. The Māhiṣmanḍala of Asoka's mission has to be referred to that district. Hence Vanavāsa,

Banavase in Dharwar the capital of the division of Banavase 12,000 was the southernmost limit of the missionary activity of Asoka.

The great centres of Buddhist activity get enumerated in another context in the Mahāvaṁśa. The Ceylon ruler Duṭṭagāmaṇi Abhaya held a great congregation on the occasion of laying the foundation stone of the Great Stūpa (Mahā Vihāra) that he constructed. To this congregation he invited the priestly communities from the various well-known Buddhist centres. This invitation was responded to by brethren of the holy order in as many as fourteen centres, the centres being:—Rajagṛha, the ancient capital of Magadha, Iśitapatana, the deer park in Benares, Jetārāma-Vihāra in Śrāvasti in Nepal-Tarai, Mahāvana in Vaisalī (North Bengal), Ghositārāma in Kauśāmbi not far from Allahabad, Dakkhiṇagiri-Vihāra in Ujjain in Malva, Aśokārāma in Pupphapura (Pāṭalīputra or Patna), Kasmir, Pallava-bhogga, probably somewhere in the region of the Indus, Alasanda of the Yonas, probably the Alexandria represented by the modern Uch in the north of Sindh, "the road through the Vindhyan forest mountains" possibly the centre Māhiṣmatī of the Mahīṣa-maṇḍala, Bodhimaṇḍa-vihāra (Bodh-Gaya), the Vanavāsa country and lastly the great Kēḷāsa-vihāra." This Kailāsa-vihāra may refer to Amarāvati in the Guntur district while it is barely possible it may refer to Ellora in the Nizam's dominions; but the trend of the description would indicate the former rather than the latter. This detailed list of Buddhist centres excludes the Tamil country altogether. Whether the representatives actually came or no is a different matter. But these were centres of holy reputation at the time in the estimation of the author. He apparently had recourse to older chronicles kept in the Mahāvihāra, the construction of which is under discussion. If the Tamil country did contain any vihāra of similar reputation it is not likely that that would be omitted in the narration. Hence the inference seems quite warranted that active Buddhist propaganda stopped short of the Tamil land both in the days of Asoka and in the centuries following almost to the middle of the century before Christ. Remembering that there was nothing to prevent individual Buddhists, or even bodies of them, following the bent of their mind in matters of religion even in the Tamil country, it is clear that the active propaganda under the imperial impulse of Asoka might still have stopped short of the Tamil country. That seems the state of things in respect of Buddhism reflected in this body of Tamil literature referring to the times under discussion.

THE NORTHERN LIMIT OF TAMIL LAND.

In the previous sections the limits of Tamil land were marked by a belt of country beginning with Pulikat on the east coast and terminating with the Kalyānpuri river, the northern limit of Kanara on the west coast. On the farther side of this frontier were the class of people regarded as robbers by profession and described in Tamil literature as Vaḍukar, who extended even southward of this frontier line in certain localities. This is just exactly the limit indicated in the Periplus for the Tamil country as all the Dakhan further north fell into a distinct category which the author of the Periplus[1] called Dachinabades (Sans. Dakshiṇāpatha). According to this author "beyond Baryagaza (Broach) the adjoining coast extends in a highland from north to south; and so this region is called Dachinabades, for Dachinos in the language of the natives means "south," *the inland country back from the coast towards the east comprises many desert regions and great mountains and all kinds of wild beasts—leopards, tigers, elephants, enormous serpents, hyenas and baboons of many sorts and many populous nations as far as the Ganges.*" The work further states that all the muslins, etc., of the east coast of this

[1] Edn. by W. Shoff, p. 43.

country had to be brought across "great tracts without roads" to the two marts of Paethana (Paiṭhān) on the Godaveri and Tagara (Ter, in the Nizam's dominions). The limit of this region is marked at "White island" on the west coast, an island situate a little to the north-west of Mangalore with which according to this author Damirica (Dramiḍaka or Tamiḻakam) began. This description of the country set against the west coast from Broach to Mangalore almost, will answer to the description of the Tamils who called the whole region, a little more or less, Danḍāraṇyam. According to the information that could be gathered from Tamil literature of this period the western boundary of this forest region would stop short somewhere near Goa on the west coast. Next the frontier on this side came the Tuḷu-Konkan territory of the Tamil Chief Nannan. To the south of this territory was the territory of Keraḷa, the land of the Chēras. One Chēra ruler of this time went by the name, rather a distinguishing epithet, "Āḍu-kotpāṭṭu-Śēral-Ādan," *i.e.*, the Chēra king who carried off cattle. This Chēra is celebrated in the sixth "ten" of the classical collection called "ten[1] tens" by a poetess by name Kakkaipāḍiniyār Nachchellaiyār; in other words "the poetess the good Śeḷḷai who sang of the

[1] Pandit Maha. Swaminatha Aiyar's edn., 98-99.

crow." In the epilogue he is said to have taken these cattle in Daṇḍāraṇyam which the commentator explains as a division of country in Āryanāḍu or Āryadēśa. Thus then it is clear that across the northern frontier of the Tamil country was a belt of land occupied by various tribes, and behind them was the great forest country of Daṇḍaka, the far-famed Daṇḍaka of the Rāmāyaṇa and the Mahākāntāra perhaps of a later time.

CHAPTER II.

BRAHMANISM IN THE TAMIL LAND.

Tamil tradition of comparatively late age describes the Tamil country as mainly composed of forests and practically uninhabited till Agastya came from the far north. In a solemn conclave on the Himalayas the Dēvas and the Rishis had assembled on one occasion. Finding the earth sinking from the weight of the august assembly and much exercised about this phenomenon, they hit upon the device of sending somebody to the south to balance the assembled weight of the north, and pitched upon Agastya, who alone of all those assembled was capable of balancing the rest of them all together. When the request was made to him he readily agreed to proceed on such a great errand of benefit to this divine humanity. Starting southwards therefore on this beneficent mission Agastya went first to the Ganges and obtained from her the river Kāveri. Then he went to the Rishi Jamadagni and took from him his son Tṛṇadhūmāgni, and from Rishi Pulastya his virgin sister Lopāmudrā. Going further onward in his journey he came to Dvāraka, and took from there 18 of the ruling family of Vishṇu (Vṛṣṇis), and 18 crores of two classes of people Vēḷir and Aruvāḷar. With such a following he proceeded south destroying the forests, and transforming the forest-region into inhabited country till he made his home in the hill of Podiyil in the southern part of the Western Ghats keeping Rāvaṇa and his Rākshasas away from that part of the country. It was then that he ordered his disciple, the son of Jamadagni to go and fetch his wife, keeping a distance of four rods' length on all sides of her in the course of their journey. As they were crossing the river Vaigai a sudden flood carried her off. Going forward to her assistance, and, putting forward a bamboo stick for her to take hold of, the dutiful pupil brought her successfully out of the water, and then took her to his master. For this transgression of instructions Agastya pronounced both of them ineligible for entry into heaven. Protesting their innocence they in turn said that he might have a similar fate also for his inconsiderate anger. It was on account of this anger of the master that he directed his disciple's grammar Tolkāppiyam, as the disciple assumed the name Tolkāppiyar, since his advent into the Tamil country, be not heard. The point in this story is that the reclamation of the forest tracts in this region is somehow associated with a southern migration led by Agastya, and among the tribes that came with him are found mentioned Vēḷir and Aruvāḷar, two well-known peoples of Tamil India. For this Tamil land the most accepted boundary given is the Tirupati hill in the north (Viḍavēngaḍam), Cape Comorin (Kanyākumārī) in the south, and the two seas on either side. Whenever this great migration took place, and whether such a migration was historical or no, there is something like the march of civilisation from the north into the south, and under northern guidance and influence. Agastya himself came and brought a disciple along with him, the son of another sage. Along with him came presumably the northern culture especially associated with the Brahman.

Leaving tradition aside we have evidence, in the earliest extant literature of the Tamil land, of the very high position ascribed to the Brahman in the literature of the south. In one of the earliest of the Tamil classics recently made available a king is described as following the path of the "Andaṇar" (Brahmans) who follow the Dharma by doing the six duties imposed upon them by immemorial prescription. These are described as learning and teaching, sacrificing and conducting sacrifices, receiving gifts made to them and making gifts to others.[1] In the same collection comes later on a reference to another monarch of the same dynasty where he is spoken of as "not knowing obedience except to Brahmans." The authors in these two cases happen to be themselves Brahmans. In the one, the author was a Brahman by name Gautama who was distinguished for composing poems in a particular mode in Tamil. He celebrated the father of Śeṁ-Kuṭṭuvan and requested as a favour that he and his Brahman wife should go to heaven. This Chera consulted other elderly Brahmans how this could be done to Gautama. Under their advice he celebrated ten *Vēdic* sacrifices on the completion of the tenth of which the Brahman and his wife ceased to be visible. The other one is the famous poet by name Kapilar. This Brahman was regarded as a model of a virtuous man and spoken of in such terms by poets who were not themselves Brahmans. He celebrates another Chera by name Śelvak-Kaḍungo. The same description of the ordinary occupation of the Brahman is given in the classical grammar Tolkāppiyam where the Grammarian lays down what were the customary occupations of the Brahmans. The same six occupations are there given as those to which they generally devoted themselves.[2] Almost the

---

[1] Padiṟṟup.attu, Poem 24, ll. 6 to 8.
[2] Poruḷ, Sūtra,75.

same language is used in referring to the Brahman by Buddhist and Jain writers in similar connections. The Śilappadhikāram, a work of the Chēra prince-ascetic Iḷangō, refers to what happened to Gautama above referred to in the account that is given of a Brahman Parāśara of the Chola country who went on a visit to the Chera "who gave heaven itself to the Brahman Gautama," having heard of his great liberality. In describing this Brahman this author[1] speaks of him as one devoted to the attainment of heaven, of two births, whose wealth consisted in the three fires, whose learning embraced the four *Vēdas*, who had special charge of the celebration of the five sacrifices and whose chief occupation consisted of the six items: learning and teaching, sacrificing and conducting sacrifices for others, receiving in gift and giving, brought in under the same epic category as the grammatical enumeration referred to in Tolkāppiyam above "of the victorious Brahman" (pārppana-vākai). Strangely enough on his return journey he came to a Buddha Vihāra[2] at a Brahman village Tangāl in the Pāndya country and halted there in the course of his journey. In the companion work Maṇimekhalai[3] also we come upon references almost exactly the same

[1] Canto XXIII, ll. 62 to 80.

[2] See Arthaśāstra.

[3] Canto XIII.

in tenor to the occupation of the Brahman although that work, true to its character, in one connection [1] holds up to ridicule the celebration of these sacrifices by inflicting pain upon the animals sacrificed. It will thus be seen that although these references are found in the literature of the first centuries of the Christian era they indicate an immigration of the Brahman in times much anterior, and the character of the Brahmanism of which we gain glimpses in this literature shows itself to be pre-Buddhistic.

The Pre-Buddhistic Character of Brahmanism in the Tamil Country.

We have already referred to the Brahmanical tradition concerning the coming into the south of Agastya. Buddhist tradition has altogether a different version of the coming of Agastya into the Tamil country. According to the Akitta Jātaka which relates to a Brahman magnate's son and daughter who renounced their vast wealth and settled down near the banks of the Ganges some leagues farther down from Benares, Agastya the brother remained in the new settlement for some time. Finding that even in the forest people came to him in large

---

[1] Canto XIII, ll. 29-38.

numbers he left the place unknown to his sister and travelled through the Tamil country (kingdom of Damila), and took up his abode in a park in Kāvēripaṭṭaṇa (the capital of the Cholas at the mouth of the Kāvēri). Even there he was not left in the isolation he desired; he therefore flew across to an island called Kāra set over against the island of the Nāgas. This Kāradīpa was also called Ahi-dīpa or the isle of snakes. In the island and in the rock-cell hermitage which he took up for his residence he could find nothing to eat except the leaves of the *kāra* tree (*Canithium Parviflorum*) that grew there which he used to wet in the water and boil and eat without salt or spices. When in that condition, Indra came in the guise of a Brahman to beg for alms. Akitta gave the prepared food each time Indra appeared, himself not taking any. It is to exhibit the merit of this gift that Buddha is said to have related the story on a particular occasion Akitta is generally taken to stand for Agastya, but there is so little common between the Brahmanical tradition concerning Agastya and this story that the identification itself would seem not to have very much to support it excepting the name. But the Buddhistic work Maṇimēkhalai has certain references to Agastya. He carried the water that flowed afterwards as the Kaveri, in his water vessel (*kamanḍala*), and at the request of a Chola king Kāndama, he let the water flow as the river Kāvēri. This king at one time was afraid of the coming of Paraśurāma, and sought asylum of Agastya having entrusted the kingdom to his illegitimate son Kākanda. Agastya gave him the asylum on that occasion. Another Chola king whose name is not specifically given was advised by Agastya to celebrate the annual festival to Indra which lasted for 28 days, during which period all the Dēvas even left their abodes and were resident in Kaveripaṭṭaṇam. The Chola capital Kaveripaṭṭaṇam had the name Champā because Champā-Patī, the goddess of Jambudvīpa, made it her place of residence. When the Kaveri began to flow through that town the name was altered.[1] In either of these two cases the connection of Agastya is with the Chola country and the river Kaveri. But the Maṇimēkhalai refers to Agastya as "the ascetic of rare austerity of the Malaya (mountain),"[2] making it clear that he is referring to Agastya of the Brahmanical tradition associated with Malaya or Podiyil hill in the southern part of the Western Ghats. The tradition connecting Agastya with the south therefore seems to be an accredited tradition of long standing; and his coming into this part of the country is symbolical of the breaking in of Aryan

[1] Maṇimēkhalai, Padikam (prologue).

[2] Canto I, l. 3.

civilisation into the Tamil land. It would therefore seem inferable that the Brahmanism such as was prevalent in the Tamil country must be Brahmanism of pre-Buddhistic character. That it was so is in evidence in the importance that is invariably attached to the position of the Brahman as the conductor of the sacrifices intended for the good of the community as a whole.

That this was the character of Brahmanism in the Tamil country is clear from a poem included in the collection Puṛanānūṛu. It is a poem by Mūlam-Kiḻār of Āvūr in celebration of the learning and character of the Brahman Kauṇiyan Viṇṇam-Tāyan of Pūm-Śā ṛūr in Śoṇāḍu (Chola country). The first part of the passage refers to his being a descendant of a family of learned men who made it their life occupation to study by means of the six auxiliary sciences (*angas*), the four *Vedas* whose one object was truth, and which was perpetually in the tongue of Śiva himself. This great learning was attained by them in order that they may be enabled thereby to beat down all those outer religions which base themselves on works which set themselves against the Vēda. Having acquired this learning they understood the false teachings of those religions which appeared like truths, and exhibiting their false character established the truth of the *Vēdic* religion by celebrating sacrifices in the twenty-one[1] orthodox ways. "Coming of such a family you wear a bit of deer skin in the thread lying across the body adorning your shoulders. Your wives constant in their chastity, wearing the jewel specifically assigned to wives of those that celebrate sacrifices, and possessed of personal charms conduct themselves in full accordance with your station. They carry out your commands by making ghee flow like water by tending the several kinds of cows whether you lived in forest or in country. With their assistance, having celebrated innumerable sacrifices and spread your fame over the whole earth, you shine by feeding largely at the end of the sacrifices those that attended. May we have the good fortune to see this exalted position of yours for ever. Let me go back to the place full of the gardens on either side of the Kaveri which brings in freshes as soon as it thunders on the Western Ghats, and thus fosters the earth. I shall enjoy your vast gifts by eating that which ought to be eaten, and riding that which ought to be ridden, and thus celebrate your liberality. You remain on earth where you are, firm as the Himalayas with high sloping sides, making like the Himalayas themselves unfailing rain." This poem is intended to celebrate the excellence

[1] This is also interpreted as the 21 methods of logic, or the 21 ways of interpretation.

in Brahmanical accomplishments and is therefore specifically intended to give an idea as to what exactly a Brahman's learning and conduct were expected to be in those times. The poet who celebrates the Brahman in this wise is, as the title indicates, not a Brahman himself, and the character that he gives to the orthodox Brahman here is supported in full by the corresponding *sūtras* of the Tolkāppiyam. The commentators of the Sūtras quote this poem as the illustration *par excellence.* It is not the Brahman alone that comes in for praise for his faithful performance of sacrifices. One of the earliest known Pāṇḍyan kings is known to fame as one that celebrated many sacrifices. The poet Neṭṭimaiyār asks the question whether the sacrificial posts he planted after celebrating various sacrifices are in larger numbers, or those enemies that live in disgrace, having been defeated and turned back by his valour.[1] A later Pāṇḍya grant known as the Vēḷvik-kuḍi grant refers to a gift by this Pāṇḍyan of the village, the title to which was established by satisfactory proof.[2] A Chola contemporary of the poetess Avvaiyār is known by the name "The Great Chola who celebrated the Rājasūya."[3]

A great Chera—the younger brother of the "Chera of the Himalayan boundary" and uncle

---

[1] Puṟanānūṟu, Poem 16, pp. 17-21.

[2] Epi. Rep., 1908, Sec. 20 (Madras).

[3] *Ibid*, poem 367 by Avvaiyār.

of the Red-Chera celebrated ten sacrifices and gave heaven itself to the Brahman Pālai Gautama [1] and his wife.

Thus we see that Tamil kings had adopted the practice of getting sacrifices celebrated—the peculiar function of the Brāhmaṇa according to the accepted canon of law of the Tamil land.

This is not altogether the only detail of pre-Buddhistic Brahmanism which we find in these Tamil classics. There are clear indications of the kind of theism which could be generally described as Bhakti where people could devote themselves to the service of the god of their heart with the assurance of salvation. Four such sections find prominent mention according to the peculiar form of god to which people composing these sections devoted themselves. Four such gods get mention in a poem by Narkīrar,[2] an early and a very prominent poet of the Śangam. Celebrating his contemporary Pāṇḍyan, he points to the special qualities in which he resembled each one of the four "world-protecting gods." These are according to him respectively Śiva of the "dark-throat," Baladēva of "white colour" with the plough for his weapon, Krishṇa of the deep-blue colour with flag of *the bird* (Garuḍa) and Subrahmaṇya (the Red-One) of the "Pea-cock carrier." Of

---

[1] Paddiṟṟuppattu-"Ten-tens," section 2.

[2] Puṟam., 56.

these the Pāṇḍya addressed resembled in anger Death himself, in strength Baladeva, in fame Krishṇa or Vishṇu, in determination in carrying out his wishes Subrahmaṇya. It must be noted that Śiva described circumstantially in the first part is equated with Death in the second, as Rudra is specifically associated in the Trinity with destruction. Almost the same four are found mentioned as the guardians of the different kinds of land in the Tolkāppiyam. The forest country is under the special protection of Krishṇa or Vishṇu, the hill country under Subrahmaṇya, the cultivated country under the protection of Indra and the coast country under the protection of Varuṇa. Here the two Indra and Varuṇa come in in place of the two Śiva and Baladēva. It is hardly necessary to describe the possible significance of these discrepancies, but it seems to imply the recognition of the six as distinct entities rather than postulating the non-existence of any two. Describing the temples that were in existence in Kaverippaṭṭaṇam, the author of the Śilappadhikāram,[1] refers to a temple of Śiva, to one of Subrahmaṇya, to one of Baladēva and to one of Vishṇu or Krishṇa in the order stated, followed by the temple of Indra the festival to whom the canto actually describes.[2]

---

[1] Canto V, ll. 169-175.

[2] Compare the deities invoked in the Nanāghat Inscription of the Sātavāhana Queen Nāganikā; No. 1112. Lūder's list of Brahmi Inscriptions, Ep. Ind., X.

This is summarised in the companion work Maṇimēkhalai by the statement that temples beginning with that of Śiva with an eye in the centre of his face, and ending with that of the guardian-deity of the public square (Bhūta of the Chatushka) "should all be tidied for the coming festival."[1] Much the same idea is found expressed in ll. 453-9 of the poem Madurak-Kānji by the poet Māngudi Marudan.

We therefore seem warranted in inferring that the Brahmanism that prevailed in the Tamil country was in character pre-Buddhistic, and had for one of its specific objects an exhibition of the heretical character of the sister religions, Buddhism and Jainism. This gives a certain controversial character to it which is not altogether strange having regard to the character of both Buddhism and Jainism. This body of literature exhibits the existence of these religions side by side with Brāhmanism, having attained to a certain amount of organisation for effective controversy.

Tamil opposition to Buddhism on behalf of Brahmanism.

We have noticed above already that Aśoka's propaganda in favour of Buddhism stopped short of the Tamil country. That it did not get into the Tamil country is clearly in evidence in the

[1] Canto 1, ll. 54-57.

fact that no important Buddhist centre indubitably referable to the Tamil country is found enumerated among those that sent delegates to the great assembly for the consecration of the Mahāvihāra in Ceylon in the 2nd century B.C. That coupled with the knowledge of the country in the period previous to the Christian era we gain from Tamil literature, would warrant the conclusion that the advance of Buddhism into the Tamil country in the fashion contemplated by Asoka was kept back by force But this is confirmed by the opposition set up in the Tamil land against the encroachment of the northerner of which we get glimpses in this body of Tamil literature. Aśoka would not have stopped short in his propagandist mission if he could have carried it into the Tamil country although it is possible that the self-abnegation that prompted desistance from war might be regarded sufficient explanation. This latter fact, however, would not explain his abstention from propagandism of the organised character that he carried through in the rest of India. Along with this has to be taken the number of references in Tamil literature to the Āryans (Vaḍavar) being beaten back. It is just likely that we shall have to take into consideration the wars against the Vaḍukar also in various localities, which would not have been undertaken by the rude tribes along the northern frontier unless there was an organised power behind them, either to incite them to it, or at least to encourage them if they did it. The early Chola, Pāṇḍya and Chēra rulers, all of them take credit for achievements against the Aryas of the north. The Chola Karikāla, the Pāṇḍya Neḍuṁ-Śeḻiyan and the Chēra Neḍum-Śēral all of them claim to have set their emblems on the Himalayas, and even the Malayamān chieftain of Tirukkōvilūr is given credit for having beaten back an Āryan force besieging his citadel of Muḷḷūr. Even omitting the references to the Vaḍukar for the time,[1] this opposition seems to have been set up not so very much in mere hostility to the peaceful pursuit of Buddhism or Jainism; but seems essentially intended for securing the freedom for the unfettered pursuit of Brāhmanism in the Tamil country. This it would be difficult to explain except by the assumption that in the empire of Aśoka, it was difficult to pursue this form of religion unmolested if not by active persecution at least by the propagandist effort at the imposition of a certain kind of uniformity, or much rather conformity.

---

[1] For actual references see pp. 95-100 of my Beginnings of South Indian History.

The Continuity of Hindu Culture in the South.

A special feature of its History.

It is this state of things, of which we gain a direct glimpse only from Tamil literature, that gives character to South Indian History—for the earliest period of the history of the Tamil country. Brāhmanism having found a welcome home in this region when Buddhism was in the ascendency in North India, pursued its path unmolested, if it did not actually occupy a position of advantage in comparison with the other two religions. This freedom made the Tamil country at this period, as it proved in other later periods, a special refuge to Aryan culture whenever it was hard pressed in the North. From this period onward Brāhmanism both in its early and in its later developments went on continuously unmolested, not uninfluenced, by the various changes that took place across the Tamil frontier. In this body of literature and in this particular period we see a certain amount of development in the *āgamic* worship of the Vaishṇava Pāncharātrins. There is nothing exactly to show that the Śaiva *āgama* did not come in along with this into the Tamil country although we have not come across any direct statement of it so far in the same manner as the Vaishṇava. That with the spread of Buddhism and Jainism there was a collateral development of the Orthodox Brāhmanism in the middle country of northern India seems warranted by the position of these religions in the Tamil country. The rise of the school of Bhakti which Sir R. G. Bhandarkar laboured hard, but successfully, to prove as a normal development from the Upanishadic culture, receives welcome support from the position of this particular school of Brahmanism in the south. This establishes an intimate connection, in the age to which this body of literature has special reference, between the north and the south. This special development could not have been on this side of the Christian era if the intimate connection of the development both in the north and in the south has to be taken as established, as we have to, on the basis of this evidence.

ITS CONNECTION WITH THE NORTH.

This special development in the south of the orthodox systems of Brahmanism of the north apparently took form with the rise of the Sungas to power in northern India. Pushyamitra's was perhaps the first organised effort for the revivification of Brahmanism in the face of a foreign enemy like the Greeks of Bactria thundering at the gates of orthodox India both in the political sense of a foreign enemy, and in the sacerdotal conception of heretics in religion. This opposition, although comparatively short-lived in the case of Pushyamitra and his successors, seems to have put a new heart into the southerners of the orthodox creed, and given them the occasion to organise themselves for any possible struggle against their rivals. Apart from the various references in Tamil literature to the north and of the claims put forward for conquest against the Āryans which ought to be referred to the period following—the period of Āndhra dominance—the period of this religious ferment and activity seems referable to the period of revival under the Sungas and Kaṇvas. That such connection was maintained even politically is in evidence in the Kharavela inscription itself.

The Kharavela Inscription.

The famous Hathigumpha inscription of Kharavela which has been recently read and re-read and published by Mr. K. P. Jayaswal in the Bihar and Orissa Research Society's Journal, and the controversy over which is not yet unfortunately over, has one detail which seems clearly to refer to the sending of tribute or presents in the shape of elephants and valuable jewels from the Pāṇḍya country. These presents were sent over-sea. In itself, communication over-sea with Kalinga is quite possible, and that raises actually no difficulty; and if presents did come from there it must be of the character described. If the reading of the inscription in regard to that particular part is put beyond a doubt, that would establish communication between Kalinga and the south. In the period following, the great Chola Karikāla went north as was pointed out already and received in his turn presents from the kings of Vajra, Magadha and Malva or Avanti. The existence of a country like Vajra in the valley of the Sone is brought to our notice only in this connection. And that possibility finds confirmation in another reference in the same Hathigumpha inscription where Kharavela is said to have married a princess of the Vajra royal family. This reference seems to give the character of historicity to the references contained in Tamil literature, in a connection to which captious objections, may, it is just possible, be raised. This inscriptional reference to a geographical detail like that puts the character of the literary reference on a somewhat better footing. We shall have to revert to this point later.

THE DAWN OF THE CHRISTIAN ERA.

The country south of the Krishna was divided among 'the three crowned Kings' and seven chieftains, with an eighth coming somewhat later. There were a host of minor chieftains of lesser dignity. It is the coast region and the more open country that belonged to the kings, while the middle regions of hills and forests belonged to the chieftains, and perhaps even a few tribes (Nāgas and others). The east coast from Pulikat to the south of Tonḍi in the Zemindari of Ramnad, belonged to the Chola, although midway between the kingdom proper and its northern viceroyalty of Kānchī lay the hill-country round Tirukkovilūr in the possession of a class of chieftains named Malayamān; and between his territory and the coast the chieftains of Oymā-nāḍu very often loyal supporters of their suzerain, occasionally turbulent and rebellious. South of the Chola kingdom lay that of the Pānḍya, which extended from coast to coast, and embraced within its borders the modern districts of Madura and Tinnevelly, and the State of Travancore, taking in also a part of Coimbatore and Cochin. This included in it the chieftaincies of Āay. (The Aioi of Ptolemy) round the Podiyil hill in the Western Ghats and the domains of Pēhan round the Palnis which come under their sphere of influence as well. North of this and along the Western Ghats on the sea-side lay the territory of the Chera; a territory stretching right across the Palghat gap through Salem and Coimbatore. South Mysore was parcelled out among a number of chieftains corresponding to the modern Pāḷayagars, whose allegiance was at the disposal of either, but the more powerful of their neighbour kings. Such were the Irungō of Araiyam, Pāri of Parambunāḍ (west of the Kaveri in Kongu), Adiyamān of Tagaḍuṛ (Dharmapuri) and Ori of the Koḷḷimalais. The first of these was within the Mysore territory proper and to the east of his domain lay the Gangas, and Kongu to the south. The northern frontier of the Tamil land was held by Nannan of the Tuḷu country and Konkaṇ in the west, and Pulli of Vēngaḍam (Tirupati) in the east, the further north having been the land of the Vaḍukar and Danḍāraṇyam (Sans. Danḍa-kāraṇyam).

These chieftaincies were the bone of contention between the Cholas and the Cheras. When the period under treatment begins, the Cholas were supreme under Karikāla, who ascended the throne, probably after defeating the Chera and Pānḍya in a battle at Veṇṇil (Koilveṇṇi as it is now called) in the Tanjore District. He was a remarkable sovereign who, in many ways, contributed to the permanent welfare of his subjects, and has consequently been handed down to posterity as a beneficent and wise monarch. He constructed the embankments for the Kaveri, and his chief port Puhār was the great emporium of the east coast. His reign was long, and, taken along with those of his two predecessors and the successor next following him, constitutes the period of the first Chola ascendancy in the south. In the reign of his successor a great catastrophe befell Puhār, and the city and port were both destroyed. This was a hard blow to the ascendancy of the Cholas. But Karikāla had, after defeating his contemporary Chēra, given probably one of his daughters (it is just possible a sister) in marriage to the son of his vanquished rival. This alliance stood the Cholas in good stead. Karikāla's successor began his reign with a victory, which his heir-apparent won for him, against the Chēra and Pāṇḍya combined at Kāriyār, probably in the Salem District. When Puhār was destroyed, at least in part, there was a civil war owing perhaps to the untimely death of the young Chola prince; and the Chēra ruler for the time being, advanced through the central region. He intervened in favour of his cousins with effect, as against the rival claimants of royal blood, and restored the Chola dynasty to some power; but the ascendancy surely enough passed from them to the Chēra.

The Chēra ascendancy under the "Red Chēra" (Śenguṭṭuvan) lasted only one generation. In the reign of his successor the Pāṇḍyas rose to greater importance, and the Chēra suffered defeat and imprisonment at his hands. This Pāṇḍya ascendancy probably lasted on somewhat longer till about the rise of the Pallavas in Kānchī. This course of the political centre of gravity in southern India is borne out in very important particulars by the Ceylon chronicle called the Mahāvaṁśa. According to this work, the Cholas were naturally the greatest enemies of the Singalese rulers. There were usurpers from the Chola country in Ceylon in the first century B.C.; and there were invasions and counter-invasions as well. On one occasion the Chola invaders carried away 12,000 inhabitants of Ceylon and set them to work at 'the Kaveri' as the Chronicle has it.[1] This looks very much like an exploit of Karikāla seeing that it was he who either built the city of Puhār, or greatly extended it. King Gajabāhu of Ceylon[2] was present at the invitation of the Red-Chēra, to witness the celebration........... of a sacrifice and the consecration of the temple to the "Chaste Lady" (Pattini Dēvi) at Vanji on the west coast.

[1] Upham's Mahāvaṁśa. Vol. i. p. 228.

[2] Śilappadhikāram, Canto. 30. l. 160. apart from the prologue.

The ascendancy of the Chēra, however, passed away as already mentioned, to the Pāndyas in the course of one single generation. The Red-Chēra was succeeded by his son or successor, "the Chēra of the elephant look," who was his predecessor's viceroy at Tondi, and figured prominently in his wars in the middle region. He was defeated and taken prisoner in a battle, which he had to fight with the contemporary Pāndyan, designated the victor at Talaiyālanganam. With this mishap to the ruler the Chēra ascendancy passes away. The Pāndyans of Madura take their turn now, and continued to hold the position of hegemony up to the time that the Pallavas rise into importance. This, in brief and in very general terms, was the political history of South India at the beginning and during the early centuries of the Christian era.

CHAPTER III.

Connection with Ceylon, Generally one of Hostility.

Ceylon was known to the ancients perhaps as early as South India itself, and Tamil literature contains a few references earlier than that in Buddhist tradition, which associate the island with the story of the Rāmāyaṇa. In one poem,[1] a poet of the city of Madura who is known by the name Kaḍuvan Maḷḷanār, who was by profession " an actor in the Tamil mode," refers to the ancient Kōḍi (Kori of the classical geographers, end of " the bridge " as the commentator renders it) of the Kauriyar (Pāṇḍyas) where in the foreshore of the boisterous sea the warlike Rama held, with his companions, a council under a big banian tree, when by a mere look he put an end to the noise that the birds were making on the tree. This " Council of Rama " is apparently the Council held for constructing the dam across the sea to reach the Lanka of Rāvaṇa. There is another reference in an early poet Ūnpodi Paśum-Koḍaiyār in a poem,[2]

[1] Aham 70, ll. 13-16. [2] Puram, 378.

celebrating the famous Chola Iḷam-Śēṭ-Śenni who destroyed Śeṛup-Pāḷi. The reference there is to the abduction of Sītā by Rāvaṇa, and the incident is brought in there for a comparison to the wondering monkeys which took up the jewels she dropped while she was being carried across in the aerial car. The next poem of the same collection refers to Lanka as the territory of one Villi Ādan. There are references in the Śilappadhikāram to three incidents of the Rāmāyaṇa. The first is Rama's going to the forest at the command of the father (XIII. ll. 63-66). The next is to divine Rama having gone to the forest at the command of the father and being put to great sorrow owing to his separation from his wife. (XIV ll. 46-49). The third relates to the going of Rama and his brother to the forest and the destruction of well-fortified Lanka (XVII, p. 401). There is a similar reference to the building of the bridge of Rama, alluding to materials thrown in going to the bottom, in the Maṇimēkhalai (XVII, ll. 9-15).

It is clear from these stray references taken along with that in Aham 70 already referred to, that to the audience of these poets the story of the Rāmāyaṇa was familiar in minute detail. But turning from the Tamil classics to the Mahāvamśa, the history of Buddhism in Ceylon, the first occasion when Ceylon is brought into communication with this part of India is in connection with the occupation of the island by Vijaya and his followers, passing over for the occasion the mythical references to the visits of the Buddha and his predecessors to the island. According to the story as incorporated in this chronicle and divesting the story for the time being of the mythical colouring, Vijaya was a prince of Bengal (Vanga). He was the great-grandson of the king of Bengal by a Kalinga Princess whom he had married. His mother the Bengal Princess was an amorous young woman and was abandoned by the parents. She joined a caravan *travelling to the Magadha country*, apparently from Bengal. The caravan was attacked in the *Lāṭa* country by a lion which killed several of the party and drove the rest. Among those that escaped was the Bengal Princess who ran away along the path the lion came by. When the lion returned to its cave it discovered the beautiful princess on the way and is said to have been charmed, according to the story, by her good looks. The result of the amorous dalliance of the lion with her was the twin birth of a boy and a girl. After various adventures both the children and the mother escaped from the guardianship of the lion which was ultimately killed by the son. In return for this good service the king of Bengal gave his " lion-handed " grandson the kingdom, having had no son. The grandson, however, made it over to an uncle of his who had married his mother and retired from there with his own sister to the land of his birth. He there built a city which he called Sīhapura, (Sans. Sīmhapura), and cleared the forest round for a great distance founding villages. This according to the story was the kingdom (of Lāṭa) where he ruled. The sister-queen bore him 16 twins of whom he designed the eldest for the succession. Finding that he was an intolerably wicked young man the king had to subject the prince and his friends to the disgrace of being half-shaved and banished from the kingdom. Vijaya, his companions, and their wives and children were all put on board a ship and sent upon the sea. In the course of the voyage they got separated, probably in consequence of a shipwreck; the children landed on an island which the Mahāvaṁśa calls Naggadipa (Sans. Nagnadvīpa) the island of the naked, the women landed in an island called Mahiḷadipaka (islet of women), while Vijaya himself is said to have landed at a haven called Suppāraka. This last place had been identified with Sopara on the west coast of India as Vijaya is ordinarily taken to have sailed from Lāṭa or Gujarat. We shall see presently that neither the one nor the other is tenable on the material furnished by the story. The Mahāvaṁśa then introduces the prophecy of the Buddha that the island of Lanka would be occupied by Vijaya coming from the country of Lāṭa and to his direction to Śakka, Indra, to do the needful, as through Vijaya Buddha's religion was going to be established in Ceylon. In the course of this narration Ceylon receives both the names Lanka and Tambapanni.

Vijaya came with 700 of his followers ; and was told by an ascetic whom he saw that the island was called Lanka which was uninhabited. Vijaya thereafter had to overcome the Yakshas in the island and take possession of it completely. The island where he first landed from the ship which carried him and his followers was called, according to this story, Tambapanni (Sans. Tāmravarṇi), because on landing their hands and feet which touched the ground became red with the dust of the red-earth, and the city founded on that spot was named therefore Tambapanni. The whole island was named Sīhaḷa (San. Simhala) from his name, Sīhabāhu (Sans. Sīmhabāhu). His followers went about founding villages here and there in various parts of the island in the northern portion of it, and got into some kind of settlement. It was then that it was felt by Vijaya that a mere body of men cannot make a country. In order to obtain the necessary complement of womenfolk he sent a special embassy to Madhura in

Southern India asking for the hand of a princess, daughter of the Pāṇḍya, who agreed and sent along with the princess a number of young women of the noble families and of the 18 guilds to go and colonise Ceylon and marry the new settlers there. They all came across apparently by way of Rāmēśvaram and landed in the port of Ceylon, Mahatiṭha (Mantota) opposite the island of Mannar almost where the railway line starts in the island now. Thus was founded civilised society in Ceylon. It is clear that the story contains elements of history in it although the historical elements are so covered over with myth that it would be difficult to believe at first sight that it contains anything historical at all. A close examination of the story, however, will exhibit that there are some elements of history undoubtedly in it. The story conveys the information that the northern parts of the island of Ceylon were colonised from Bengal,—to be more accurate, Gangetic Kalinga. That comes out clearly from the story itself, and we find it confirmed from a somewhat overlooked circumstance in the story itself. The Bengal princess that was banished from her father's capital joined a caravan *going to Magadha*, which would mean, she left some town in Bengal which might have been on either side of the Ganges, and went along the road to Bihar. If the story is to be taken as authority at all, it was in the course of this journey that the caravan was attacked by the lion, it may be an animal lion, or more probably a tribe of wild people with a lion for their *totem*. The *region where they were attacked is called Lāṭa.* This has been apparently too readily equated with Lāṭa (Gujarat) which also becomes Lāḍa in Tamil. It certainly would be far more reasonable to equate it with Rāḍha which in the eastern Prakrit would appear Lāḍha, or by a further modification Lāḷa, *ḍha* and *ḷa* interchanging usually. The Asoka edicts give us authority for this, as oftentimes the term "Rāja" is in the language of these parts represented by [1] "Lāja," and Rajjuka by Lajjuka. One of the inscriptions referable to the period of the Kushanas refers to a district in this region as Rāḍha. Mr. Bannerji[2] identified this Rāḍha, at least northern Rāḍha, with Burdwan and the southern Rāḍha, must be south or south-west of it, in either case towards Kalinga.

Both the Bhagavatī Sūtra forming the fifth of the Jain Angas and the Āyārānga Sūtra contain references to the meeting of Mahāvīra with the Ājīvaka Makkhali Gosala in Nālanda, and their residence in Paṇiyabhūmi together for six years. This last place is said to have been

---

[1] *Vide* Kalsi, Dhauli and Jaugada versions in Rāmāvatara Sarma's Edition of the Asoka Edicts.

[2] R. D. Bannerji's Pāla Kings of Bengal, pp. 71-75, Memoirs of the Ben. A. S., V. 3.

in Vajjabhūmi, one of the two divisions of Lāḍha, which is describded as a forest country difficult to travel and inhabited by rude people who set their dogs upon mendicants wandering in the country.[1]

This location confirms what Tamil literature has to say of Vajra-nāḍu already referred to as being country in the basin of the river Sone. Vajra-bhūmi and Śvabhra-bhūmi constituted two divisions on the basis obviously of the peculiar geographical features. It must also be noted that this part of the country contains many other divisions up to the present time ending in "bhūmi," such as Manbhum, Singbhum, and Birbhum.

In a subsequent part of the story Simhabāhu gave up the Bengal kingdom to his mother and her cousin-husband, and took himself away to an uninhabited region where he cleared a kingdom for himself in the forest and settled with his queen-sister to rule there, having founded the capital Simhapura. On the basis of the story therefore there was a kingdom known as the kingdom of Lāḷa which was on the high-road between Bengal and Magadha where Simhabāhu cleared the forest of the savage tribes and constituted for himself a kingdom with a capital Simhapura. That this was either a part of

[1] *Vide* the Ājīvakas by Mr. Barua, pp. 57 and 58 (Calcutta Univ. Publication).

Kalinga itself, or not very far from the frontier of it, is in evidnce in both the Śilappadhikāram,[1] and Maṇimēkhalai,[2] which refer to a fratricidal war between two cousins of Kalinga. They ruled respectively over two parts of the kingdom with their capitals "Singapuram" (Sans. Simhapura) and Kapilai (Sans. Kapilā). The only detail that has to be satisfactorily accounted for on this hypothesis is the islands where the banished party, men, women, and children respectively landed. Naggadipa, where, according to the story, the children landed is certainly the Nakkavaram of the Tamils (the modern Nicobars) Mahiḷadvīpa may have to be looked for among the innumerable islands in the same region. The Ptolemaic name Maniolai is near enough in sound to Mahila. The Suppāra where the men landed may be another island about the same region, and for a guess Sabadeibai islands of Ptolemy on the west coast of Sumatra might very well answer the purpose. It is certainly matter for great doubt whether Suppāra of the West coast has anything to recommend it for identifying it with this place. As a matter of fact, if the party set sail from the Gangetic region, it must have been very near Damlok at the mouth of the Rupnārayan river, wherefrom other missions to Ceylon started. For that region of Bengal

---

[1] Canto. 23, ll. 138-158.

[2] Canto. 26. ll. 15-25.

this port or somewhere near seems exactly the starting point ; and then if they went adrift they must have gone towards this island region rather than sail all the way round. The identification with Suppāra on the West coast of India became possible, once Lāḷa was equated with Gujarat for which there is absolutely no warrant whatsoever in the tradition as embodied in the Mahāvaṁśa. Suppāra would mean merely the good shore, the shore that offered safe anchorage in a storm almost like the cape of Good Hope. Any place that afforded a good landing might have been so named. If the Mahāvaṁśa story is to be accepted as containing any history, Lāḷa will have to be Rāḍha a region of Kalinga (Bengal), and other places will have to be looked for in the Bay of Bengal and none whatsoever on the Arabian sea side of India. Vijaya is said, in the story again, to have landed in Ceylon at a place which he named subsequently Tambapanni where he laid the foundations of a town. This ultimately gave one of the names to the island itself. The whole party went in a ship and the landing was effected by Vijaya with 700 men and no more. It would be difficult to identify the Ajanta painting which ordinarily goes by this name with the landing as described in the Mahāvaṁśa itself. What is to our purpose here is that Vijaya had to find womenfolk for himself and his companions from Madura. If he came from Bengal or Kalinga, settled in the island and entered into wholesale marriage relations with the Pāṇḍya country—the geographical details of this narration work out correctly—it is clear that the northern part of the island of Ceylon, in fact the earlier civilised part, was colonised partly from Bengal and partly from the Tamil country. What actually was the date of Vijaya's occupation of Ceylon and in consequence the migration from the Pāṇḍya country does not rest upon so clear a foundation. The Mahāvaṁśa claims that Vijaya landed in Ceylon as the Buddha was passing into Nirvana in the Nepal Tarai, and according to the Chronology of the Mahāvaṁśa it would be sometime in 544-543 B.C. But the extraordinary length of the reigns of the immediate successors of Vijaya make it suspicious that Vijaya's landing took place so early. It is likely that it took place much later, but sometime anterior to the conversion of the Ceylon king to Buddhism and the establishment of regular relationship between Asoka and his contemporary Devānām-Piya Tissa. The edicts of Asoka mention the name Tambapanni for Ceylon. Tambapanni is a name unknown to the Tamils. It is certain therefore that the colonisation from Bengal came in some time anterior to the period of Asoka, may be at least about the time of his grandfather Chandragupta Maurya when people in

Patalipura had some knowledge even of distant Madura. It is in connection with Vijaya that the Pāṇḍya country first comes in contact with the history of Ceylon.

On this occasion, however, the connection, it must be remembered, is entirely of a friendly character. So far as the Mahāvaṁśa or the Dīpavaṁśa is concerned South India is not brought into contact again with Ceylon subsequently to Vijaya's coming, but it is stated that when Vijaya died without leaving a successor he had to direct his ministers to go for a successor to his father to send in his stead his brother, Sumitta (Sans. Sumitra) to be king. Before, however, the embassy could arrive the father had died and the said Sumitra was actually ruling; and this Sumitra had married a Madra (Maddha) princess and had three sons by her. He directed his younger son Pāṇḍu Vāsudēva to go and succeed the uncle in Ceylon. He reached Ceylon with 32 followers and was much in the same predicament for lack of a consort as Vijaya himself. He looked about himself for a suitable bride in the daughter of a Śākya chief who had settled on the other side of the Ganges when the whole clan was destroyed by the Magadha ruler. He had a beautiful daughter by name Bhaddakaccana who was so warmly wooed by seven princes that to save her and himself from their importunities, the father sent her with 32 attendants on a ship down the Ganges. The ship sailing safely arrived in Ceylon. Pāṇḍu Vāsudēva married her and made this princess his queen. In course of time all of her brothers followed excepting one, and they settled in various localities in Ceylon and founded communities of their own. It is by him that the dynasty was founded and there was a continuous succession of rulers, among whom was one who brought about the conversion of Ceylon to Buddhism. In this part of the story again the indication is fairly clear that the emigrants came from the region of the Ganges rather than from anywhere near Gujarat.

During the period of rule of Dēvānām-piya Tissa embassies went backward and forward several times and the connection indicated is with the Gangetic delta naturally enough, and in all the transactions in connection with the establishment of Buddhism in Ceylon and all the doings of Mahinda and Sangamitta in connection therewith, there is no mention direct or indirect with South India. Sangamitta sailed straight from the mouth of the Ganges, Mahinda came up to Vidisa in eastern Malva, and therefrom is supposed to have come by way of air. Asoka himself is said to have sent Sangamitta and the branch of the Bodhi tree down the Ganges while he himself came down to the port of embarkation over the Vindhya mountains.

It is very doubtful if Mahinda's aerial passage took him over the region of the Tamil country at all. Except for this possibility there is no mention of South India till we come to the year 177 B.C. according to the Mahāvaṁśa. Dēvānām-Piya Tisa died leaving three brothers to succeed him one after the other and the period of their rule covered about twenty years. At the end of the third reign however, the administration had so far gone in ineptitude that two horse traders from the Tamil country were able to overthrow the ruling dynasty; which part of the Tamil country they came from is not stated. After a reign of twenty-two years the usurpers were overthrown by a member of the ruling family who occupied the throne for a period of ten years.

It was after this that a Tamil of noble descent came from the Chola country, seized the kingdom and ruled for a period of forty-four years "with even justice towards friend and foe on occasions of dispute at law." This Tamil chief is named in the Mahāvaṁśa Elara, but is known to Tamil tradition as Elēlasingam; but this tradition however, tells us little that could be brought into connection with the story as told of him in this work. Some of the stories recorded of him in the Mahāvaṁśa in regard to his acts of extraordinary justice are several of them, traceable in the accounts of the semi-mythical

Cholas. While confirming the Chola origin of the chief, these do not lead us to any definite kind of connection with any of the ruling kings of the Chola dynasty so far as we know at present. So much, however, seems clear from the Mahāvaṁśa itself that he continued throughout his long reign in the religion of his fathers and did not adopt Buddhism even though in regard to the Buddhists themselves he exhibited the same beneficent liberality as to his own co-religionists. The Mahāvaṁśa itself admits of this heretic from their point of view, that "only because he freed himself from the guilt of walking in the path of evil did this (monarch) though he had not put aside false beliefs, gained such miraculous power" as to regulate and control rain. The connection this time is with the Chola country as is clear from the account, and is admittedly of a hostile character. The most powerful usurper who had a comparatively long reign was a man who continued to be other than Buddhist, and has evoked the admiration of the hostile witnesses to his equitable rule. The description in circumstantial detail of the war between the usurper Elara and Duṭṭhagāmaṇi gives one a feeling that the event is of a historical character. The hostility thus started between the Tamils of the Chola country, which for some reason or other appears to have been nearest for this purpose, and the Ceylonese of northern Ceylon continued permanently ever afterwards, so much so that this hostility had become more or less the normal relation between the two Kingdoms.

In the consecration of the "great Vihāra" it was already pointed out, the Tamil country proper took no part. None of the localities from which representatives came to take part in the consecration, with the doubtful exception of the representative from Mahishamaṇḍala, is it possible to locate in the Tamil country. It is impossible to refer this Mahishamaṇḍala to the Mysore territory to which there are a number of references in early Tamil literature from which I have drawn so largely. None of the references however gives us even a hint that the country was Buddhist, or that there was a Buddhist establishment in it. It seems likely that the Mahishamaṇḍala from which Buddhist representatives did come was the Mahishamaṇḍala dominated by Māhishmatī on the Narbada, the country of the Mahishakas round Māndhāta (an island in the Narbada river). The hostility therefore between the Hindu Tamils and Buddhist Ceylon that is inferable gets indirectly supported by this significant omission.

The next time that Ceylon comes into connection with the Tamils is under the rule of Vaṭṭagāmaṇi about 44 B.C. In his reign there was a rebellion set up by a Brahman by name

Tissa, who according to the Buddhist account, instigated by the prediction of an astrologer set up in rebellion against the newly installed King Vaṭṭagāmaṇi. At the same time seven Tamil chieftains landed at Mahatitha (Mantota) with their troops apparently in alliance with the rebel Tissa. Vaṭṭagāmaṇi skilfully appealed to the Brahman by telling him that the kingdom was already his and that he might exert himself to get the Tamils out. The Tamils easily won a victory against the Brahman first, and then attacked the king himself and defeated him in a battle near Kolambalaka. For fourteen years afterwards the king remained in exile. During this period five Tamils ruled one after the other, the remaining two having gone back with such booty as they could lay hold of, one of them carrying Somadēvi the queen, and the other the Buddha's alms-bowl, from Anuradhapura. One Tamil chief by name Pulahattha reigned for three years; his commander-in-chief Bahiya after killing him, ruled for two years. Bahiya was succeeded in his turn by his commander-in-chief who slew his master. The succession passed on to Pilayamāraka and from him to Dathika. After fourteen years and seven months of exile Vaṭṭagāmaṇi was able to overcome the last Tamil usurper Dathika and entered his capital again. His great work was the construction of the Abhayagiri

Vihāra after having destroyed a Jain *ārāma* (park or garden). He is said to have brought back his queen Somadēvi from the Tamil country and restored her to her position as queen. He built in her honour the Maṇisōma-ārāma. In these doings of Vaṭṭagāmaṇi Abhaya the Tamils again came into contact with him as enemies, having come apparently in support of the Brahman usurper and ending in usurping the kingdom for a period of nearly fifteen years.

After the death of Vaṭṭagāmani two successors followed, the second of whom was Vaṭṭagāmaṇi's son Choranāga. He was followed by Tissa. Choranāga made himself unpopular with the Buddhists by destroying a number of their monasteries which refused him asylum while he was a fugitive rebel. His queen murdered him and set up a changing succession of her lovers on the throne, among whom was a Tamil by name Vaṭuka who occupied the position of a city carpenter. Another of this infamous queen's lovers was also a person named Niliya, a Brahman palace priest as he is described, who had a short reign of about six months. She changed her mind and got rid of him as she did the others before him. These Tamils apparently were people that had settled in Ceylon, and their connection with the throne does not bring Ceylon into any connection with the Tamil country. Then we pass over a succession of rulers whose doings do not bring them into connection with the Tamil country till we come to the reign of Chanḍamuka-Siva who ruled from A. D. 101-110. His queen was named Damilā-dēvi. Whether she was a princess from any of the Tamil countries in the neighbourhood is not made clear. Chanḍamuka-Śiva was assassinated by his younger brother, Tissa by name, who ruled for a period of about eight years. He indulged a fancy of his by setting on the throne a gate watchman who looked like him and enjoyed the joke from his place as a watchman instead, when his courtiers in succession made their obeisance to the watchman on the throne. The watchman took advantage of this unseemly conduct of the king in the watchman's guise, and ordered his being slain for such bad conduct. The rule of the gate watchman apparently-became unpopular and a person named Vasabha of the Lambakanna race, and belonging to the northern provinces of Ceylon, apparently Jaffna, set up a rebellion and overthrowing Vasabha in battle occupied the throne for the long period of 42 years. The term Lambakanna designating the class of people to whom this ruler belonged, it seems as though the Lambakanna rulers were Tamils as well. Lambakarṇa means merely pendant ear. Whether that name was given to them because of the physical deformity, though brought` about artificially, of ears lengthened by making big holes in the lobes seems just possible. In the later period of the history of Ceylon and even of the Pāṇḍya country these Lamba-karṇas play an important part, and a number of chieftains in the present-day district of Ramnad are described as Lambakannas in the Ceylonese account. They had a specific function to discharge on occasions of royal coronation though what exactly the function was is not made clear. *A Lambakanna-dhura*, apparently the chief of the Lamba-kannas, along with a number of chiefs of that class was sent by the victorious Ceylon general Lankāpura to officiate at the coronation of a Pāṇḍya King in the twelfth century. If they belonged to the community of chieftains in that part of the district which is peculiarly the district of the so-called Nāṭṭukoṭṭai Chetties, the term Lambakanna may well apply to them. The Lambakanna usurpation therefore would mean the usurpation by the warriors of the Lambakanna race who must have formed a recognised part of the military forces of the state of Anuradhapura in Ceylon. This ruler is described in the Mahāvaṁśa as having been a particularly pious monarch, who anxious to extend the short life that was predicted for him, did make very large donations to the Buddhist priests and institutions, and earned the grateful encomiums of this class of people. This Lambakanna chief was succeeded by his son for a short term of three years; and his son Gajabāhuka Gāmaṇi, or more briefly Gajabāhu, succeeded to the throne. His rule, according to Geiger's chronology, beginning in 483 B. C. lasted from A.D. 171 to A.D. 193. The Mahāvaṁśa itself has very little to say of him except that he built a *Vihāra* in honour of his mother and a *stūpa*. He is also given credit for having constructed a tank and a few other minor works of merit to the Buddhist shrines. His reign is, however, of great importance in South Indian History as he was the ruler of Ceylon who was present at the completion of the ceremony of the institution of the temple to Pattini-Dēvi in the Chēra capital of Vanji. The Śilappadhikāram refers to him definitely as among the kings who were present, along with others, on the occasion; the other rulers mentioned being the Aryan princes who were just released from prison, other Kings that were similarly set at liberty, the rulers of Western Kongu, the kings of Mālva, and king Gajabāhu of Lanka "surrounded by the sea." All of them prayed that the goddess might honour their territory as she did that of the Chēra, which was answered by a voice from the air proclaiming assent.[1]

---

[1] Śilappadhikāram, Canto 30, ll. 151-164.

This is in a way confirmed by a statement prefixed to the work either by the author himfelf or more likely by the author's friend or preceptor or disciple, who usually write the introduction to the poem. The statement in this part follows that in the body of the work, and states that these temples were built in the Chola, Pāṇḍya, Kongu and Lanka, and duly consecrated as a means of expiation for the suffering to which, at any rate, the Pāṇḍya country was subjected as a result of the miscarriage of justice which constituted the seed of the tragedy. The statement in the text is a prayer, and the statement in the preface is a record of the accomplishment of all that was prayed for; but the statement in the text itself is very clear and leaves no doubt as to the contemporaneity of the "Red-Chēra" with Gajabāhu of Ceylon. The introduction of the supernatural in the poem leads some scholars to doubt the historicity of several of its statements. These scholars forget that the author was a younger brother of this selfsame Chēra. He refers more than once to the contemporary poet, his own friend and a much valued friend of his elder brother the king, Śāttan, the author of the companion work Maṇimēkhalai, apart from the reference in the introduction to both the works. As a *kāvya* the two works together constitute one, as otherwise this work alone would deal with only the first three of "the four ends of life" (chatur-vida-purushārtha). If Gajabāhu then went as far out as the court of the Chēra and constructed a temple to Pattini-dēvi why does not the Mahāvaṁśa say so? The Mahāvaṁśa is essentially a history of Buddhism in Ceylon, and not a secular history of Ceylon. It deals with those kings of Ceylon whose benefactions to Buddhism were the greatest, and passes over those with rare exceptions, who were not Buddhists with comparatively short notice. The establishment of the temple to Pattini-dēvi would go just against the grain of Buddhist tradition, and the Buddhist priests of the Mahāvihāra therefore apparently felt disinclined to record this particular incident. There are other histories of Ceylon however, which have much more to say of this Gajabāhu. They ascribe to him an invasion of the Chola country for the recovery of a large number of the Ceylonese who were taken prisoners and who were detailed for work at "the city of Kaveri in the country of Soli," which apparently means they were set to work as prisoners in the city of Kaveripaṭṭaṇam, the Chola capital. He is said to have taken back some of the Buddha relics and Buddha's begging-bowl which, according to this account, was carried away before his time. We know from tradition on this side of the channel that the great Chola

Karikāla it was that constructed, or vastly enlarged the Chola capital Puhār or Kavēripaṭṭaṇam. We have noted already that one of the Tamil usurpers among the seven carried away "the alms-bowl of the master endowed with the ten miraculous powers" that was in Anuradhapuram in the period B.C. 44-29, according to Geiger's Chronology. One of these other accounts of Ceylon actually does state that the King of Ceylon on that occasion brought away the "foot ornaments of Pattini-dēvi" and also the four arms of the gods. Thus the evidence on both sides seems inevitably to lead to the conclusion that it was Gajabāhu I of Ceylon that came into connection with the Tamil country.[1]

We have a date for Gajabāhu which we have not for the others. On the basis of the date of Buddha's *nirvāṇa* being 544-43, the Ceylon dating for Gajabāhu would be 112-132; with 483 B.C. for the Buddha's *nirvāṇa*, the date in Christian era would be 171-193. Overlooking for the moment the discrepancy of 60 years, Gajabāhu and his contemporaries must be placed in the middle of the second century A.D. which is exactly the conclusion to which we have arrived without this specific chronological datum. Gajabāhu's

[1] For fuller reference in regard to this particular incident see pp. 363-367 of my "Ancient India." The Rājāvaḷiya translated by Guṇasekhara is quoted below.

relations with India as is clear from the above account was of a friendly character. He appears to have been one of those monarchs who like the monarchs of India in general patronised all religions alike, and this latitudinarianism of the monarch was not quite approved of by the monkish chroniclers of the Mahāvihāra, on whose accounts the Mahāvaṁśa is professedly based. The omission in the Mahāvaṁśa proper of the details regarding the temple to Pattini-dēvi is perfectly natural from the point of view of the orthodox Buddhists, but that is no evidence that that incident is not historical.

The following extracts from the Rājāvaḷiya contains a fuller account of Gajabāhu's doings[1] which it would be interesting to note here:

"His son King Bapa, surnamed Vannesi or King (1) Vannēsinambapa, (2) Sinnanambapa, reigned 3 years. During his reign the king of the Soli country landed on this island with an army of Tamils and carried away 12,000 prisoners."

"Gajaba, son of King Bapa Vannēsi, succeeded to the throne. One night, when walking in the city, he heard a widow weeping because the king of Soli had carried away her children. He said within himself 'some wrong has been done in this city,' and having marked the door of her house with chalk, returned to his palace.

[1] Edn. by B. Guṇasēkhara, Colombo, pp. 47-48.

In the morning he called his ministers and inquired of them what (they knew of any) acts of justice or injustice in the city. Thereupon they replied, 'O Great King, it is like a wedding house.' The king, being wroth with his ministers. sent for the woman, the door of whose house he had marked with chalk and asked her (why she wept). The poor woman replied, 'I wept because among the 12,000 persons taken captive by the Soli king were my two sons.' On hearing these words the king expressed anger against his royal father, and, saying 'I will go tomorrow and to the Soli country,' assembled an army and went to Yapapatuna,[1] thinking 'I will (myself) bring back the people forcibly carried off by the king of Soli,' and having declared it openly, he dismissed the army. Taking the giant Nila with him he went and struck the sea with an iron mace, divided the waters in twain, and going quietly on arrived at the Soli capital, struck terror into the king of Soli, and seated himself on the throne like King Śak; whilst the giant Nila seized the elephants in the city and killed them by striking one against another.

"The ministers informed the king of Soli of the devastation of the city thus being made. Thereupon he inquired of Gajaba, "iṣ the Sinhalese host come to destroy this city."

---

[1] Yāḷpāṇapaṭṭaṇam, or Jaffnapatam, modern Jaffna.

Gajaba replied "I have a little boy who accompanied me; there is no army," and caused the giant Nīla to be brought and made to stand by his side. Thereupon the king of Soli asked "why has your Majesty come alone without an army?" Gajaba replied, "I have come in order to take back the 12,000 persons whom your royal father brought here as prisoners in the time of my father." To this the king of Soli saying, "a king of our family it was who, in times past, went to the city of the gods and gained victory in the war with the "*Asuras*," refused to send for and deliver the men. Then Gajaba grew wroth and said "forthwith restore my 12,000 people, giving 12,000 more besides them; else will I destroy this city and reduce it to ashes." Having said this, he squeezed out water from sand and showed it; squeezed water from his iron mace and showed that. Having in this way intimidated the king of Soli he received the original number supplemented by an equal number of men as interest making 24,000 persons in all. *He also took away the jewelled anklets of the goddess Pattini* and *the insignia of the gods of the four dēvala*, and *also the bowl-relic which had been carried off in the time of king Valagamba*; and admonishing the king not to act thus in future.'

'On his arrival he landed the captives, sent each captive who owned ancestral property to his inherited estate and caused the supernumerary captives to be distributed over and to settle in these countries, *viz.*, Alutkuruwa, Sarasiyapattuwa, Yatinuwara, Udunuwara, Tupane, Hewahata, Dansiya, Pattuwa, Egoda Tiha and Magada Tiha. This king reigned 24 years and went to the world of the gods.'

There is an interesting reference to a famine in the short reign of Kunchanāga of two years. This would correspond under the Geiger scheme to the years A.D. 243-44, but under the scheme of Ceylon chronology beginning B.C. 543, it would be A.D. 183-4. This latter dating would bring it over close to the date of a great famine in the Pāṇḍya country which figures in traditions concerning the history of Tamil literature. The famine in Ceylon is called Eka-Nāḷikā famine, which means, under the ordinary acceptation of similar expressions, that the staple grain, apparently rice, was sold at one Nāḷikā (one-eighth of the standard measure) for each main unit of currency. The next reign of importance in this religious history of Ceylon that brings Ceylon into connection with India is that of a Tissa known generally by his surname Vohārika-Tissa, the adjunct Voharika is the Pāli form of Vyavahārika meaning, "knowing the law because he put an end to physical injury as a penalty under law." His reign is of importance in this particular connection as it was then for the first time that the heretical sect of the Buddhists following the Vētulya[1] doctrine is said to have assumed importance in the island. This heresy under Vohārika Tissa was suppressed by the king by means of a minister of his named Kapila. The king is said to have followed the orthodox doctrine as a result of the discourses of the *thera*-Dēva who was a resident of Kambugama. This heresy of the Vētulya is said to have originated in A.B. 752, the equivalent of A.D. 209 in the first year of the reign of Vohārika Tissa, according to Turnour the translator of the Mahāvaṁśa; the peculiarity of the doctrine of these heretics consisted in regarding (1) the Buddha as a supernatural being, and (2) the doctrine (Dharma) as having been preached not by the Buddha himself but by Ānanda his chief disciple.[2] This

---

[1] Kern's Indian Buddhism, pp. 121-126.

[2] I-tsing's Record, p. 14, Takakasu's Trans.

"Both (Mahāyānists and Hinayānists adopt one and the same discipline (*Vinaya*), and they have in common the prohibition of the five *skandhas* (groups of offences), and also the practice of the "*Four Noble Truths*."

"Those who worship the Bodhisattvas and read the Mahāyāna Sūtras are called Mahāyānists (the great), while those who do not perform these are called the Hinayānists (the small). There are but two kinds of the so-called Mahāyāna. First the Mādhyamika; second the Yōga. The former profess that which is commonly called existence is in reality non-existence and every object is but an empty show, like an illusion; whereas the latter affirm that there exist no other things *in reality*, but only inward thoughts, and all things exist only in the mind (lit. all things are but one mind)."

seems to give us a clear indication of the connection between this school of Buddhism and the school of *Bhakti* in Hinduism, thus apparently harmonising somewhat with this rising school of Hindu thought, such harmonising being one of the special features of Mahāyāna Buddhism. Tārānātha makes a statement of value in this connection as, according to him, Nāgārjuna's preceptor, the Brahman Rāhuḷa-Bhadra, the Mahāyānist is said to have been " much indebted to sage Krishna, and still more to Gaṇēśa." This would ordinarily mean no more than that Mahāyānism was indebted to special schools of Bhakti, both Vaishṇava and Śaiva, rather more to the latter than to the former. What minister Kapila did for suppressing this heresy we are not told. What exactly was the occasion that called for any special preaching on the part of the *Thera*-Dēva we are left in equal darkness about; but so much is clear that the Vētulya heresy had assumed such importance and had apparently shown itself to be so aggressive that the attention of even the judicially-minded monarch was called for for keeping it under control. If the date 209 A.D. could be regarded as the correct equivalent, it will lead us a long way towards settling the date of Nāgārjuna. The Dēva who discoursed effectively to this Vohārika Tissa and kept him in orthodoxy, it is very probable, was the rival of Nāgārjuna, who could not have lived very long anterior to this actual date. The importance of the connection between the coast region of India and Ceylon will appear later. The successor of this monarch became a fugitive from the country as a result of an intrigue of his brother with the queen, and was sometime resident in the Tamil country. He returned from there at the head of a Tamil army and overthrowing his brother ruled as monarch. He was succeeded on his death by his elder brother's son who ruled for another two years followed by a short reign of one year of his son. Then there was a Lambakanna usurpation by three officers of this race. There is record of another famine in the reign of Srī Śanghabodhi of two years, A.D. 300-302 under the Geiger scheme. He was followed by the third of the Lambakannas Abhaya by name, who is known otherwise as Goṭhāhaya or Mēghavannābhaya who had a reign of 13 years. There is a story regarding the last days of this Abhaya's predecessor which resembles the story of the Tamil patron Kumaṇa and his younger brother, and which is recorded in poems 158-165 of Puṛanānūru. In either case the story has reference to a prize put upon the head of a fugitive. In either case likewise, the fugitive offered to take off, and actually took off, his own head to gratify a friend by enabling him to get the prize.

In this Abhaya's reign the Vētulya heresy comes into great prominence. He is said to have suppressed the heresy which had found great strength in the community of the Abhayagiri-Vihāra, and had to exclude from the community 60 of the heretical priests who went to the opposite shore of the continent and found asylum there. A Bhikshu by name Sangamitta in the Chola country attached himself to one of these excommunicated priests and came to Ceylon with a bitter hatred of the orthodox community of the Mahāvihāra. He is said to have been an expert in the exorcism of spirits and such other black-art. Having defeated one of the chief monks of the Tūpārāma, apparently of the orthodox school, he attracted the attention of the monarch and rose so high in his favour as to be eventually appointed tutor to the sons of the king. Goṭhābhaya's eldest son Jeṭṭa-Tissa when he succeeded set up a persecution of such of the heretical ministers as would not take their place in the funeral procession of his late father. Fearing for his own life the chief heretic teacher Sangamitta had to go back to his country and await the accession to the throne of his other pupil Mahāsēna, the younger of the two sons of Goṭhābhaya. At the death of the elder brother the heretical *thera* Sangamitta came back to Ceylon for the purpose of the consecration ceremony of the young ruler. At his instigation the orthodox community of the Mahāvihāra got to be so far thrown into neglect that they abandoned the Vihāra and left it vacant for a period of nine years. The Vihāra and its properties were appropriated by the state as unclaimed property. This persecution of the orthodox community led on to the proportionate rise of the community of the Abhayagiri-Vihāra into importance chiefly through the instrumentality of the *thera* Sangamitta and minister Śoṇa.[1]

The orthodox minister by name Mēghavannābhaya set up in rebellion, and, on the field of battle, made it up with the monarch and came to an understanding with him. In the meanwhile Sangamitta and Sona were put to death through one of the King's wives who was an orthodox devotee of the Mahāvihāra. One of the great offences that Mahāsēna gave to the orthodox community seems to have been the setting up of numbers of images of the Buddha and the building of regular temples for them, the Mahāyānist practice apparently. This time he must have set up the images of the Buddha within the Mahāvihāra itself at the instigation of another priest Tissa. This heretical temple in the near proximity of the Mahāvihāra was called Jotivana-Vihāra in the garden called Joti.

---

[1] This is briefly alluded to in the Dīpavaṁśa as well. Verses 66-76. The names of these two are somewhat altered in shape; Sangamitta is referred to as Dummitto and minister Sona as Papa-Sono.

This action caused the vacating of the Mahāvihāra for some time, and the matter was settled actually in favour of the orthodox community by the high judicial minister in spite of the wishes of the king to the contrary. The king is also said to have founded three other *Vihāras* destroying the temples of the Brahmanical gods. When this king Mahāsēna died the Mahāvihāra of the orthodox community and that of the Abhayagiri occupied positions practically of equal strength and uncompromising rivalry, so much so that the Chronicler closes the account of him with the following statement "thus this monarch Mahēsēna by his connection with ill-disposed persons having performed, during the whole course of his existence, acts of piety and impiety, his destiny (after his death) was great to his merits." The inference from this statement is clear, namely, that Mahāsēna whatever his own private predilections (which apparently inclined towards the heretical) let the two sections grow side by side, and perhaps even ceased to exhibit any special favour to the community of the Mahāvihāra. This attitude was naturally unacceptable to the orthodox community of the Mahāvihāra whose account actually constitutes the Mahāvaṁśa.

CHAPTER IV.

SOUTH INDIA, THE SEAT OF ORTHODOX HINDUISM.

This brings us to the year A. B. 808 to 835 equal to A. D. 325-352 according to the Geiger scheme or 60 years less on the basis of 543 for A. B. 1. So up to the commencement of the fourth century the actual connection between Ceylon and South India may be described as one of hostility often political, but always to a certain degree religious in the sense that Buddhism which commanded the most influential clientele in Ceylon did not command the support, or gain even the sympathy, of the Tamils who came into occupation of Ceylon from across the sea. We have already noticed that the religious condition of South India was one of complete freedom. From such evidence as is available to us, there were Buddhists and Jains pursuing peacefully each sect its own particular persuasion though it undoubtedly seems that Hinduism was the dominant religion. In the headquarters of the Chola Kingdom as well as of the Pāndya, of both of which we get elaborate descriptions in works written by Buddhist, Jain and Hindu, we find all of these co-existing, so much so that it would seem ordinarily to be difficult to infer what exactly was the particular leaning of the monarch for the time being. The *Vaidic* learning which was held in high esteem and of which we gain glimpses even in the writings of authors professing religions hostile to the claims of the *Veda* seems, on the evidence of the poem from Puṛanānūṛu quoted above, specially organised here for controverting what was regarded by this school as the false learning of those who ceased to hold the *Veda* in high esteem. That is not all. Puram 166 quoted above translates (ll. 1-10). "Hail! descendant of a family of first among wise men who enjoy the reputation of having perfected without defect the twenty-one kinds of sacrifice; who were learned in the ancient *Veda* which is habitually much cultivated and which is unceasingly in the tongue of the venerable Śiva of long-matted locks; which has for its sole object Dharma which is four-footed and learnt, with the aid of the six auxiliary sciences, with a view chiefly to controvert with success the truth-like convictions of those whose persuasions lie outside the *Veda*, and to put a stop to their increase by imposing upon people; understanding the actual truth of these seemingly true convictions, these ancestors of yours succeeded in exposing their hollowness and thus prevented their increase. Of such distinguished ancestry have you come into the world."

Whether the stimulus actually came from the north or no, there is nothing in the evidence for an inference either way; but Brahmanism in the Tamil country took the same development that it did take according to Sir R. G. Bhandarkar, in the orthodox middle country of Hindustan. We see already the coming into prominence of the cult of particular gods such as Śiva, Vishṇu or Krishṇa, etc. The four gods, Śiva, Baladēva, Krishṇa and Subrahmaṇya referred to already as having been regarded as the guiding divinities of the world on the authority of a poem by Narkīrar are the divinities whose temples the Śilappadhikāram describes as having existed in Madura and even Kaveripaṭṭaṇam. It may be that the existence of the temples of a prominent character to these four in Madura was the reason for Narkīrar's conviction in the poem quoted above. We have already pointed out the importance that was attached, in the prevalent Hinduism of this part of the country, to sacrifices such as the Buddhists and even the Jains condemned. In the society of Tamil India of those days the Brahman found the celebration of these sacrifices normally allotted to him. The function and the celebrant alike came to be treated with great honour by the community as a whole as benefactors of society. While therefore it would be safe to assert that the heterodox sects of the

Buddhists and Jains were allowed to prosper peacefully and there was no persecution in the country, it would still, on the evidence available, bear assertion that the orthodox Hinduism was the religion of the south. This Hinduism had already undergone a certain degree of modification towards subordinating the purely ritualistic part of the Brahmanic religion by a very strong infusion of the devotional element in it. While the Brahman was expected rigorously to conform to his duties as the sacrificer for the community, the rest of the community could look forward, in the security that the Brahman was discharging his duties to the community as a whole, to the attainment of earthly prosperity here in this world and salvation in the next by the comparatively easier method of devotion, each to the god of his heart. The notion of god and that of a ministering priest to stand between God and individual man already come into relief. This peculiar feature of devotion to god under the right guidance of a preceptor is a feature peculiar to *Bhakti* on the one side and to the development of Buddhism of the *Mahāyāna* form in its more abstruse aspect on the other. This feature seems to have been the peculiar feature of the heterodox Vētulya followers (of the Abhayagiri Vihāra) of Buddhism itself, and be it noted it is a development of Buddhism which as noticed by the Ceylon

Buddhists is peculiar to the continental part set over against their own coast; in other words, the Tamil country and the region adjoining. It would seem therefore as though the *school of Bhakti* and the *Vētulya heresy* of Buddhism alike were the developments of Brahmanism and Buddhism respectively as a result of the same or similar influences. If Nāgārjuna's association with Śrī-Śailam should turn out to be historical, and if he were the contemporary of Arya Dēva it is quite likely that Nāgārjuna's responsibility for this feature of Mahāyāna Buddhism is easily understandable. Ārya Dēva the rival of Nāgārjuna seems the same as Dēva who preached the Ceylon Vohārika-Tissa into orthodoxy. The term Ārya may after all mean in that particular connection no more than *Āchārya*.[1]

At the end of this first stage of our enquiry into the history of Brahmanism in South India we have come to this state of things before the rise of the Pallavas in the south. Brahmanism of the *Vedic* character came from the north and established ready superiority over such indigenous systems of religion as existed, if these could be called systems at all. The Brahmans that came in small colonies must have been comparatively few in point of number, but impressed

---

[1] The Mahāvaṁśa has a reference to reading on particular occasions, of what is called Ārya-Vaṁśa, *i. e.*, a sort of an Āchārya-Paramparā which was being publicly read on stated occasions.

the whole society by a certain degree of austere simplicity and of loyal discharge of their duty to the community which involved a sacrifice of all their time and energy in the doing. The system of ritual they brought with them was very complicated and required more or less complete detachment for performance. They did perform this duty, and there was a widespread notion that the performance of his sacrifice and the maintenance of the holy fire were essential to the prosperity of the community. Hence it was enjoined upon him as a duty that he owed to the community to do this laborious and troublesome task faithfully. Remissness in detail, or failure in the performance, either of them involved some kind of calamitous visitation for society, and his service therefore was regarded as of peculiar value to the community. Thus we see how he arrived at the first two of his duties, the performance of sacrifice, and getting others to perform such.

Learning got associated with the Brahman probably from the days of the Rig Vēda itself. At any rate in the next stage of development when the hymns got to have a ritualistic significance a class had necessarily to be detailed for the preservation of this learning. While therefore learning, even holy learning, was the common property of all the twice-born, its development and growth naturally required a special section of the community to be set apart for the pursuit of it, and either that community became Brahman or the Brahman took up that duty along with the one already described. Thus by a process almost of natural selection he became the custodian of learning. Not content merely with being the custodian he added the important function of dispensing this learning, so that he became not merely the special student who learnt all that was worth learning at the time, but he also regarded it as his duty to hand down the torch of learning undiminished, if not improved and extended. This brings us to the other two of his functions in the Tamil country, learning and teaching. This double function gave him, as it were, the natural right to be the authority for consultation and guidance in matters relating to conduct in society. It was not merely teaching of book-learning that he took upon himself, but the far more serious duty of "perfecting the people" (*janapakvatā*). This "perfecting of the people" which, in more modern language would mean civilizing the people, involved in the peculiar circumstances of the times the free gift of education and the free acceptance of rewards therefor. One was not to teach for fees but having been taught there was the moral obligation on the part of the taught to contribute his mite to the continued maintenance of the beneficent office. It was not merely an obligation on the part of the taught, but became gradually to be felt as an extended obligation upon the whole of the society. Those that were capable of being taught should have the opportunity to teach themselves, and thus arose the obligation to maintain the Brahman on the part of society. That brings us to the third pair of his functions, the giving and the receiving in gift. He taught freely and laboured hard to elevate society. The people gave freely and maintained him in comfort in order that he may pursue the good work untrammelled by considerations as to his maintenance. We thus find that the duties specially allotted to the Brahman and the privileges to which he became specially entitled were both alike the natural development of his position in society and the function that he allotted to himself. The following passage from the Śatapatha Brāhmaṇa puts the whole of his duties and responsibilities in a nut-shell:

"The study and teaching (of the Veda) are a source of pleasure to him, he becomes ready-minded, and independent of others; and day by day, he acquires wealth. He sleeps peacefully; he is the best physician for himself; and (peculiar) to him are the restraint of the senses, delight on the one hand, growth of intelligence, fame and the *task of perfecting people.* The growing of intelligence gives rise to four duties attaching to the Brahmanas—Brahmanical descent, a befitting deportment, fame and *perfecting of the people*; and the people that are being perfected guard the Brahman by four duties—by (showing him) respect and liberality, and by (granting him) security against oppression and security against capital punishment."

Much the same idea is conveyed in a far more simple way when the Tamil poet speaks of a royal family as the one which had never known to do anything that would cause pain of mind to a Brahman.

On Brahmanism so constituted came to bear new influences for the rudiments of which we have to go back to times much earlier, and that influence is the rising cult of *Bhakti*. *Bhakti* involves the notion of a personal God who intervenes in the affairs of man for the benefit of humanity. We can see the emergence of the notion of the personal God in the Śatapatha Brāhmaṇa[1] itself in the strident Vishṇu. This theistic notion of personal God and of service to him comes in its further development to be known as *Bhakti*. This was the orthodox answer to the rising of agnostic cults of Buddhism and Jainism, and in its further development it influenced both Brahmanism and Buddhism vitally as we saw. The modification of orthodox Brahmanism of the *Vedic* kind by the influence of this new and still orthodox cult of *Bhakti* we shall trace in the next section.

---

[1] I. 5, 3, 14 and I. 9, 3, 10. Also Kaṭha Up. I. 3, 9 and MacNicol's Indian Theism. p. 33.

CHAPTER V.

THE SCHOOL OF BHAKTI.

A theistic system of Bhakti consists in the worship of a personal God who is the Creator and Lord of the Universe. Devotion to him by unremitting service is the best way to the attainment of salvation or release from the ever-recurring cycle of births and deaths, and as such become recognisable as a system in the age of religious ferment of the Upanishads. The natural development of this religious ferment led to the rising of Buddhism and Jainism in the east. A more legitimate and orthodox system also grew simultaneously in the home of orthodoxy in the middle country of Hinduism. This system is represented both in the Nārāyaṇīya section of the Mahābhārata as well as in the Bhagavat Gītā. Both of these Sir R. G. Bhandarkar traces to a period anterior to the rise even of Buddhism and Jainism, but not in an organised form. He would regard the Gītā as a system which came into existence as a protest against the atheistic systems which resulted from the intellectual ferment of the age of the Upanishads. The following is Sir R. G. Bhandarkar's summary of the position: "The state of things which must have led to the evolution of the religion of the Gita seems to me to be this. About the time when the systems of religion we have been considering arose, there was a tendency amongst the people which often worked itself out, as is evident from the Pāli birth-stories, to give up worldly life and betake themselves to residence in forests or mountains. Even Buddhism, Jainism and other like systems considered an ascetic life to be a *sine qua non* of religious elevation. There is reason to believe that Śramaṇas existed before the rise of Buddhism. The religious systems that had sprung up were mostly atheistic. The Indian mind had become prone to indulge in mere moral discourses and thoughts on moral exaltation, unassociated with a theistic faith as appears clear from Buddhism and other systems, and also very dry moral dissertations of which the Mahābhārata is full. Such a system as that of the Bhagavat Gītā was therefore necessary to counteract these tendencies. Theistic ideas were so scattered in the Upanishads, that it was necessary for practical purposes to work them up in a system of redemption capable of being grasped easily. These appeared to be the conditions under which the Gītā came into existence.

I am not inclined to dissolve Vāsudēva and Arjuna into solar myths ; Vāsudēva could not have been living when the Bhagavat Gītā was composed as a discourse delivered by him, any more than Buddha was living when his discourses were reduced to the form of books. It is worthy of remark that both of them are called Bhagavats when speaking. Vāsudēva must already have been deified before the Bhagavat Gītā was written." The School of Bhakti therefore can go back to *Vedic* beginnings reaching back to the Upanishads certainly and may be traced even anterior to this particular stage of development. As a system it may be regarded as pre-Buddhistic judged by the Gītā alone. Bhakti consists as was already pointed out in love of God and complete devotion to Him. Such a notion is traceable in some of the Upanishads themselves. As a system the school of Bhakti regards Vāsudēva as the supreme soul, the internal soul of all souls. He is regarded as the supreme creator. All living beings are represented by Sankarshaṇa, who is a form of Vāsudēva. From Sankarshaṇa sprang Pradyumna, the mind and from Pradyumna, Anirudha, self-consciousness. From him sprang Brahma. The first four are regarded as the four *Vyūhas* of the supreme. A similar hier archy of gods is found in connection with the school of the *Tantra* only instead of

Vāsudēva, Māhēśvara has to be substituted and perhaps even behind this the great mother or Parāśakti. On a detailed consideration of references in literature Sir R. G. Bhandarkar arrives at the conclusion "Still it is doubtful, and it may be taken for granted that the two *Vyūhas* Vāsudēva and Sankarshaṇa only were known up to the time of the earliest inscription which is to be referred to about the beginning of the first century before the Christian era, so that the system of four *Vyūhas* was not fully developed up to that time." From this he draws the further inference that as the Bhagavat Gīta has no specific reference to the four *Vyūhas* it must have been composed at a time anterior to this period and to a period up to which we could trace references to the *Vyūhas* in literature reaching back to the 4th century B. C. The worship of Vāsudēva and Baladēva, among the very large number of deities including even animals and trees, is referred to in a passage in the Buddhistic Niddēśa[1] referable to the 4th century B. C. There is a reference to a shrine to Sankarshaṇa in the Arthaśāstra. Patanjali refers to Vāsudēva as God in his comment on Pāṇiṇi IV, 3, 98. In an inscription at Ghasundi in Rajputana there is a reference to the temple for Sankarshaṇa and Vāsudēva. This inscription

---

[1] Sir R. G. Bhandarkar's Vaishnavism, etc., p. 3.

is dated about 200 B. C. on Palæographical grounds alone.[1] The Bẹsnagar inscription refers to the erection of a Garuḍadhvaja "in honour of Vāsudeva the God of Gods." That was constructed by one who bore a Greek name Helio-dora who describes himself as the son of Diya and as a Bhāgavata. He further states that he was a native of Takshaśila and was an ambassador of the Yavana Antalikita to Bhāgabhadra, probably ruler of eastern Mālva. This inscription is referable to the second century before Christ. There is a reference to Sankarshaṇa and Vāsudēva in the Nanaghat[2] inscription No. 1, dated the first century of the Christian era on palæographical grounds. The particular way in which the name Vāsudēva occurs in the Sūtra of Pāṇini and the explanation that Patanjali offers support, the presumption that Vāsudēva was regarded as a divine person even in the days of Pāṇini. Clearly historical references therefore take back the worship of Sankarshaṇa-Vāsudēva to the 4th century B.C. Sir R. G. Bhandarkar however doubts whether the four *Vyūhas* were known so early and concludes "It may be taken for granted that the two *Vyūhas*, Vāsudēva and Sankarshaṇa only were known up to the time of the latest inscription which is to be referred

[1] Ludder's List of Brahmi Inscriptions, No. 6.

[2] Luddor's List of Brahmi Inscriptions, No 1112.

to about the beginning of the first century before the Christian era, so that the system of four *Vyūhas* was not fully developed up to that time."[1] Apart from these however the learned doctor would regard the essential teaching of the Bhakti school traceable in the Upanishads themselves. He gives reference to two passages from the Upanishads, which contain according to him, "a verse to the effect that this supreme soul is not to be attained by lectures (from a teacher), nor by intelligence nor by much learning; *He is to be attained by him whom the supreme soul favours*; to him he discloses his form. Again we have the doctrine that *the supremely wise Being*, the life of all, leads a man to do good deeds, whom he desires to elevate (K. U. II, 8); and another that God dwelling in the heart of all beings controls them which latter forms the subject of a celebrated passage in B. U. III, 7. From this it is clear that the doctrine that the individual soul is dependent on the Supreme and that the latter alone works out the salvation was acknowledged in Upanishadic times." We shall show later on that this is exactly the doctrine of the Southern school of Bhakti.

---

[1] On the whole of this see Mr. R. P. Chanda: Arch. Memoirs, No. 5, 1920.

South India, its Special Home, though not its Origin.

This idea of Bhakti or devotion to a personal god is traceable in the earliest extant pieces of Tamil literature. Some of the oldest poems contain references to theistic gods both Vaishṇava and Śaiva, and what is more to the four *vyūhas* for which Sir R. G. Bhandarkar could find no clear reference in Sanskrit literature before the 1st century B. C. The Paripāḍal an ancient poem of the Śangam collection contains among one of its oldest pieces an unmistakable reference to the four *vyūhas* of Vishṇu. Its poem 3 is devoted entirely to Vishṇu, for whom there are a number of other poems in the same collection where various other *Vēdic* aspects of the God are adverted to, but nothing so clear as this to the four *vyūhas.* The worship of Krishṇa and Baladēva seems to have been quite an ordinary feature of Tamil civilization in the earliest periods of which we have knowledge. One of the oldest of South Indian [1] shrines for which we have a reference is devoted to the worship of Krishṇa. This feature of that temple seems to have continued till about the 8th century A. D. Among the numbers of temples mentioned as having existed in Kaveripaṭṭaṇam,

---

[1] Tirumālirunjolai near Madura.

the capital of the Cholas in the first century of the Christian era figure temples to Krishṇa and Baladēva. Temples to these two are found mentioned among the four principal shrines of Madura, namely those to Śiva, Krishṇa, Baladēva and Subramaṇya. These are again the four deities celebrated by the poet Narkīrar the President of the Third Śangam in Madura. A number of minor deities do of course come in for reference particularly among the deities to whom temples were found in Kaveripaṭṭaṇam. This multitude of gods and godlings to whom temples were in existence in the same city is referred to in the Buddhistic work Maṇimēkhalai in general terms; all temples beginning from that to Him with *an eye in the forehead and ending with that to the Bhūta in the* public square. A similar sentiment in Maduraik-Kanji was already referred to. The early grammatical work Tolkāppiyam referring to the presiding deities over the various divisions of a country refers to the forest country presided over by Krishṇa, the hill country presided over by Subrahmanya, the plain country presided over by Indra (the king), the country on the sea-shore presided over by Varuṇa; the *Vēdic* gods Varuṇa and Indra being brought into line with Subrahmaṇya and Krishṇa. We see therefore the germs that fructified into the school of Bhakti, both Vishṇu-Bhakti and Śiva-Bhakti, in the Tamil country already, and they exhibit the features which the northern school of Bhakti does in all its detail. In the course of development South India came to be regarded as the special provenance of Bhakti although the *Vēdic* form of ritualistic religion was maintained by the colonies of Brāhmanas who had come and settled down, and who were countenanced and maintained by the ruling powers and society as a whole. The unmistakable beginning of this development we could see already in early Tamil liteature. Several of the features peculiar to the Gīta itself are found in the poems devoted to Vishṇu, and even some of those more abstruse features for the worship of God, reaching behind the Bhagavat Gīta itself to the Upanishads.

The Aryan Character of its Literature.

This makes it clear that the literature of the the South taking into consideration only the literature extant, is essentially Āryan in character, exhibiting, no doubt, occasional features other than Āryan which get absorbed into the system. Buddhist and Jain works must necessarily have this character of the northern literature by the very necessities of their origin ; not so the Hindu part of the literature of the Tamils. These show unmistakably their Brahmanical character, not because they necessarily originated from or were handled by the Brahmans,—and this feature is to a great extent true—but because of something deeper still than that. Writers who were Buddhists and Jains, writers that were not Brahman exhibit this special character of the literature that has come down to us. It is possible to refer to numbers of poems in any collection referable to this period and known collectively as the Śangam collection which show this tendency very plainly. We shall examine the most characteristic of Tamil works with a view to this end and see how far there is any Āryan influence traceable in it. Before proceeding to that examination, however, it is worth while pointing out at once that it is acknowledged on all hands by common tradition that the Tamil language originated with Śiva and that its grammar was put into systematic form first by Agastya and then by his disciple the author of the Tolkāppiyam on the model of the Aindra School of Grammarians. The earliest tradition regarding the emigration of these people exhibits Āryan lead also. It was Agastya that led the emigration. The bulk of the people belonging to the ruling and agricultural classes were led forward by him in a colony from south-western Hindustan, the land of Krishṇa. It is they that destroyed forests and turned these into arable land; in other words, introduced the first elements of civilization from the north. This tradition no doubt states that Agastya's grammar preceded that of Pāṇini and that the division of the *Vēdas* accepted in the Tamil country is based on the older *Śākas*, rather than the division into four recognised groups by Vyāsa. The only authority extant for all these traditions however, it must be noted, is tradition preserved for us by the commentators of a much later period; and the one that is preserved which offers full details is that preserved by the Brahman commentator Nachchinārkiniyar who lived in the twelfth or the thirteenth century. We are not however dependent upon this late tradition for our authority. We can trace innumerable details in the body of the literature in original that has come down to us, and if these details should be put together it becomes fairly clear that so far as literary Tamil is concerned it is undoubtedly of Āryan character with equally indubitable traces of other than Āryan features in it, features which are far too primitive in comparison.

CHAPTER VI.

THE KUṚAL : A CHARACTERISTICALLY TAMIL CLASSIC.

Among the number of works and collections that have come down to us from this remote period, most of which have a character of their own, the Kuṛal of Tiruvaḷḷuvar stands easily pre-eminent as a peculiarly Tamil classic. The word "Kuṛal" means no more than short literally, because the whole work is composed of stanzas in the aphoristic couplets of 4 and 3 feet respectively; hence the name Kuṛal. It is actually composed of 1330 of these stanzas divided into 133 chapters. These are again thrown into three larger groups which give another name for the work *muppāl* (*tṛvarga*, three kinds). This division into three consists of three out of four divisions which go by the name "objects of life" (*purushārtha*). This is supposed to be a peculiarity of that work. It is a peculiarity no doubt, but not so characteristic of Tamil as there is a corresponding division known to the Sanskritists who speak of the *tṛvarga* which is the exact equivalent of *muppāl*. It can be described as a didactic work the purpose of which is to enforce the teachings of ethics common to all religions then obtaining in India, so that whatever might be the actual persuasion adopted by the individual he would still find a guide for conduct in life in this work. Being thus eclectic in character, Buddhists, Jains and Brahmans claimed the work as relating to their particular form of religion, while there are not people wanting who would see in the work an anti-Brahmanical character, recognising it at the same time as relating to the religion of the Hindus.

The four objects of life are, as is well-known, Dharma (righteousness), Artha (wealth), Kāma (Love) and Moksha (Salvation). The work of course gives Tamil names for these respectively Aṛam, Poruḷ, Inbam and Vīḍu, which are the exact Tamil equivalants of the corresponding Sanskrit terms. The author omits any elaborate treatment of the last for the very logical reason that that is not a subject which lends itself to didactic treatment, being unearthly in its character. If the first three objects of life are attained by adopting a moral life, the other follows inevitably in consequence. Hence the omission of the fourth in this. The book devotes 34 chapters of the 133 to righteousness taking into it all the four stages of disciple, householder, a retired life and that of the hermit, the four well-known Brahmanical divisions of life.

Of these the life of the house-holder comes in for elaborate treatment naturally in 20 chapters. Then follows forest life treated in 10 and lastly comes the life of renunciation dealt with in 3 chapters; one chapter is devoted to the study of fate. Following this comes the part relating to life in society which presupposes some kind of Government. In this section particularly, the indebtedness to the Arthaśāstra of Chāṇakya stands out clear. Almost the same division of treatment happens to be followed as in Kāmandaka's Nīti Śāstra if not the Artha Śāstra itself.

The section on King is treated in 25 chapters, ministers in 10, the country, fortifications and royal wealth each in one chapter, army in two, alliance in 5, enmity in 6 and other miscellaneous matters relating to the conduct of the king, the conduct of subjects, the conduct of agriculture, etc., in 19 chapters making a total of 70 chapters for this section out of the 133. Coming to the section on love the division follows the characteristic flora, the feelings evoked and the actions resulting therefrom. These are all treated in the remaining 25 chapters. That the author of the Kuṛal knew the Artha Śāstra is very clearly in evidence. One Kuṛal, as pointed out by the commentator Parimēl Aḻahar, is not capable of interpretation properly and has actually been misread for want of knowledge of the Arthaśāstra text.

Therefore then it must be posterior to the Artha Śāstra. It is quoted with acknowledgment in the Maṇimēkhalai, and, without the explicit reference, in a few places in the Śilappadhikāram, thus referring it to a period before the two. There is a collection of poems in appreciation of this work ascribed to the members of the "Third Tamil Śangam," including in it one stanza each by "the voice in the air," Sarasvati, Śiva and the contemporary Pāṇḍya Uggrap-Peru-Vaḻudi, the other 49 by the forty-nine members of the famous Academy. The fact that one of the members Śattanār actually quotes from it implies that the work had already attained to a certain amount of vogue among the learned.

Strong Infusion of Sanskrit Culture; Ethical and Political.

We have already pointed out that the peculiar feature in the Kuṛaḷ of dealing with only the first three of the four objects of life is not altogether so peculiar, having regard to the notion exhibited in Manu in regard to *tṛvarga* in Chapter II, Sloka 224. The author of the Kuṛal apparently adopted the same principle as the śloka of Manu above referred to. That that was the principle adopted, and the actual details of the division of the whole work on those particular lines, taking into consideration even the *Vaidic* four stages of life are found explained in an old manuscript which contains an introduction to the commentary by Parimēl Aḻahar. This authority considers the first four sections, namely, invocation, celebration of rain, celebration of those that renounce the world and the celebration of conduct as purely introductory, and the following chapters take up, one after the other, conduct in household, in forest life and lastly in renunciation, thus taking up 34 of the chapters. Then follow the 70 chapters dealing with politics in the widest sense of the term being synonymous with all that constitutes earthly prosperity. Then follows the chapter bearing on the kind of life dealing with the relation between man and woman. In this he adopts to a far more prominent degree the customary divisions of land in Tamil along with much that may be found in the northern lore. To show how far this didactic work, the professed purpose of which is to enforce moral conduct of an eclectic kind so as to provide a general rule of conduct for all, whatever their religion, is indebted to the Artha Śāstra, we have only to refer in some little detail to chapter 51 of the work dealing with the selection of ministers by the king. The first verse of this chapter contains an expression which indicates unmistakable affinity with Kauṭilya's Artha

Śāstra. The substance of the verse is that a man before being selected for admission into the body of ministers should be tested by the four ways of righteousness, wealth, love and *fear of life*. This is subjecting the man to temptation in the various ways to which a minister is peculiarly liable. In these four items the first three are common enough, but the last one is an expression which according to the commentator was misunderstood and altered into a wrong reading for lack of knowledge of the original source of inspiration, that source being Book 1, Ch. 10 of the Artha Śāstra (translation) or Chapter 6, page 16 of the text, referring to what Chāṇakya calls *upadā*. The last expression in Tamil is *uyir achcham* literally fear for life. The second of these two words has been altered into "*èch-cham*" meaning "that which remains." These are the four *upadās* that Chāṇakya refers to. That the commentator is not drawing from his imagination is fully in evidence in the following eight out of nine verses constituting this chapter. Each one of them refers directly to the various objections of schools of politicians referred to in the Artha Śāstra, Chapter VIII of the translation or Chapter IV of the original. Except for the difference in the name of two of those quoted, which may be after all alternative names, the whole chapter agrees point for point with Chapter VIII of the Artha Śāstra. The last verse winds up the discussion by agreeing with the conviction arrived at by Kauṭilya. The only pity of the whole is that these authors are not so named in the text itself. We have no right to expect it having regard to the fact that the whole of this work is thrown into the form of aphorisms which have necessarily to be very brief, and, as was pointed out already, each one of these verses could contain only 7 feet, four and three each, in two lines. But to any dispassionate reader the similarity of idea is quite clear, detail for detail, so that there is no reasonable doubt left that the author of the Kuṛal had full knowledge of the Artha Śāstra and adopted several of its conclusions strangely enough. It is to the credit of Tamil scholarship of an elder age that this similarity had already been pointed out by a commentator who preceded Parimēl Aḻahar in this work.[1] It is possible to refer to a number of other verses in which the relation between the Kuṛal and the Nīti Śāstra of Kāmandaka appears very plainly, and it is a well-known fact that the Kāmandaka is only an abridgment of the Artha Śāstra of Chāṇakya, and the author acknowledges his indebtedness to this latter work and its author. We shall indicate the similarity, only in respect of just a few other Sanskrit works.

[1] Quoted by Paudit R. Raghava Aiyangar in Sen-Tamil, Vol. 1, pp. 46-48.

Kuṟaḷ 259 where the author says "It is better by far not to kill for eating than celebrate a thousand sacrifices" may be compared with Manu, Chapter V, Śloka 53. "He who during a hundred years annually offers a horse sacrifice, and he who entirely abstains from meat obtain the same reward for their meritorious 'conduct.'" Kuṟaḷ 166 which says that he that grows jealous of another's making gifts will himself with all his relatives suffer without food and clothing is found in the Dāna Chandrika. Kuṟaḷ 256 which says if there were no people in the world that would kill for eating there would be none in the world to kill at all is an idea embedded in the Bhīshmaparva of the Mahābhārata. Kuṟaḷ 58 again: "If women only conducted themselves faithfully and dutifully they would lead a much respected life in heaven." This may be compared to Chapter V, Śloka 155 or 156 of Manu "no sacrifice, no vow, no fast must be performed by women apart (from their husbands); if a wife obeys her husband *she will for that (reason alone) be exalted in heaven.* A faithful wife who desires to dwell (after death) with her husband must never do anything that might displease him who took her hand whether he was alive or dead." It is hardly necessary to multiply quotations. Surprising as it may seem at first sight that there is such an intimate connection between the two cultures the Āryan and the Draviḍian in Kuṛaḷ, we would be no less surprised if it had been otherwise having regard to the historical circumstances under which this remarkable work had been produced in the Tamil land. A close study of the work in intimate connection with Sanskrit literature goes to heighten our admiration of the extraordinary learning of the commentator Parimēl Aḻakar, who in many of these matters exhibited these features most accurately. That his judgment that the author of the Kuṛaḷ set before himself a work which would give to everybody a practical rule of conduct in life irrespective of his peculiar religion, and therefore it is a work eclectic in character and liable to be claimed by the various sections of people as belonging peculiarly to themselves is fully justified. The work has reference to the Hindu society of South India and that the author had much respect for Brahmans and Brahmanism as an integral part of the social order is unmistakably in evidence in the following three verses: Kuṛaḷ 134 states briefly that the Veda if forgotten could be learnt again, but the Brahman loses his character if he falls off from conduct peculiar to his station. Kuṛaḷ 543 lays down that the righteous rule of a monarch stands as the main support of the learning of the Brahman and righteousness; and Kuṛaḷ 560 similarly states that if the king ceases to render protection cows will cease to yield and Brahmans who have to do their six-fold duty will forget their learning, the Veda. In each one of these cases the consequences are regarded as nothing short of calamitous to society. It may not be possible positively to assert that the author was of the Brahmanical persuasion, as other than Brahmans, even Buddhist and Jain authors often speak in the same strain of the Brahman as a member of Hindu society; but on a dispassionate examination of the work there seems justification for the assumption that the author of the Kuṛaḷ though undoubtedly belonging to a lower caste was Brahmanical in religion.

CHAPTER VII.

The Rise of the Pallavas.

The question who the Pallavas were is one which can hardly be described as being out of the stage of discussion yet. The theory that held the field till recently almost unchallenged was that they were a tribe of foreigners supposed to be of Parthian origin who having effected a lodgment in the part of the country near the mouth of the Indus, moved southeastwards gradually till they came to be found in possession of the region dominated by Kānchī. The main reason for this contention is that a class of people called Palhavas figure among the lists of tribes on that frontier in the Rāmāyaṇa, the Mahābhārata and other such sources of information. They are also found to figure among the enemies overthrown by the Sātavāhanas, namely Gautamīputra Sātakarṇi and his son. The Ceylon chonicle also mentions a tract of country which seems to be located in that region which is named in the Mahāvamśa, Pallavabhogga. This collection of references to the Pallavas is held to justify the conclusion that they were a body of foreigners who entered India by way of Baluchistan, and moved on till they hinduised themselves so far as to forget their foreign origin and raise no suspicions among the peoples over whom they imposed their authority. There are, however, grave difficulties in the way of accepting this apparently satisfactory account as we have some information in Tamil literature which militates strongly against this view of their origin. We have already pointed out that in the days of the early Cholas, Kānchī was a Chola Viceroyalty, Palatine Viceroyalty though it was. We have already given a number of references to show that the Tamils regarded Pulikat as their northern boundary, and the people or the tribes that inhabited the region immediately north of it have invariably been referred to as speaking a language different from that of the Tamils. Those people are invariably referred to as Vaḍukar, which is the name by which the Telugus are ordinarily known in the Tamil country to-day. But in that early age the term Vaḍukar seems to have been invariably applied both to the Telegus and the Kannaḍa people across the Tamil frontier.[1]

Even the Periyapurāṇam a work of the early 12th century observes this classification as it

[1] For references see ch. I above.

speaks of the Karnāṭakas as Vaḍukar.[1] That designation is still preserved in the name of the Badagas of the Nilgiris. The region on the eastern side of this portion of the Peninsula occupied by this people is the region where we find the earliest memorials of Pallava rule. When the Pallavas emerge into the full light of history we find them in possession of Kānchī. Whether they were Tamils or Telugus they are people we find along the region between the lower course of the Krishna and the river Pālār. To begin with, this region, at least the major part of it, was designated Tonḍamanḍalam in those days. In regard to their origin and their previous habitat we have already exhibited a certain number of references from the old classical collection Ahanānūṛu referring to what actually constituted Tonḍanādu ; both Kānchī and (Tirupati) were alike included in this territorial division Tonḍamanḍalam. We have also quoted an old passage, from Nachchinārkiniyar's commentary, by an author whose name is not quoted, giving the important equation that the people called Tonḍaiyar, people of Tonḍamanḍalam, were treated as the same as the Pallavas. During the period to which this reference must be held to relate the words Tonḍaiyar and Pallavas, were considered to be synonymous.[2]

---

[1] See Mūrti Nāynārprāṇam, stanza 11.

[2] Nackhhinārkkiniyar's comment on Sutra 54, Poruḷadhikaram Tolkāppiyam.

On this basis alone there is good reason for regarding the Toṇḍaiyar as the name of the people living in the country who were subsequently called by a Sanskrit translation of the same. This inconvenient position is sought to be got round, by votaries of the foreign origin of the Pallavas, by bringing the Chola occupation of Kānchī and of the literature bearing on the period to a comparatively short period of interregnum that is supposed to have existed between one of the early dynasties of the Pallavas and the later great dynasty; in other words by bringing the Śangam age itself to the fifth century A.D. We have already demonstrated clearly that it would be impossible for a variety of reasons to move the period down by about four centuries in that arbitrary fashion. The question rests still upon the specific Gajabāhu synchronism supported by so much of valuable historical evidence that it would require a very strong case on the other side to turn it upside down, not to speak of the insuperable difficulty in detail that would have to be confronted in any attempt at constructive criticism. Kānchī figures in this body of early literature as a viceroyalty of the Cholas and the only Toṇḍamān that figures in the whole body of this literature as the ruler of this part of the country is the Toṇḍamān Iḷaṁ-Tirayan of Kānchī who ruled over Conjeevaram not so much in his own right but by right of his

Chola ancestry. We shall come to this point a little later.

The Pallavas. Native to South India.

Among the large number of places in which the Pahlavas get mention in Sanskrit literature they are found mentioned with the well-known tribes of the north-western frontier such as the Śakas and the Yavanas. It would be difficult to find any clear reference to these anywhere in South India. There are a certain number of places in which the south Indian kingdoms are mentioned. We do not find anything corresponding to the Palhava state or tribe in the south. The Asoka edicts do not mention any. Even where the reference occurs in classical Sanskrit literature the Cholas, the Pāṇḍyas, the Keralas are referred to and where we should, from geographical position, expect the Pallavas a class of people by name Drāviḍa is mentioned. Drāviḍa or Darmida is generally taken to be the equivalent of the Tamil, Tamiḻa in Tamiḻakam (Sans. Dramiḍaka), the whole of the Tamil country. It is also used in a somewhat narrower sense as indicating one of the four kingdoms, a kingdom that would correspond to, and that gets to be known to later history as, the Pallava kingdom with Kānchī for its centre. It would be rational therefore to regard the Pallavas native to South India, and as the people who were before then known by the name Toṇḍaiyar more generally. There are some objections to be met before taking this particular position. By a careful study of the available Pallava records that epigraphy has unearthed, we are able to throw the early Pallavas into three groups. They are found first of all as tribal chieftains ruling their various little states, three or four of them could be specifically mentioned, in the region extending from the lower course of the Krishna to almost the Pālār, Daśanapura, Pālakkada, Mēnmāttura and Kānchī. The records of some of these rulers happen to be in Prakrit and the others in Sanskrit ; and they are found scattered across from the west coast to the frontiers of the Godaveri district in the east, the actual belt of country constituting the Vaḍuka frontier of the Tamils of the classical Tamil literature. Their association with Amarāvati, the discovery of certain statues of Roman workmanship as it is thought and the statement that one of these early rulers attained to his royal dignity by marriage, are all brought into requisition to give them a marriage alliance with the Āndhras, to give their art a Roman origin and to make these a foreign people who imposed themselves as rulers over the vast region extending almost from the Godaveri to at least Pālār in the south. The matter requires therefore careful consideration.

In the region which these later inscriptions indicate as peculiarly the Pallava Province we find in the days of the Sātavāhanas certain records which called it peculiarly the district of the Sātavāhanas. The Myakadoni inscription refers to the region round Adoni as Sātāhani Āhāra, and the person responsible for the government of it is named Khanda Nāga (Skanda Nāga), the Mahāsēnāpti (great general). If the āhāra or district of the Sātavāhanas in this record meant anything it must refer to the district which was the fief of the Sātavāhanas peculiarly, the Sātavāhanas being a clan of the powerful race of the Āndhra people as a whole. This interpretation of the term Sātavāhana is quite in keeping with what we find in Tamil literature. The Hirahadagalli copper-plates found in the Bellary district would confirm the same position, but being on copper-plates, it is likely that the record had travelled before it reached its final resting place at the village named above. This spread of the Sātavāhanas from east to west along the region which the Tamils called Vaḍuka region would make the Sātavāhanas, Āndhras, and give the region the character of an Āndhra frontier province. The name Khanda Nāga itself shows a family likeness to the early Pallava names that we know of from other records. Along with these must be considered the records of another class of Sātavāhana officers who give themselves Nāga names and symbols in their records, and are associated with the district which went by the name of Nāgara Khaṇḍa afterwards. That is the region along the western ghauts with Bānavāse for its capital. The expanded cobra-hood at the beginning of the inscription and the very name Çūṭu being Tamil and old Kanarese for crest, in this case the crest of the cobra, would make them Nāgas clearly. This interpretation can be supported by a familiar use in classical literature of Śūḍu, being frequently associated with cobra hoods; and *Çūṭukula* can, without violence, be taken to stand for Nāgakula, a family of the Nāgas. We find this chieftain and his records associated with the western part of the belt of the country extending from the east coast to the west which the Tamils of the classical age invariably called the country of the Vaḍuka. There is also the feature that the Āndhra coins bearing on the obverse the representation of a two-masted ship and found extending in the Toṇḍamaṇḍala country proper would argue the possession of this tract by the Sātavāhanas at least for a time. The representation of a ship on the Sātavāhana lead coins found in this region is very appropriate as the more important section of the people who inhabited this tract of country is known to Tamil literature as the Tiraiyar (lit. sea-people). It is one of their chieftains, the son of a Chola king by a Nāga Princess, that figures in clasical Tamil literature as the first Viceroy, other than a royal prince, of Kānchī. He is invariably given the name Toṇḍamān, great one among the Toṇḍar or Toṇḍaiyar. The classical passage quoted by Nachinārkiniyar already adverted to equates the Toṇḍaiyar with the Pallavas. Naturally therefore if the region occupied by the Toṇḍaiyar or the Pallavas passed under the authority of the Sātavāhanas, and if they appointed Governors for this particular region from among them, these Governors would be governors of the Toṇḍamaṇḍalam or the Pallava country, and would get to be known popularly as Pallava Governors. The name of the great general in authority round Bellary having a family likeness to the names of the early Pallavas would warrant the assumption that it is these Mahāsēnāpatis of the south-eastern territory of the Sātavāhanas that were the division of the family which came to be known to history as the Pallavas. They extended their authority from Amarāvati in Guntur southwards to Kānchī itself and the territory dependent thereon extending to the banks of the south Pennār. The Nāga or snake as one of the ensigns on the banners of the Pallavas would argue some intimate connection with the family of the Nāgas, and that is what we find in an examination of such records of theirs as are so far accessible to us. There might have been foreigners in the region of the Guntur district. That is something different from calling the dynasty a dynasty of foreigners. So far as the available evidence goes they were a dynasty of officers of the Āndhras probably related, or even springing out of the clan of the Sātavāhanas. When the power of the latter extended southwards as the result of constant struggle on this frontier, the Governors of the Guntur district extended their sphere of authority so as to take in the newly acquired territory. When the Sātavāhana dynasty broke up in the middle of the third century these apparently set up independently and founded the new dynasty of the Pallavas as distinct from the older chieftains, the Toṇḍamāns of the region. As the Tamils did not note any distinction between these Vaḍukas and those that lived to the westward of them along their northern frontier they must have been near of kin to each other in many respects. Belonging to the same clan as the ruling dynasty of the Dakhan it is nothing strange that they should have entered into marriage alliance even of an important character. All these circumstances would only be natural in their particular position. Hence the conclusion seems warranted by the known facts in relation to these people, that they were natives of South India, and are not a dynasty of foreigners.[1] The conquest of the Tondamandalam by the Sātavāhanas would amply account for the eclipse of the Chola power in that particular region which had hitherto remained unaccounted for. When the Pallavas emerged into importance we find them engaged in a two-faced struggle one against the Cholas of the south in alliance often with the other Tamil powers, and the other against the newly rising power of the Chālukyas in the north-west. In the beginning of this struggle we find the Cholas not the great political power that they were, but comparatively insignificant and depending upon the support of the Pāṇḍyas.

Pallavas: Patrons of Northern Culture.

We find in the earliest known inscription of the Sātavāhanas that they were votaries of the well-known Hindu Gods—Visnṇu and Śiva. The Nanaghaut inscription refers to some of the names of the Lokapālas (the guardian deities of the directions), the *Vyūhas* (forms) of Vishṇu, and Skanda or Subramaṇya. The Myakadoni inscription itself is the record of the gift of a village by a queen to a Vishṇu temple. If therefore, as was pointed out in the preceding

[1] Rajaśēkhara, the great poet and critic who lived in the Courts of Mahendrabala and Mahīpāla of Kanauj gives the account of the Geographical divisions and peoples of India in his time. He distinguishes between the Southern *Pallavas* and North-Western *Pahlavas*. In his time the Pallavas of Kanchi were just losing their ascendency in South India or had just lost it. (See Introduction to Kāvyamīmāmsa, Baroda Sanskrit Series.)

section, the dynasty of the Pallavas was native to the locality and were in close association, official and personal, with the ruling family of the Sātavāhanas, we should find them devoted to the same cult generally as the main branch of the Sātavāhanas, their religious culture being naturally northern, probably in both forms Vaishṇava and Saiva. We find in the Āndhra country, even a foreigner like the Śaka Rishabhadatta, a votary of this comprehensive cult of the Āndhras themselves as we are enabled to understand from the inscriptions recording his various donations. It is that broad culture that the Pallavas carried into the Tamil country when they moved into the northern part of it. Although we find evidence of the prevalence both of the cults of Śiva and Vishṇu in the Tamil country already, the patronage of this northern culture generally seems to have been associated with the Pallavas. Their inscriptions till late in the history of the dynasty happened to be either Sanskrit or Prakrit; their earliest temples, even the cave ones, are devoted to Śiva and Vishṇu, and to none of the other deities known to the somewhat miscellaneous pantheon of the early Tamil classics. Hence the advent of the "foreign Pallavas" into the Tamil country not only meant the rule of the foreigner to the Tamils but also carried along with it the special patronage of the new culture of the north. The hostility between the Pallvas and the Tamil kings of the farther south seems to be accounted for to a certain extent at any rate by this partiality apart from their character as barbarian foreigners in the eye of the Tamil. Throughout the period of Pallava history which may extend from A. D. 200 to almost the last quarter of the 9th century the Pallavas and the southern powers were in constant hostility if they were not always at war. The hostility between the early Chāḷukyas and the Pallavas, which is a prominent feature of the history of both the powerful dynasties, is due to the effort of the Chāḷukya successors of the Āndhras to extend their authority over the whole of what was once the Āndhra Empire, and the correlative effort of the newly founded dynasty of the Pallavas to make good their own possessions against these new claimants. It is the necessities of this struggle on the northern frontier that sometimes gave respite to the southern frontier but otherwise the normal state of relationship seems to have been one of hostility between the Pallavas and the Tamils all through this long period of close on seven centuries.

PALLAVAS: NOT GREAT PATRONS OF TAMIL LITERATURE.

This long period of Pallava dominance, as it may well be called, was a period of no doubt considerable activity and output in regard to Tamil literature. A large number of Tamil works are referable to this period, but in none of them do we find the Pallavas as patrons of Tamil literature in the sense that we find the kings and the petty chieftains of the age preceding are. Several of these poets were contemporaries of some of the great sovereigns of the Pallava dynasty. The Tēvāram hymner Appar, a Jain first and a Śaiva afterwards, was a contemporary of the great Pallava Mahēndra Varman whose conversion to Śaivism is said to have been due to him. His companion but a much younger man, Sambandar, was a contemporary of his son and successor Narasimha Varman; but neither of these rulers can be considered as a special patron of either of the authors that the kings or chieftains of the Śangam age could be said to be ; and the works of most of these writers have reference not directly to the celebration of the exploits of the patrons. They devote themselves more or less to other themes and such references as we get to these rules are merely incidental. It is only one work so far known that can clearly be considered to have had their patronage, and that is the work Nandikkalambakam dedicated to a Nandi Varman victor at Teḷḷāṛu, a late Pallava of the 8th or 9th century. So far as is known therefore the Pallavas do not show themselves to have been in any special sense patrons of Tamil literature as their predecessors could.

CHAPTER VIII

EARLY HISTORY OF THE PALLAVAS.

What was said of the origin of the Pallavas in the previous sections would have made it clear that they were in all probability a family of feudatories of the Sātavāhanas of the Dakhan. These feudatories are clearly described as belonging to the family of the Nāgas, whatever that may mean to us now. Northern Mysore and the country set over against it up to the western sea which later on became a fief of the Kadambas was in the possession of a Nāga family of Maharatis belonging to the Chūṭakula, apparently a Nāga designation. The Sātavāhana Rāshṭra proper, set over against the territory of Kānchī further to the east of this division, was the fief of the great commander (Mahāsēnapati-Skanda Nāga). In the days of the greatest expansion of the Āndhra empire under Pulumāvi II and his immediate successors the whole of the southern frontier of the Āndhra country, the region of the Vaḍukas according to Tamil literature, was held by powerful families of these Nāgas. When the Āndhra empire broke up early in the third century these powerful feudatories made themselves independent in the regions under their government. Toṇḍamaṇḍalam which in the reign of the great Pulumāvi was under the Sātavāhanas should have fallen to the lot of the Mahāsēnāpati referred to above, or his successors in the same region, the district which was called peculiarly the district of the Sātavāhanas. The advance of the Sātavāhanas themselves under Pulumāvi must have put an end to the authority of the Cholas in this particular region. When the Governors set up independently of the Sātavāhanas, a generation or two later, the Mahāsēnāpati Skanda Nāga himself or one of his successors became heir to this region of the Toṇḍamaṇḍalam as well.

According to the available inscriptions of the Pallavas, the Pallavas could be divided into four separate families or dynasties. The connection of some of these to one another we know, and of others we do not know. We have a certain number of charters in Prakrit of which three are important ones. Then follows a dynasty which issued their charters in Sanskrit; following this came the family of the great Pallavas beginning with Simha Vishṇu; this was followed by a dynasty of the usurper Nandi Varman, another great Pallava. We are overlooking for the present the dynasty of the Ganga-Pallavas postulated by the Epigraphists. The earliest of these Pallava charters is the one known as the Mayidavolu[1] (Guntur district) copper-plates.

These plates contain the charter issued by the heir-apparent (Yuva Mahārājah) Śiva Skanda Varman making a grant in the division Dhannakada, that is Amarāvati, in the tenth year of the reign of his father whose name is not given.

The next record is what is known as the Hirahadagalli plates (Bellary District).[2] This record is dated in the 8th year of Sivaskanda Varman and confirms the gift made by his father who is described merely as "Bappa-dēva" (revered father). Another copper plate charter found in the Guntur district, is dated in the reign of a Vijaya Skanda Varman and is the record of a grant made by Chārudēvi,[3] wife of the Yuvamahārāja Vijaya Buddha Varman and mother of Prince Buddhyankura. There is no doubt that the Yuvamahārāja of the first record is the same as the ruling sovereign of the second, the name and circumstances of the two records giving us full warrant for the identification. The question is a little less certain in respect of the sovereign mentioned in the third record, namely Vijaya Skanda Varman. Is he the same as the Śiva Skanda Varman of the

[1] Eph. Ind., Vol. VI, p. 84.

[2] Ep. Ind., Vol. I, p. 2.

[3] Ep. Ind., Vol. VIII, p. 2, 143.

previous two records? Among the records of that age Śiva, Vijaya and sometimes even Vijaya-Śiva, are used as prefixes indicating the regard or respect in which the ruler was held. Apart from this the use of the attribute Vijaya before Skanda Varman does not alter the name, but only gives an additional circumstance of importance. It would not be therefore doing any particular violence to identify the Vijaya Skanda Varman of the third record with the Śiva Skanda Varman of the other two. These three charters all of them refer t , the region which was peculiarly the district of the Sātavāhanas. If this identification of Vijaya Skanda Varman turns out true the succession could be arranged in the following table :

"Bappa-Dēva"
|
(Śiva or Vijaya) Skanda Varma
|
Yuva Mahārāja, Buddhavarman. — Vijaya Chārudēvi
|
Prince Buddhyankura.

The Mayidavol grant was issued, from Conjeevaram (Kānchī) by the heir-apparent, to the Governor at Amarāvati, and the village granted is described as being in the Āndhrapatha (Vaḍukavaḷi of the Tamils, the Andhra country). Thus it is made clear to us that Kānchī was already the capital of a region taking in naturally the Toṇḍamaṇḍalam and the districts north of it at least as far as Amarāvati or the River Krishna. In the second charter the ruler Śiva Skanda Varma lays c'aim to having performed the Agnishṭoma, Vājapēya and Aśvamēdha sacrifices. Of these the last could be performed only by a conquercr, or one who set up as such. The way that he addresses his grant to the lords of provinces royal princes, generals, rulers of districts, customs officers, prefects of countries, etc., gives us an insight into the distinct Asokan character of the organization of the government and its affiliation even to the Arthaśāstra. What is more important it exhibits an organization which is northern in character, perhaps quite distinct from that of the Tamils of the farther south. There is another interesting detail in it that the father of this king, whatever his name, had granted many crores of gold, and what is more important to us in connection with the origin of this dynasty *one hundred thousand ox-ploughs.* This, if it means anything, indicates undoubtedly the effort made by this ruler for the conversion of the great forests into arable land. It would be well to remember in this context that this part of the country was known to the Tamils as Daṇḍāraṇyam, the same as the Sanskrit Daṇḍakāraṇya where cattle-rearing was the principal occupation, and cattle-raiding the principal sport. It was apparently this "Bappa-dēva" that made an effort, with what success we are not told, to transform the forest into cultivated country. It will thus be clear that this dynasty of the Prakrit charters beginning with "Bappa-dēva" were the historical founders of the Pallava dominion in South India. It is taken here that all the ruler whose charters in Prakrit have come down to us are to be regarded as members of a single dynasty while there is the possibility that they were members of two dynasties which may not after all be connected with each other ; but there is little doubt, if this alternative should turn out true, that the two dynasties followed each other without much interval.

Passing on to the Pallavas of the Sanskrit charters we come to a number of dynasties which would at first sight appear to be so many separate dynasties. According to the Uruvapalli copperplates the succession is as follows :—

Skanda Varman
|
Vīra Varman
|
Skanda Varman II
|
The Yuvamahāraja Visnṇugopa
|
Simha Varman II
|

The Darśi fragment refers itself to the time of the great-grandson of Vīrakorcha Varman, that is Vīra Varma, referring apparently to Simha Varman, son of Yuvamahārāja Vishṇugopa. The Chendalūr Plates issued from the "victorious Kānchīpura" gives

Skanda Varman
|
Kumāra Vishṇu
|
Buddha Varman
|
Kumāra Vishṇu II.

The Udaiyendram grant similarly gives :—

Skanda Varman
|
Simha Varman
|
Skanda Varman II
|
Nandi Varman.

The newly discovered Ongōḍu-Plates give :—

Kumāra Vishṇu
|
Skanda Varman
|
Vīra Varman
|
Skanda Varman

These four separate genealogies were apparently not altogether separate in respect of the fact that several of these grants were issued from Kānchī, and others from places like Daśanapura, Pālakkada.

and Mēnmāttūra. There are considerations which would lead us to consolidate these four separate genealogies into one genealogical table.

The Uruvapalli copper-plates record the grant of Yuva Mahārāja Vishṇugopa, but the grant is dated in the reign of a king named Simha Varman. If Vishṇugopa issued the grant as Yuvamahārāja and dates it in the reign of a Simha Varman, Simha Varman must have been the Mahārāja, either the father or an elder brother of the donor. According to the grant itself Vishṇugopa's father is a Skanda Varman. The only other alternative therefore is that Simha Varman was in all probability an elder brother of Vishṇugopa. So the genealogy will have to be extended by the addition of Simha Varman and would stand—

```
                    Skanda Varman
                          |
                     Vīra Varman
                          |
                   Skanda Varman II
                          |
          ----------------------------------
          |                                |
   Simha Varman I              Yuvamahārāja Vishṇugopa
                                           |
                                   Simha Varman II.
```

The Chēndalūr genealogy contains four names beginning with Skanda Varman. Dr. Hultzsch from palæographical considerations held that these rulers must have come in between

Simha Varman II and Simha Vishṇu. There are considerations however which would lead to the identification of the Skanda Varman of these plates with the Skanda Varman the father of Yuvamahārāja Vishṇugopa. This arrangement would make Kumāra Vishṇu another brother of Yuvamahārāja Vishṇugopa, with a son Buddha Varman and his son Kumāra Vishṇu II. The genealogy of the Udaiyēndram grant gives again at the top a Skanda Varman followed by three other names ending in Nandi Varman. The Vēlūrpāḷaiyam plates introduce what appears a gap with Kumāra Vishṇu II and brings in a Nandi Varman before introducing Simha Varman, the father of Simha Vishṇu. The only Nandi Varman referable to this period would be the last name mentioned in the Udaiyēndram grant. Therefore it is possible to include this genealogy in that of the line of Simha Varman, the elder brother of Vishṇugopa; Skanda Varman being the father, Simha Varman his eldest son and the elder brother of Yuva, Mahārāja Vishṇugopa, his son Skanda Varman and his son Nandi Varman. This last will, according to the Vēlūrpāḷaiyam plates bring us on to the line of Simha Vishṇu. The Ongōḍu plates discovered in the year 1915 introduce us to yet another line beginning with Kumāra Vishṇu. The last of these Skanda Varman issued the document not from Kānchī but from Tāmbrāpa.

None of these names figure in the Vēlūrpāḷaiyam plates in this order; nor does the Vāyalūr Pillar contain the four names in this order as given in the Ongōḍu plates. The Kumāra Vishṇu at the head of the table therefore may be Kumāra Vishṇu I or Kumāra Vishṇu II, and the whole dynasty, a local dynasty having had nothing to do with the regular succession of the main line. If it should actually have been so we get the final genealogy as follows:—

- Skanda Varman I
  - Vīra Varman
    - Skanda Varman II
      - Simha Varman I
        - Skanda Varman III
          - Nandi Varman
      - Yuvamahārāja Vishṇugopa or Vishṇugopa Varman
        - Simha Varman II.
      - Kumāra Vishṇu I
        - Buddha Varman
          - Kumāra Vishṇu II

Verse 10 of the Vēlūrpāḷaiyam plates introduces then, without specifying any connection, Simha Varman, father of Simha Vishṇu and that introduces us to the line of the well-known Pallava dynasty. Before proceeding to a consideration of that dynasty we have to consider one or two questions that arise in respect of the dynasty of the Sanskrit charters, and Vishṇugopa of Kānchī, the contemporary of Samudra Gupta. Incidentally also we shall have to consider the question whether the dating of the

Uruvapalli, Mangalūr and Pikīra grants respectively from Pālakkada, Daśanapura and Mēnmāttūra, all of them places in the Guntur district, warrants the assumption of a Pallava interregnum in Kānchī; if there had been such an interregnum, whether that is the time to which we could refer the ancient Cholas, Karikāla and others.

AN INTERREGNUM IN THE PERIOD OF THE PALLAVAS.

The question of this interregnum is so closely connected with the question of the origin of the Pallavas that the one cannot be separated from the other for any clear understanding of the early history of the Pallavas. The late Rai Bahadur V. Venkayya made an excellent contribution on the subject of the Pallavas to the annual report of the Archæological Survey of India for the year 1906-07. This article was an elaboration of his presidential address to the South Indian Association on the same subject. He states it as his opinion, on page 221, that 'the Pallavas with whose history we are concerned, may, until their origin is satisfactorily established by indisputable evidence, be supposed to be identical with the Pahlavas, Palhavas and Pahnavas of the Purāṇas. This identification is based on etymological grounds and supported by the fact that alhavas formed a distinct element in the population of Western India early in the second century A.D. Their movement from Western India to the East Coast is not only possible but rendered likely by known historical facts. Future researches must disclose the actual circumstances which led to the movement of the Palhavas to the East Coast and to their assumption of sovereignty.'

'As I have already remarked, the Pallavas were the political successors of the Āndhras in the Godaveri and Kishna deltas and consequently, the former must have acquired sovereignty soon after the latter ceased to be the ruling power. The Āndhras probably lost their dominion about the middle of the third century and the Pallavas may be supposed to have taken their place about the end of the same century.'

The late Mr. Venkayya arrived at these conclusions by dismissing the consideration that the Toṇḍamān Iḷam-Tirayan, who is known to Tamil-literature as the Viceroy of Kānchī, was the Toṇḍamān who was the son of the Chola King by a Nāga Princess "as it is not stated anywhere specifically." The connection is however clearly enough indicated in lines 29 to 37 of the Tamil poem Perumbāṇāṟṟuppaḍai, a work of Kaḍiyalūr Rudran Kaṇṇan. This same poet has celebrated Karikāla in the Paṭṭinappālai. Both the poems are included in the collection Pattuppāṭṭu. But Mr. Venkayya would bring down Karikāla to the period of interregnum, and Iḷam-Tirayan will therefore naturally go also to that period according to his arrangement.[1]

He was led to this consideration by the fact that in the eastern Chāḷukya grant of Vimalāditya of the early 11th century, a Trilochana Pallava is mentioned. This Trilochana Pallava Mr. Venkayya takes to be the feudatory of the Chola King Karikāla, and therefore Karikāla must be brought down to his period.

"Though this story is found only in records of the 11th century and is not corroborated by earlier inscriptions, it is evidently based on the belief current in the 11th century that the Pallava dominions extended in those early times to the modern Ceded Districts." If this consideration is due to a grant of the 11th century, it is hard to understand why a commentator who might have followed, it may be a century after, should not be shown similar consideration in regard to the connection of Iḷam-Tirayan of Kānchī with a Chola, as the Perumbāṇāṟṟuppaḍai makes it certain. The learned scholar admits that there is no evidence of the eastward movement of the Pallavas, and still would postulate that the Pallavas got into the country and imposed themselves upon the people of the locality. We have already quoted references from early Tamil literature to the territory of the Toṇḍaiyar, that is

[1] A.S.I., 1906-7, note on p. 224.

Toṇḍamaṇḍalam, dominated by Kānchī, the capital of Iḷaṁ-Tirayan. We have also quoted one passage in which the hill Vēngaḍam (Tirupati) is said to have been in the territory of the Toṇḍaiyar. What is more we have referred to a passage apparently from the ancient classics, though the actual source is not known at present, from the commentary of Nachinārkiniyar on the Tolkāppiyam that these Toṇḍaiyar were also known to these early Tamils by the name Pallava. These cogent considerations would make it certain that the terms Pallava and Toṇḍaiyar were synonymous in the estimation of the early Tamils. If therefore we have to look for the origin of the Pallavas, here are the people from among whom they must have sprung. The region of the Toṇḍamaṇḍalam, the more extended division, was known to the Tamils by another name. The Toṇḍamaṇḍalam proper was called Aruvā-Nāḍu, the northern portion of which dominated by Tirupati was apparently known Aruvā-vaḍa-talai. The people were also called Aruvāḷar, people with the bill-hook. The two descriptions therefore of these people as Toṇḍaiyar and Aruvāḷar are descriptions based the one upon the totem of the tribe, the creeper *Toṇḍi*; and the other a professional name from the scythe which must have been their weapon as cattleherds. We have pointed out already that the whole border land of the Tamils beyond this was occupied by a race of people known to them by the generic name Vaḍukar whose profession was cattle-rearing. That this region was divided among a number of petty chieftains is also known. These chieftains were called by the Tamils Kuṟumbar, sometimes also "Kuṟunila manner," petty chieftains. They are also classed as cowherds (Iḍaiyar). Among these one name comes out prominently, and that is the name of a chieftain Kaḻuvuḷ who was very troublesome on this frontier, perhaps on the western side of it, and a victory against whom by the early Chēras is made much of in poem 88 of the Padiṟṟupattu. That same passage taken along with poem 71 of the same collection makes it clear that Kaḻuvuḷ was a chieftain among the cowherds.[1]

It is apparently these people that are referred to in poem 88 as Anḍar. Anḍar is a term in Tamil which is taken as synonymous with cowherds. The index to the work makes Anḍar mean enemy. In that sense the penultimate syllable must have been shortened for which process there is no need as the metre of the poem does not require it. It seems therefore open to the interpretation that the term Anḍar is a modification of the Sanskrit Ändhra which Ptolemy renders Andara, apparently Āndhra (Vaḍukar of the Tamils). Iḍaiyar would be a term applied

[1] Compare poems 135 and 365 of Aham.

to them as cattle-rearing was their main occupation. That that region was remarkable for cattle-rearing, and that even southern kings undertook expeditions against that region and its petty chieftains for the purpose of bringing in their cattle are in evidence in two pieces. One of the early Chēras is described as the Chēra who carried off the cattle from Danḍāraṇyam (Aḍukōṭpāṭṭu-Śēran). There is a reference of a similar character to the cows from this country being carried off to the headquarters of Pulli of Tirupati. There is some justification therefore for Sir Walter Elliott's classification of certain early coins as those of the Kuṛumbar of this region, but anything like a dynasty of Kuṛumbar would seem unwarranted as the Pallavas never gave themselves that name, and the Kuṛumbar chiefs never seem to have advanced to the dignity of founding dynasties. Hence it is a far cry to connect the Pallavas of the Tonḍamanḍalam with the Yavanas, Śakas and Pahlavas of the west till more evidence of a specific character becomes available to justify the hypothesis of a migration of the foreigners southeastwards from the region of Guzarat and North Konkan to the Ceded districts part of the Tonḍamanḍalam.

Evidence of Tamil Literature.—The validity of evidence from Tamil literature would be admissible only if the chronology of the latter could be fixed with some degree of certainty. If with

Mr. Venkayya we should believe that Karikāla and Iḷaṁ-Tirayan lived in the 5th or 6th century, the period of the interregnum he finds warrant for in the Sanskrit charters of the Pallavas, we shall have to demonstrate that all the region that came into the literature of the Tamils of this period had, in the 5th or 6th century, the general political division and the distinct character that could be gleaned from this body of literature. I have elsewhere thrown into relief the political condition of South India in this period. It does not require very much of argument to show that this is not the political condition of South India in the 5th or 6th century as we know it from such information as is at our disposal. For one thing, the social organisation of the region as portrayed in this body of literature is too primitive for these data. Other specific facts which would fix the age of this body of literature to the 1st and 2nd century A.D. have all been indicated, and they relate to a period anterior to the rise of the Pallavas both of the Prakrit and the Sanskrit charters. It is the Sātavāhanas under Pulumāyi that made the first conquest of the Toṇḍamaṇḍalam as the coins of this Sātavāhana ruler find their provenance in the Toṇḍamaṇḍalam region. The type of the lead coins with a two-masted ship found in this region is appropriate for the locality of the Tiraiyar ; and it is probably this invasion of the Sātavāhanas that deprived the Cholas of the Viceroyalty of Kānchī which must have followed immediately the rule of the Chola Kiḷḷi referred to in the Maṇimēkhalai. This inference is supported by a number of references in the same body of Tamil literature which relate to invasions of the south by the Āriyas and Vaḍukar which were beaten back with great exertion by the Tamil chieftains. One of the Cholas is praised for having subjugated the Paradavar in the south and Vaḍukar in the north.[1] Another Chola claims credit for having broken up the Āriya forces on the field of Vallam.[2] The Malayamān chieftain Kāri is said to have beaten back single-handed the Āriya forces besieging Tirukovilūr, his capital.[3] Similarly a Chola king, probably the same as the one already referred to, is said to have beaten down the heads of the Vaḍukar at Pāḷi or Śeru-Pāḷi [4] a place very likely on the West Coast or at least in the western part of the Tamil country. The fact that Danḍāraṇyam was a forest in the country of the Āriyas according to the Tamils would make the Āriyas under reference the people of the country named Ariake in the Periplus, or their rulers, and the region in their occupation the country included in the name, the Dakhan. It may be as the ultimate result of this struggle that Chola assistance was called

[1] Puram. 378. [2] Aham 336. [3] Naṟṟiṇai 170. [4] Aham 375.

in, and the Cholas constituted the Viceroyalty of Kānchī under Karikāla. There is clear evidence from the Ahanānuru that one chieftain by name Tiraiyan ruled over the Toṇḍamaṇḍalam from Kānchī, and Vēngaḍam included in it. It is doubtful whether he was the same as Iḷam-Tiraiyan; but the fact that the latter takes the attribute "*Iḷam*" (young) is a clear indication that there was another Tiraiyan before him. This would make it possible that the Sātavāhana conquest under Pulumāyi came in after the disappearance of the Chola ascendency. In any case it is clear that the Sātavāhana hold on this region could not have lasted long.

This seems the condition of things reflected in the latest Pallava grant, the Vēlūrpaḷaiyam-plates. This document together with a few others of quite recent discovery seem to make the interregnum hardly called for. It seems quite possible from the known facts relative to the genealogy of the Pallavas of the Sanskrit charters to arrange them in a continuous line, and even bring them into connection with the Simhavishṇu line. The late Mr. Venkayya himself and the epigraphists consider it impossible that the Prakrit charters could be brought down to a date after the middle of the fourth century, the date of the invasion of Samudragupta and his victory over Vishṇugopa of Kānchi. The Prakrit charters therefore and the dynasty or dynasties evolvable from them must be anterior to about A.D. 350. As we have nothing to lead to the identification of Samudragupta's Vishṇugopa of Kānchī with either of the two known Vishnugopas of the later Sanskrit charters we shall have to regard him as a separate person distinct alike from the dynasty of the Prakrit charters and of the dynasty of the Sanskrit charters. We shall have to find room therefore for the dynasty or dynasties of the Sanskrit charters after this particular period. This arrangement seems warranted by one circumstance which may fix the chronology. The Vēlūrpaḷaiyam plates state it clearly that Skandaśishya, Skandavarma I of the genealogical table, seized from King Satya Sēna the "*Ghaṭika*" of the Brahmans. This Satya Sēna seems to be the same as Swāmi Satya Simha, a Mahākshatrapa who is known to us from the coins of his son Mahākshatrapa Swāmi Rudra Simha III.[1]

The transcript of the legend may be read Satya Sēna but it is rendered by the learned Professor, Satyāsimha. It might as well be

[1] Prof. Rapson, pp. 191-92 of Catalogue of the Indian Coins in the British Museum., Āndhras, etc. In regard to the reading of the coin legend suggested above, Prof. Rapson is of opinion "The letters of the coin legends are so minute and so carelessly formed (at this period—the close of the Kshatrapa Dynasty) that I consider it quite possible that the true reading may be Satyasēna and not Satyasimha, as given by me on page 192 of the B. M. Catalogue of the Āndhra Dynasty." On a kind reference by the obliging Professor in my behalf, Mr. John Allan of the British Museum examined the coin in question and gives it as his opinion, "I certainly think you would be justified in reading the name as Satyasēna and not Satyasimha."

Satya Sēna. His son would be Rudrasena as well. Names ending in Sena are not unknown among the rulers of this dynasty. The date of this Satyasēna would be sometime anterior to A.D. 388. If Skandaśishya's date be 388, the three generations before him would have for them about 40 years if all three of them did rule. It is Skandaśishya's father who according to the Vēlūrpālaiyam plates "simultaneously with the daughter of the chief of serpents grasped also the complete insignia of royalty and became famous."

Passing on now to the Vēlūrpāḷaiyam plates themselves we are provided with the following succession of the early Pallavas up to Simhavishṇu:

Kālabhartṛ
|
Chûtapallava
|
Vīrakūrcha
|
Skandaśishya
|
Kumāravishṇu
|
Buddhavarman
|
Nandivarman
|
Simhavarman
|
Simhavishṇu.

Along with these have to be taken the table provided by the Chūra plates.

Skandavarman
|
Mahārājah Vishṇugopa Varman
|
Simhavarman
|
Vijaya Vishṇugcpa Varman.

The two Ongōḍu plates give us two genealogies :—

I. Mahārāja Kumāra Vishṇu
|
Mahārāja Skandavarman
|
Vīra Varman
|
Mahārājah Vijaya Skandavarman

II. Mahārājah Vīravarman
|
Mahārājah Skandavarman
|
Yuvamahārājah Vishṇugopa
|
Simha Varman.

These separate genealogies are obviously intimately connected with each other and have to be worked up into one table as many of the names are common and are apparently connected with each other. This is to a certain extent facilitated by the full list of Pallava succession given in the so-called Vāyalūr Pillar Inscription. Rao Bahadur Mr. Krishnasastrigal proposes to identify Kālabhartṛ with the Kāṇagopa of the Kaśākuḍi plates, and also with Mahārājah Kumāra Vishṇu of the Ongōḍu plates I. Similarly in respect of the second name Chūtapallava which would mean a "tender twig of the mango," he would regard it as a surname of Skandavarman I of the Uruvappalli grant, the Ongōḍu plates I, also giving the name Skandavarman. The names that follow do not differ. Vīrkūrcha and Vravarman are not so different, nor Skandaśishya and Skandavarman. He is led to this identification of the genealogy of the Ongōḍu plates with those of the Vēlūrpāḷaiyam ones as he finds the palæography of the Ongōḍu plates No. 1 older in point of character, and almost the earliest known record of the Pallava dynasty of the Sanskrit charters. The Mahāraja Vijaya Skandavarman, the donor of the grant would be Skandavarman II, Skandaśishya of the Vēlūrpāḷaiyam plates. If this is agreed to, there is no difficulty in accepting this except for the first name Kumāravishṇu which has no affinity with Kālabhartṛ or Kāṇagopa. One part of the genealogical tree gets then settled. The genealogy in the Ongōḍu plates No. II amounts to almost the same as the Mangalūr plates giving the genealogy from Vīravarman to Simhavarman II as in the table below. The Chūra plates add to this and carry the genealogy to Mahārāja Vijaya Vishṇugopa Varman the son of Simha Varman II, the donor of the Ongōḍu grant No. II and Mangalūr grant.

The point that the donor's grandfather Vishṇugopa is given the title Mahārāja in this may be overlooked as a similar discrepancy is noticeable between the Ongōḍu plates I and II in respect of Vīravarman, the first grant omitting the adjunct Mahārāja. The fact that the first Ongōḍu grant was made from the victorious camp of Tāmbrāpa is taken to warrant the conclusion that it was a subordinate family, by M. Jouveau-Dubreuil, and, taking advantage of the name Kumāravishṇu, he would make the members of the Pallava dynasty whose names are found on this table another line of descendants of Kumāra Vishṇu I. That would make a difference of three generations between the Epigraphist's estimate of time and the Professor's, both of them based on Palæography and nothing else. Three names being in agreement we are rather inclined to accept the epigraphist's dictum on a questin of palæography. We arrive then at a consolidated table of Pallavas somewhat as under.

(I) Kālabhartṛ (Kāṇagopa)
|
(II) Chūtapallava
(perhaps a surname of Skandavarman I, mentioned in the Uruvapalli grant)
|
(III) Vīrakūrcha (Vīrakōrchavarman or Vīravarman)
|
(IV) Skandaśishya (Skandavarman II).

(V) Simhavarman I	Yuvamahārājavishṇugopa or Vishṇugopavarman	VI. Kumārvishṇu I.
(XI) Skandavarman III	(IX) Simhavarman II.	VII. Buddhavarman
XII) Nandivarman.	(X) Mahārāja Vijaya Vishṇugopa Varman	VIII. Kumāravishṇu II.

Turning now to the Vāyalur Pillar the names 31 to 36 are in the recognised order of the later dynasty. The name 30 is a Vishṇugopa which may be the Vishṇugopavarman of the Chura plates in which case we go on to the Simhavarman II in No. 29. No. 28, Simhavarman seems an additional name. 25, 26 and 27 may be the names Simhavarman I, Skandavarman III and Nandivarman I of the table. No. 24, Skandavarman then would be Skandavarman II on the table. Then comes in a Vīravarman, No. 23, who may be the Vīrakūrcha of the table. He is preceded by a Simhavarman No. 22 for whom and for three preceding names we can find no equivalent on the table. Then follows the names Skandavarman preceded by three names Skandavarman, Kūmāra Vishṇu, Buddhavarman which may be the names Skandavarman II, Kumāravishṇu I and Buddhavarman; but the same three names repeat from 12 to 14. These are preceded by two other names 10 and 11, Kāṇagopa and Vīrakūrcha; then from 9 to

1. Vimala.
2. Konkaṇika.
3. Kālabhartṛ.
4. Chūtapallava.
5. Vīrakūrcha.
6. Chandravarman.
7. Karala.
8. Vishṇugopa.
9. Skandamūla.
10. Kāṇagopa.
11. Vīrakūrcha.
12. Skandavarman.
13. Kumāravishṇu.
14. Buddhavarman.
15. Skandavarman.
16. Kumāravishnu.
17. Buddhavarman.
18. Skandavarman.
19. Vishṇugopa.
20. Vishṇudāsa.
21. Skandavarman.
22. Simhavarman.
23. Vīravarman.
24. Skandavarman.
25. Simhavarman.
26. Skandavarman.
27. Nandivarman I.
28. Simhavarman.
29. Simhavarman.
30. Vishṇugopa.
31. Simhavarman.
32. Simhavishṇu.
33. Mahendravarman I.
34. Narasimhavarman I.
35. Mahendravarman II.
36. Parmēśvaravarman I.

3 there is a considerable agreement with the table here except that No. 6 Chandravarman has to be taken as a mistake for Skandavarman. The name Karāḷa does not appear in any of the grants at all and the connection of the first two names Vimala and Konkaṇika do not find reference in any of the grants available to us. In respect of this list of 36 names, it must be borne in mind that it is a list made up in the reign of the later Pallava Narasimhavarman II, and in all probability the list was put together from a comparative study of the various tables discussed above from some record of these various grants; what is worse, put together perhaps without any accurate knowledge of the connection of the various members to each other, or their actual position in the succession. This seems the only explanation for the repetitions and variations that one notices in the list in comparison with the genealogies of the grants. It would be safer to guide ourselves by the various tables discussed above rather than by this one omnibus list which otherwise provides us with no details whatsoever.

CHAPTER IX.

THE HISTORY OF THESE PALLAVAS.

Having arranged the various genealogies in the Sanskrit charters of these Pallavas in a consolidated table, we might now turn to enquire what exactly it is possible for us to know of the Pallavas from these records and other sources of information available to us. Turning to the the Vēlūrpāḷaiyam plates we can pass over the document till we come to Kāḷabhartṛ described as the head jewel of his family like (Vishṇu) the husband of Indira (Lakshmī). This perhaps give us a hint that he bore the name Kumāra Vishṇu as the Ongōḍu plates No. 1 would make us infer. No information of a historical character is given in regard to him. Then follows his son Chūtapallava identified in the table with Skandavarman of the Uruvapalli and other grants. Even that name seems to be a mere eponymous name, the later tables giving instead the name merely Pallava. It is in his son Vīrakūrcha that emerges the first historical character. He is said to have grasped the complete insignia of royalty together with the hand of the daughter of "the chief of the serpents" thereby becoming famous. Put in ordinary language this would mean that he married a Nāga Princess and thereby acquired title to sovereignty of the region over which he ruled. This obviously has no connection with the birth of Toṇḍamān-Iḷaṁ-Tiraiyana who, according to the tradition embodied in the classical poem Perumbāṇārṟuppaḍai, was the son of a Chola king by a Nāga Princess whose union with him was not exactly what Vīrakūrcha's union as described is intended to be. The former is purely an affair of love which may even be regarded as a liaison. Vīrakūrcha's is a regular marriage to a Princess and, through her, the acquisition of sovereignty. Neither the detail of the marriage nor the acquisition of sovereignty will agree with the story of Iḷaṁ-Tiraiyan. The explanation of this apparently is that the Pallava chieftain, whoever he was, contracted a marriage with a more influential Nāga chieftain in the neighbourhood and thereby acquired his title to the territory which came to be associated with the Pallavas. We have already noted that the Sātavāhana Viceroy of the region round Adoni was the great commander Skandanāga. We also noted tha even before his time the territory round Chittaldrug, extending westwards to the sea almost, was in the possession of a family which went by the name Çuṭukula the members of which family sometimes described themselves as Sātavāhanas also. This would mean that they were a clan of the Sātavāhanas other than that which held rule over the Dakhan, but connected by blood and perhaps even by alliance with that clan. At one time under the rule of the later Sātavāhanas these Nāgas appear to have extended their authority and even acquired a considerable portion of the kingdom of the Sātavāhanas themselves. If the Pallava chieftain in the neighbourhood made himself sufficiently distinguished and contracted a marriage alliance with these Nāgas from whom came the early Sātavāhana queen Nāganikā, it would have been possible for him to have become recognised a feudatory sovereign of the region of either the Sātavāhanas themselves nominally, or of their successors the Nāgas. This hint, vague as it is in the inscription, seems to let us into the secret of the rise of this dynasty of the Pallavas to power, and may give us even a clue to the time when these Pallavas should have risen to the kingly position. This must have happened at a time when the Sātavāhanas as a ruling dynasty had passed away, and the attempt at the assertion of the Gupta power over this region under Samudra-Gupta had in a way shaken the authority of the older dynasties and left the field open for new dynasties to spring up. The character of the invasion of Samudragupta itself makes it clear that the whole of the western portion of the empire of the Āndhras was in the hands of a power whom for some good reason Samudragupta did not attack. One such reason might have been that they held possession of the territory with some power. It is likely that their authority was not readily acquiesced in by the smaller chieftains, feudatories of the Sātavāhanas along the east coast. If this surmise should turn out correct it is possible to conceive that the western portion was held by the powerful family of the Nāgas, relations of the Sātavāhanas, and the Pallavas were among the feudatories who showed a ready inclination to throw off the Sātavāhana yoke. When Samudragupta had come and gone, the western power, whatever that was, might have entered into a marriage alliance with the Pallavas and recognised them in the position to which they had already risen by their own efforts. This state of affairs seems supported from what is said of Vīrakūrcha's successor. Skandaśishya, son of Vīrakūrcha succeeded the father and is described as "the moon in the sky of his family"; in other words the most distinguished member of the family. He seized from King Satyasēna the "*Ghaṭika*" of the Brahmans. We already indicated the possibility that the Satyasēna here referred to may be Mahākshatrapa Svāmi Satyasēna of the coins whose time would be the ninth decade of the 4th century A.D. We do not know definitely that the power of the Mahākshatrapas extended as far south as to come into contact with the Pallavas. The probability seems to be the Pallavas co-operated with the dynasty of the Western Dakhan in a war with the Kshatrapas of Malva who might, it is possible, have made an effort to extend their authority southwards into the region of of the Dakhan.

Decadence of the Āndhra Power.

The state of things foreshadowed in the previous section is confirmed by the history of the decadence of the power of the Āndhras who held sway for more than three centuries in the whole of the Dakhan extending even into the Tamil country round Kānchī. According to Professor Rapson an elaborate study of the coins and inscriptions relating to this dynasty leads to the conclusion that after the long reign of Yagña-Śrī Sātakarṇi the empire broke up into two. The Purāṇas mention only three names after this Sātavāhana. One of the names Śri Chandra could be read on coins found in the Āndhradēśa proper. There are three other names also traceable in the coins of this region and in the Chanda district of the Central Provinces. The coins of neither of these groups have been found in western India. This distribution of the coins of the later Āndhras seems to justify the conclusion that the Empire was divided.

What is more, this investigation seems to confirm what the Matsya Purāṇa has to say regarding the dynasties that succeeded the Āndhras. This portion of the dynastic list according to the version common to several manuscripts of the Matsya, Vāyu and Brahmāṇḍa Purāṇas begins, "*Āndhrāṇām Samasthitē rājyē tēṣam bhṛty ānvayā nṛpāḥ Sapt-aiv-Āndhrā bhaviṣyanti,*" meaning that while the Āndhras were still ruling a family of their servants who were themselves Āndhras ruled for seven generations. One version of the Matsya Purāṇa, however, has "*Āndhraḥ Śrīparvatīyas ça tē dvi-pançaśatam samāḥ,*" that the Śrī Parvatīya Āndhras ruled for 52 years. Taking the two together we get to this. That one section of the Āndhras who could be designated Śrī Parvatīya Āndhras who were subordinate to the authority of Yagña-Śrī asserted their independence and ruled for 52 years in the region round Śrī Parvata, that is, the home territory if it may be so called, of the Āndhras. There is no mention in that list of what had happened to the western portion of their territory unless we take the next following passage to refer to what probably happened to that part. Ten Ābhīras, servants of the Āndhras as the others, ruled for 67 years. We have an Ābhīra governor of the Mahākshatrapa Rudra Simha, son of Rudra Dāman with a date 103 which is equivalent to A.D. 181. The Ābhīra concerned here is the General Rudra Bhūti, son of the general Bapaka, the Ābhira'.[1]

The Purāṇas seem to be correct to this extent that the Ābhīra feudatories in the region of Gujarat set up rule on their own account in the later years of the Āndhras, in all probability in the years following Yagña-Śrī. This would have reference to the early years of the third century A.D., and if the Ābhīras ruled for 67 years it would bring them practically to the end of the third century. The inscription of the Ābhīra king Iśvara Sēna at Nasik is a clear indication that that part of the Āndhra country was under the rule of the Ābhīras. Iśvara Sēna himself was the son of the Ābhīra Śivadatta. If with Professor Rapson we can take these Ābhīras to be identical with the members of the Traikūṭaka dynasty, the Traikūṭaka era beginning A.D. 249 would be the era of the Ābhīras as well. The Ābhīra Iśvara Sēna may therefore be referable to about the same time. The inscription found in Jaggayyapetta of one Śrī Vīra-Purusha Datta of the family of Ikshvāku, and dated in his 20th year shows that even the eastern territory of the Āndhras was passing into other hands. This inscription is referable on palæographical grounds to the period of the later Āndhras. What is most

1 'Lüder's list of Brahmi inscriptions. Ep. Ind., X., No. 963. (Southern list.)

important to our present purpose here is that the southern portion, and perhaps by far the largest portion of the Empire of the Āndhras, passed into the hands of a family of feudatories who called themselves Śātakarṇis as well, and had for their capital Banavāse (Vaijayantī). This is the famous Çūṭu dynasty who give themselves the name Nāga as well, and who have for their crest an extended cobra hood. Their inscriptions are found in Kanhēri, in Kanara and in the Shimoga district of Mysore. From their inscriptions so far made available to us we know of three generations of these and two reigns, namely, that of Hārītīputra Vishṇukada Çuṭukulānanda Śātakarṇi and his grandson by the daughter Śivaskanda Varman, also called Śiva Skanda Nāga Śrī in the Banavāse inscription, and Skanda Nāga Sātavāhana in the Kanhēri inscription. These two rulers appear to have preceded the Kadambas almost without any interval. It would appear as though the Kadambas made the conquest of the territory which became associated with them from this Śiva Skanda Varman himself. The inscriptions of this dynasty at Kanhēri may be taken as an indication of the extent of the territory to which they had become heir when the Sātavāhana power decayed. These were themselves Śātakarṇis, and almost from the commencement of the rule of the Sātavāhana held possession of the southern viceroyalty for them. Their ascent to independent power would again support the statement of the Purāṇas that it was the Āndhrabhṛityas that ascended to power and independence while yet the Āndhras were still ruling. It is these Cūṭukula successors of the Āndhras in the territory immediately adjoining that of the Pallavas that must be the Nāga family by a marriage alliance with which Vīrakūrcha was able to make good his position as ruler of the south-eastern viceroyalty of the Āndhras. Probably the Pallavas in the locality of the Prakrit charters fought and took possession, of the territory from the later Āndhras. It may be that the Śrī Parvatīya Āndhras and the Pallavas of the Sanskrit charters, at least the early members among them, either felt it necessary, or considered it advantageous, to get their possession validated by this alliance with, and countenance of, perhaps the most powerful among the successors of the Āndhras. It may be possible even that the Princess mother of Śivaskanda Varman Skanda Nāga had married the Pallava chieftain perhaps a Mahābhōja, as holding an important viceroyalty of the Āndhras. If this surmise should turn out correct, as we have as yet no direct evidence to confirm it, Śivaskanda Nāga Śrī of the western inscriptions would be the Skandaśishya of the Pallava inscriptions. Such a position for Skanda Varman would be in accordance with the tradition associated with the foundations of the dynasty of the Kadambas.

LIGHT FROM KADAMBA INSCRIPTIONS.

According to the tradition as we find it recorded in the inscription of Kakustha Varman, it was a Brahman by name Mayūra-Śarman who went to complete his Vēdic studies to the "Brahman settlement," (Ghaṭikā) of Kānchī. There he got into a quarrel with either some cavalry men, or an important officer of the cavalry of the Pallavas, and gave up the life of a Brahman and assumed that of a warrior. He was so successful in his new life when he acquired possession of all the forest country up to Śrī Parvata, laid the great Bāṇa under contribution, and otherwise made himself a very considerable obstacle to the pretensions of the Pallavas who were just then rising into importance. The Pallava monarch for the time being considered it prudent to recognise the redoubtable Brahman as a military officer of his with the government of a considerable province extending from the sea in the west to the eastern limit of "Prēhāra."[1] Who were the Pallavas to appoint this Brahman to the Governorship of the province whose capital was Banavase? The Pallavas must have

[1] Could this be Pērur in the Cuddapah district with which the origin of the Ganga dynasty is connected?

possessed the territory which the Brahman perhaps made his own, and then the Pallavas rightfully conferred it upon the Brahman as his fief. If it had not been so, there is no sense in a Kadamba inscription claiming this as the rightful foundation of their title to the province. It seems therefore that the alliance between the Nāga and the Pallava which gave the title to the Pallava for the possession of the whole of the territory means nothing more than an alliance between the Pallavas and the Cūṭus. This alliance resulted in the Pallavas becoming ultimately rulers not only of the Pallava territory proper but of practically the whole Empire of the Āndhras, as much of it at any rate as had not gone into the possession of others like the Ābhīras and the Ikshvākus of the east. This assumption would satisfactorily explain the setting up of the Kadamba power in the region which was peculiarly the province of the Cūṭus. If that should turn out to be so, the statement regarding Skandaśishya that he took from Satyasēna the *ghaṭika* of the Brahmans would become not merely possible but very likely. It is perhaps a subsidiary branch of this family of the Cūṭus that ultimately overthrew the Kadambas in this region, and founded the dynasty of the Chāḷukyas.

CHAPTER X.

THE PALLAVAS AND THE GANGAS.

It has already been shown above that the Pallava overlordship of the territory associated with the Kadambas indicates that the Pallavas succeeded to the whole of the southern portion of the Āndhra Empire. This accession of territory to the Pallavas is explained by the fact of a marriage alliance between the Pallavas and a race of the Nāgas who held the southern viceroyalty in behalf of the Sātavāhanas, and claimed to belong to the same clan of the Śātakarṇis as well. A similar position of overlordship over the Gangas is given to the Pallavas in the so-called Penukonḍa-plates [1] of the early Ganga, Mādhava, the third of the name according to the complete list of Mr. B. L. Rice. These plates record the gift of a number of villages adjoining Parigi about seven miles north of Hindupur in the Anantapur district, and therefore quite on the borders of the Kolar district with which the rule of the Gangas is peculiarly associated. The document being undated the late Dr. Fleet, who held that most of the Ganga plates hitherto known were

[1] Ep. Ind., XIV, pp. 331 ff.

spurious, records it as his opinion that these plates must be regarded genuine, with the remark that "A.D. 475 seems a very good date for it." The plates give a genealogy:

Konkaṇivarman
|
Mādhava
|
Ayyavarman
|
Mādhava

In regard to the first two there is nothing worthy of note except that according to other records of this dynasty Konkaṇi-Varman had the name Mādhava and was the uncle of the other Mādhava rather than the father. This difference may be explained on the ground that the table given here is a list of succession not necessarily from father to son. Ayyavarman may be Ariyavarman, and may be synonymous with Ari-Varman and Hari-Varman, and even possibly with Krishnavarman as Mr. Rice suggests. What is of peculiar importance in regard to him in connection with the Pallavas is that he was installed by a Mahārājah Simhavarman, "the Indra of the Pallava kula" 'in a literal sense' (yathārtham). His successor, according to this record, Mādhava, had the alternative name Simhavarman, and he is said to have been similarly installed 'in the literal sense' by Mahārāja Skandavarman of the Pallavas. According to the other records of these Gangas however a Vishṇugopa comes after Ayyavarman. Mr. Rice who is the editor of the Penukoṇḍa plates finds it possible that there is an omission of the name in these plates by the fault of the engraver. It seems likely however from the unanimity of the records in respect of this ruler Vishṇugopa, that a ruler by name Vishṇugopa, did precede Mādhava, the last of the name in this pedigree, whether he was the latter's father or grandfather; or there is still the possibility that he might have been an uncle for which assumption there is no authority in any of the records. The fact that Simhavarman installed Ayyavarman and that he was followed by a ruler with the name Vishṇugopa, and that this Vishṇugopa was followed by a ruler who was installed by a Pallava Skanda Varman seem to imply a Pallava overlordship over the Gangas. If as suggested above Vishṇugopa, happened to be an uncle or granduncle of Mādhava the name Simhavarman given to Mādhava would be an honour done to Simhavarman who installed Ayyavarman on the throne. There is therefore reference to a Pallava ruler Simhavarman who must have had a successor following, either immediately or in the next generation, by name Skandavarman with just the possibility that the Vishṇugopa of the Gangas was a name given to the ruler in honour of a Vishṇugopa, the Pallava overlord. If this possibility should turn out a fact then we have this Pallava succession: Simhavarman, Vishṇugopa and Skandavarman. According to the Udaiyēndram grant we have had a succession Skandavarman, Simhavarman, another Skandavarman followed by a Nandivarman, and we have for good reasons regarded this Simhavarman as the son of Skandaśishya, father of Yuvamahārāja Vishṇugopa. The possibility of connection therefore between the Pallava sovereigns of the Penukoṇḍa plates and the succession list of the Pallavas we have arrived at seems clearly indicated to the period following the reign of Skandaśishya or Skandavarman II; but the identification of the actual rulers is not thereby made easy. Simhavarman I, his younger brother Vishṇugopa and Skandavarman the son of Simhavarman may be one set of names, if that is the order in which they ruled; for our present purpose it would quite do if Simhavarman was followed by Skanda Varman, Vishṇugopa being a mere Yuvamahārāja. There is another alternative; the three names referred to may be Simhavarman II son of Yuvamahārāja Vishṇugopa, his son Mahārāja Vishṇugopa of the Chūra plates followed by the name Skandavarman, the son of Simhavarman I, if this had been the order of the Pallava succession. Whichever of the two alternatives should ultimately turn out correct the three Ganga rulers Ayyavarman, Vishṇugopa and Mādhava, the second or third of the name, must have ruled in the period between Skandaśishya or Skandavarman II, and Simhavarman the father of Simhavishṇu of the dynasty of the great Pallavas that, for good reasons, we have ascribed to the period A.D. 380 to A.D. 500. Even the approximate date of these rulers would depend entirely upon the arrangement of the Pallava order of succession. After Skandavarman II we might take it almost certain from the Uruvapalli plates that Simhavarman I succeeded the father, Vishṇugopa being the Yuvamahārāja under him. If Vishṇugopa did not rule Simhavarman was probably followed by Simhavarman II Skandavarman perhaps having been very young. It is also likely that he was followed by Vishṇugopa II of the Chura plates, he in turn being succeeded by Skandavarman III; then must have followed the dynasty of the other son Kumāra Vishṇu I. If we can safely follow the Vēlūrpāḷaiyam plates, Kumāravishṇu must have been succeeded by Buddhavarman, Nandivarman following then. The fact however that the Vēlūrpāḷaiyam plates speak of a host of rulers following Buddhavarman before Nandivarman at last succeeded would indicate that Simhavarman I was probably followed by Kumāravishṇu; he by his son Buddhavarman perhaps followed for a short while by Kumāravishṇu II. The succession perhaps passed then to Simhavishṇu II of the table; then Vishṇugopa II; then Skandavarman III and lastly Nandivarman. We may accept this order of succession tentatively till we get more clear lead as to the actual order of succession of these. If we turn to the Vāyalūr plates for this lead it would be difficult to find any. Simhavarman the father of Simhavishṇu is preceded by Vishṇugopa whom we might take to be the second of the name. He is preceded by a Simhavarman which is so far correct. He is preceded by another Simhavarman and the only Simhavarman available is Simhavarman I of the table. He is preceded by five names 23 to 27 which are the names found in the Udaiyēndram plates already referred to, of which No. 28, Simhavarman must be one. Nos. 15 to 22 seem difficult of adjustment on the table; some of the names are new and there is also confusion in the order. As was pointed out already this list seems to be a jumble of various genealogies collected and put together as the order of succession without a correct knowledge of the actual succession. It would therefore be better to accept the arrangement last suggested namely Simhavarman the eldest son of Skandaśishya being followed by Kumāravishṇu I and then by Buddhavarman and perhaps even by Kumāravishṇu II, the succession going back to the son and grandson of Vishṇugopa I, and then on to a son and grandson of Simhavishṇu. That will bring Simhavishṇu, Vishṇugopa and Skandavarman of the Penukonḍa plates late in the succession making the date A.D. 475 for the plates possible. It may even be somewhat later. Skandavarman was according to the Vēlūrpāḷaiyamplates followed by Nandivarman; then comes in a break in the succession as far as our present knowledge of it goes. Then follows the line of Simhavarman, father of Simhavishṇu; Nandivarman, Simhavarman, Simhavishṇu and Mahēndravarman occupying almost a century, and perhaps a little more, between Simhavarman of the Penukonḍa plates and Narasimhavarman the great Pallava whose accession might be dated approximately about 600 A D.

It was already pointed out that the Ganga territory lay in the Anantapur and Kolar districts particularly, and later on extended to take in practically the whole of the Mysore district as well with an alternative capital at Talakāḍ. Kolar however is regarded as the ancestral capital of this dynasty even when the capital was actually at Talakāḍ; and the hill Nandi is regarded as peculiarly the hill of the Gangas. According to one traditional verse defining the boundaries of Tonḍamanḍalam, the Pallava territory proper, the western boundary is fixed at Pavaḷamalai (coral hill); according to another it is taken westwards to Rishabhagiri. The former apparently denotes the foot hills of the Eastern Ghauts that skirt the foot of the plateau and have a westward trend till they strike the Western Ghauts beyond the Nilgiris; while the latter is obviously the hill Nandi. This latter boundary perhaps explains the overlordship which was clearly admitted by the Gangas themselves according to the Penukoṇḍa plates. It is clear from this that the original territory of the Gangas, at least the eastern part of it, formed a portion of the Toṇḍamaṇḍalam and the Pallava claim to overlordship rested upon a sound historical basis. The overlordship claimed in regard to the territory specially associated with the Kadambas was already explained as being due to the Pallavas becoming heir to the territory by virtue of a Nāga marriage, that is, the marriage of Vīrakūrcha with the Nāga princess which gave him a wife and a kingdom together. This historical union has nothing whatever to do with the period of the Toṇḍamān Iḷaṁ-Tiraiyan of Kānchī. We thus see that the period extending from the latter half of the fourth century down to almost the commencement of the seventh is occupied by what seems a continuous succession of Pallava rulers. Anything like an interregnum postulated by the late Mr. Venkayya, within which has to be brought of not merely the great Chola

Karikāla, but the succession of political changes centering round his name and that of his successor for a generation or two at the lowest seems impossible.

The Theory of Interregnum Baseless.

After all this theory of a Chola interregnum in the fifth century rests upon the flimsy foundation of the eleventh century information that a Trilochanā Pallava reclaimed the forest country of the ceded districts and started a dynasty of the Pallavas from whom the later rulers of the locality claimed descent. This reclamation of the forest country is clearly indicated to have been the achievement of the first important member of the Pallava Prakrit charters who is given no name and who is credited with having bestowed crores of money and a hundred thousand ox ploughs. Nothing could be clearer than this statement in regard to the reclamation of the forest country by him. The fact that he is referred to only by the term Bappadēva (revered father) and not by any other specific name points to the fact that his services were specially distinguished in regard to this matter, and that he left such a deep impression upon the people that it was hardly necessary he should be defined by a specific name. Although Dr. Hultzsch attempted another explanation of the expression occurring in the Uruvapalli plates in regard to Simhavarman II that he was "a worshipper at the feet of the Bhaṭṭāraka Mahārāja Bappadēva" as meaning his father, it will bear the interpretation that the Bappadēva described as the Bhaṭṭāraka Mahārāja is the Bappadēva of the Prakrit charters, the founder of the authority of the Pallavas in the Telugu districts. The objection to Dr. Hultzsch's interpretation quite justifiable in regard to later documents, is, in regard to this particular document, that Vishṇugopa was not a Mahārāja and could not perhaps exactly be described as Bhaṭṭāraka Mahārāja. There is no indication of a reason for the departure in respect of him particularly. If Trilochana Pallava were regarded by later tradition to be credited with having cleared the forest country to turn it into occupied land, here was Bappadēva's work which later tradition might indicate as that of Trilochana Pallava. It is just possible that Bappadēva's name was some equivalent of Tṛilochana (Śiva) taking the fact that his son called himself Śivaskanda-Varman into consideration. If he bore anything like the name Śiva he could be spoken of as Tṛilochana and the late tradition seems to be an echo of the achievement of Bappadēva himself.

On palæographical considerations above the Prakrit charters have to be regarded earlier than the southward march of Samudragupta, that is about A.D. 350; Samudragupta's date being known it is impossible to bring either of the two Vishṇugopas that figure in the genealogical table to a date about A.D. 350. Vishṇugopa of Kānchī, the contemporary of Samudragupta, must have been a ruler different from the two Vishṇugopas of the later table. Therefore then after the Sātavāhanas, we have the Pallava dynasty or dynasties of the Prakrit charters, then follows the reign of Vishṇugopa, and then the dynasty of the Sanskrit charters to whose history actually we shall now turn.

The Chronological Datum in the Lōkavibhāga.

The Archæological Department of Mysore discovered a manuscript of a Digambara Jaina work named Lōkavibhāga of which an account is given in their report for 1909-10. The subject treated of is Jaina cosmography. The work was supposed to have been first given by word of mouth by Vardhamāna himself, and is said to have been handed down through Sudharma and a succession of other teachers. Rishi Simhasūri or Simhaśūra made a translation of it, apparently from the Prakrit into Sanskrit. The work is said to have been finally copied some considerable time before the date of the copy (*purā*) by Muni Śarvanandin in the village named Pāṭalika (Tiruppādiripuliyūr; Cuddalore New Town) in the Pāṇarāshṭra (Bāṇa country); then follows the date of the completion of this task. It was in the year 22 of Simhavarman, the Lord of Kānchī, and in the year 80 past 300 of the Śaka year; in other words Śaka 380. This piece of information is confirmed by two other manuscripts of the work since discovered. The late Dr. Fleet, who was suspicious of early Śaka dates, after having examined the date carefully, and making a correction in respect of the month and date, has arrived at the conclusion that it is equivalent to the year A.D. 458. The Simhavarman under reference therefore must have begun to rule in A.D. 436. Unfortunately for us there are two Simhavarmans according to our genealogical table, Simhavarman I and Simhavarman II. As we have arranged it on the table three reigns come between the one and the other. It is just possible that the reference is to Simhavarman I except for the fact that Skandaśishya's reign would be very long having regard to the Satyasēna datum already examined. If the Simhavarman referred to in the Penukonḍa plates is Simhavarman II as we have shown reasons that he was the person referred to, the Lōkavibhāga was a work that was composed in the reign of Simhavarman II having regard to the fact that the Penukonḍa plates are datable about A.D. 475. A.D. 436 to 475 is a period of 40 years, and might be regarded long enough for the reign of two kings and of part of the reign of a third. After the Skandavarman referred to in the Penukoṇḍa plates there should have followed three rulers before we come to Mahēndravarman whose date would be somewhere near A.D. 600; namely, Nandivarman, Simhavarman, the immediate successor of Nandivarman according to Vēlūpāḷaiyam plates, his son Simhavishṇu followed by Mahēndravarman. One century might be considered too long a period for three reigns on an average computation; but there is nothing impossible about it if one had been an unusually long reign or if any two of them had been fairly long reigns. The possibility of anything like an interregnum, in which we could work in the kings and potentates associated with Karikāla and intimately connected with the so-called Śamgam literature, would then be obviously impossible.

As a result of this somewhat detailed investigation the trend of Early Pallava History may be described as follows: While yet the Cholas were ascendent in the south holding Toṇḍamaṇḍalam under their control with Kānchī for its capital the later Sātavāhana under Vāsishṭīputra Pulumavi made an effort at conquering the country answering exactly to the Toṇḍamaṇḍalam extending from North Pennār to South Pennār. This effort is reflected in Tamil literature by references to various incidents in the struggle between the Āriyar or Vaḍugar on the one side and the Tamil rulers, particularly the Cholas on the other. Among these rulers stands out the name of Iḷaṁ-Śenni who is given credit for having defeated the Paradavar of the south and the Vaḍugar of the north in one context. In another he is similarly credited with having crushed the Vaḍugar at Pāḻi on the west coast. That these Vaḍugar should be no other than the Andhras is in evidence in a passage of the Paṭṭinappālai where Karikāla is said to have brought under his control the Oliyar and then the Aruvāḷar and then the Vaḍugar, these last being interpreted by the commentator as those next north to the Aruvāḷar.

The region indicated by this reference is the region which would correspond exactly to the south-east frontier province of the Andhras dominated by Dhanakaṭaka (Amarāvati). In this region at one time the Sātavāhanas had so far succeeded as to create a frontier province under a Nāga general Skanda Nāga who is described as a Mahāsēnāpati. Under Pulumāvi therefore the war had gone on for a considerable time. After the death of Karikāla, owing apparently to the civil war that raged in the Chola country, the Cholas lost hold on the country almost up to the banks of the southern Pennār as the ship coins of the Andhras in this region indicate. It was during that period that the

Andhras felt the necessity of a viceroyalty in the south-east of an important character to which none other than a great general and possibly even a blood relation of the ruling family was considered necessary. After some time, probably in the reign of Yagña Śri, they felt the viceroyalty so far settled as to appoint a local chieftain of some influence to the position. This apparently was the Bappadēva referred to in the earliest Prakrit inscription accessible to us. His gift of money and a large number of ox-ploughs seems to be a continuation of the good work begun by Karikāla of destroying jungle and creating arable land from it, and digging tanks and providing for irrigation. This chieftain is of the Bhāradvāja Gōtra like the later Pallavas, and both he and his son ruled over Kānchī as their headquarters. Whether these were in any manner connected with the Toṇḍamaṇḍalam of Iḷaṁ-Tiraiyan, Viceroy of Kānchī, in the age immediately preceding is not known. Iḷaṁ-Tiraiyan's viceroyalty passed on to Chola Iḷaṁ-Kiḷḷi, the younger brother of Neḍumuḍi-Kiḷḷi. After the viceroyalty of this prince we do not hear of Kānchī being under the Cholas. It is very probably then that it passed into the hands of the Pallavas. As was already pointed out there were four generations of these rulers, it may be two dynasties of two rulers each, who ruled over this territory.

Whether the territory passed to another dynasty, or whether it was the same dynasty that continued, we do not know for certain; but it is clear that the territory of the Pallavas had broken up at least into three as in the Hariśēna inscription of Samudragupta three rulers at least are said to be governing the territory under the early Pallavas. That inscription refers to Hastivarman of Vengi, Ugra Sēna of Pālakka and Vishṇugopa of Kānchī. This probably was the result of a struggle between the new dynasty of the Ikshvākus who came from the north and occupied the eastern portion of the Sātavāhana territory, and the Pallavas of the south. The rulers of Pālakka and Vengi may have been offshoots of this intruding dynasty of the Ikshvāku king Śrī Vīra Purusha Datta. If that is so, Vishṇugopa of Kānchī would represent the native Pallava as against the new dynasty of intruders from the north. Samudragupta's defeat of these rulers seems to have brought about a change in Kānchī. Vishṇugopa's power was apparently undermined by the defeat and his throne was usurped by the founder of the Dynasty of the Sanskrit charters. This seems the actual course of events as Vishṇugopa's name is not mentioned in any of the charters, and Vīrakūrcha is the man who is said first to have acquired possession of this territory along with the hand of the Nāga princess. This clearly indicates a struggle, and the struggle must have been between Vishṇugopa himself and a collateral branch of the family, it may be, who sought the alliance of the powerful Nāgas in the immediate west. Vīrakūrcha or Vīravarman who, we have pointed out, might be the unnamed son-in-law of the Cūṭu chief of Banavase whose son is named Skanda Nāga in one of the records and Skandavarman in the other. This Skandavarman was apparently the Skandaśishya of the Sanskrit charters. In other words Vīravarman became heir alike to the south-eastern Viceroyalty of the Sātavāhanas held by the Nāga general first in behalf of the Sātavāhanas and later by the usurping local dynasty of the Pallavas of the Prakrit charters, it may be by right of birth, but certainly by an act of policy. Through his wife he became alike heir to the most powerful south-western viceroyalty of the Cūṭu family of the Śātakarṇis, thus uniting under one ruler the whole southern block of Sātavāhana territory about the time that the northern most part of that kingdom was being disputed for by the Nāgas from the south, and the reviving power of the Kshatrapas from the north. Either Vīrakūrcha himself or his son Skandavarman was able to reassert the authority of the Pallavas over the territory extending as far north as Vengi. Several of the Sanskrit charters were issued from their victorious camp in various of the well-known localities along the lower course of the Krishna. Skandaśishya's son Simhavarman, perhaps much more the younger son Vishṇugopa, probably took part in this reconquest of the north for the Pallavas. Another son Kumāra Vishṇu who probably ascended the throne after his elder brother Simhavarman is given credit for the conquest of the Chola country; that is the first effort at expansion southwards by the Pallavas. The history of the next following generations is somewhat obscure, but when we come to Simhavarman and his son Simhaviśhṇu we are more or less on firm historical ground. There was a reassertion of the Pallava authority over the Chola country under Simhaviśhṇu, and Mahēndravarman was able to make very much more of a permanent advance.

The Rise of the Chālukyas.

In the meanwhile changes of a momentous character had taken place to the west of the Pallava territory. The region of the Nāga chieftains, cousins of the ruling Sātavāhanas, had been taken either in the reign of Skandavarman himself or his somewhat feeble successor by an enterprising Brahman who succeeded almost as a rebel in putting an end to the Pallava power in the northern half of their territory extending southwards from Śrī Śailam. He extended his power so far as to levy contributions from the territory of the Bāṇas immediately to the west and south of the Pallava territory proper. The Pallavas apparently recognised his hold upon his native country by conferring it as a fief upon him thereby purchasing peace and perhaps a restoration of the Pallava territory of the Ceded Districts. This achievement of Mayūra Śarman, the Veda Scholar, must have taken place in the reign of Skandavarman himself or in that of his son Simhavarman. A certain number of generations of these had actually ruled. We find the Pallavas slowly gaining strength and reasserting their authority over the Gangas by successively annointing and thus ratifying the succession of two Ganga rulers. The inference of a weakening of the power of the Kadambas at that time seems possible and this was taken advantage of by a feudatory dynasty of the Kadambas, themselves a dynasty connected with them by blood and perhaps similarly claiming authority from the Sātavāhanas themselves. These are the western Chālukyas who like the Kadambas claimed to belong to the Mānavyasa Gotra, and described themselves as Hārītiputra. Their, later charters trace their descent from the rulers of Ayodhya and lay claim, in their behalf, to belong to the family of Ikshvākus ; the Cholas laid claim to the same descent as did Śrī Vīra Purusha Datta, the interloper in the eastern half of the

Āndhra territory. By the time that Simhavishṇu had placed himself firmly on the throne of Kānchī, the Chāḷukyas had so far established themselves in power first in the north-western part of the Āndhra dominions gradually extending downwards to occupy what belonged to the Çūṭu Nagas, the cousin-viceroys of the Āndhras. It is in this frontier that they came into contact with the Pallavas necessarily hostile as it meant an expansion of Chāḷukya power and territory in that direction. It is then there began the war between the Chāḷukyas and the Pallavas which is the feature of their later history.

CHAPTER XI.

Kanchi, the Centre of the Pallavas.

During the whole period of their history extending from about A.D. 200 to the end of the 9th century the Pallava power centred round Kānchī, which became definitely associated with them, at any rate from the days of Samudragupta onwards, though a very much earlier ruler states in a charter that he issued that he ruled from Kānchī. Kānchī was the centre and capital of the region known to the Tamils as Toṇḍamaṇḍalam and the Pallavas came into possession of that region exactly. They show almost from the beginning of their history, to have brought along with them the culture of the north, that is Āryan culture as distinguished from what may be called Dravidian. Their charters were all issued either in Prakrit or in Sanskrit. It may even be regarded that during their age Sanskrit literature came in for some encouragement in the region which must be regarded Pallava. The Jain work Lōkavibhāga already referred to is a work which was composed in Cuddalore in the fifth century. That is not all.

Patrons of Religion and Art.

They seem to have been great patrons as well, of religion and art. With the accession to power of the great dynasty of the Pallavas beginning with Simhavarman and his son Simhavishṇu they extended their power southwards and brought it up to the banks of the Kāvēri. As a matter of fact, Simhavishṇu is stated to have taken possession of the country of the Kāvēri. Throughout this region we see evidence of the work of his son Mahēndra-Varman, otherwise called Mahēndra-Vishṇu. The tanks, the cave temples, and some even of the smaller temples are ascribable to him. A Sanskrit burlesque ascribed to him and called Matta-vilāsa-prahasana is not merely evidence of what may be regarded as partiality for Sanskrit literature, but it also throws considerable light upon the religious condition of the times. The purpose of the work is to bring into ridicule the votaries of the various cults that prevailed at the time. An ascetic Pāśupata, a Kāpālika and his wife, and a Buddhist mendicant are brought into colloquy in the play and held up to ridicule. The omission of the Jain in this group may lead to the inference that at the time he composed the work Mahēndra was a Jain, and might thus lend support to the Śaiva tradition that rather late in his life he was converted to Śaivism by the Saint Appar.

That a work of the character of Matta-vilāsa-prahasana should be composed in Kānchī for the purpose for which it should have been intended, is evidence of a certain degree of prevalence of Sanskrit learning. This position of Kānchī is supported by its having been a *Ghaṭika* of the Brahmans at an earlier period, and by the fact that Mayūra Śarma of the Kadambas found it necessary to go to Kānchī to complete his *Vedic* studies. Mahēndra seems to have been a patron of music as well, and a short musical treatise referable to his time is inscribed on the face of the living rock in the great Śiva temple at Kuḍîmiyāmalai in the Pudukotta state so that Mahēndra in particular was a patron of art as well as of religion.

Sanskrit Literature during the Period.

Among the finds of manuscripts brought to light by the search-parties sent out by the Government Oriental Manuscripts Library are two works ascribed to Danḍin, the author of the Kāvyādarśa. This last work has a verse illustrating a particular kind of composition. The verse which has to be of a recondite character takes for its illustration the city Kānchī and its rulers the Pallavas. This reference alone would lead one to suspect that Danḍin had something to do with Kānchī. These manuscripts newly brought to light relate to the subject-matter of the prose-work Daśakumarā Charita generally ascribed to Daṇḍin. The poetical work seems to be called Avanti-Sundari-kathā-sāra, and of the original prose version a few fragments alone are yet available, but the substance of the story is put in poetic form and contains an introductory chapter which gives some information regarding Daṇḍin himself and his ancestry. The matter of peculiar importance to our subject at present is that Daṇḍin calls himself the great-grandson of Bhāravi, the author of Kirātārjunīya, and Daṇḍin seems to refer himself to the reign of Rājasimha or Narasimha II among the great Pallavas. This seems supported by the fact recently brought to notice by Rao Bahadur R. Narasimhachariar that a Ganga king by name Durvinīta lays claim to having written a commentary on the fifteenth canto of the Kirātārjunīya of Bhāravi. In this account Bhāravi is also brought into contemporaneity with the Chālukya Vishṇuvardhana, an ancestor of Jayasimha I, who became famous afterwards as the founder of the Chālukya dynasty. This would make Bhāravi a contemporary with either Mahēndra Pallava himself or his son Narasimha I. In either case Bhāravi's Kirātārjunīya may account for the great popularity that this particular incident, in the epic tradition of the manifestations of Śiva, attained in this part of the country. Apart from its being one of the most oft-quoted instances of Śiva's beneficence, the cutting out of this particular episode on the face of the big rock in Mahābalipuram which remained somewhat inexplicable till now finds a satisfactory explanation. Though we have another instance of a sculptural illustration of this in distant Behar in Chandi Mau, still it was matter which could not readily be explained why the Tēvāram hymners should have pitched upon this particular incident among a large variety, and the sculptors of Mahābalipura should have chosen this for an illustration. If Bhāravi and Daṇḍin flourished in Kānchī, Kānchī must have been a very important centre of Sanskrit learning at the time.

Great Religious Ferment in the Country.

This period must also have been one of great religious activity. Many of the existing temples came into existence during this period and most of them in Kānchī and the surrounding locality received encouragement and extension. The town of Kānchī itself is so full of these Pallava monuments that it would be possible for one to make a complete study of Pallava art and architecture without going out of it. The great renaissance of religion and literature characteristic of the age of the Guptas in the north found a reflex during the age of the Pallavas in Kānchī.

Both Śaivism and Vaishṇavism, the two offshoots of the school of Bhakti, took form and shape during this period. Literature bearing upon both of these in Tamil is almost entirely the product of the age of the Pallavas. Of the 63 Śaiva devotees one of the earliest is the Chola king Ko-Śengaṇ who must have followed the age of the Śangam very closely. We have shown elsewhere[1] that the earliest of the Vaishṇava Āḻvārs were in all probability contemporaries of the Toṇḍamān-Iḷaṁ-Tiraiyan himself. It is not at all unlikely that some of the sixty-three Śaiva Aḍiyārs may be referable to an age as early as these. The latest among the Āḻvārs is Tirumangai Āḻvār, who lived as certainly as it is possible for us to know the fact, in the middle of the eighth century. The latest of the Śaiva Aḍiyārs, Sundaramūrti, lived perhaps a generation later in the closing period of the Pallava dominance in the south. The greatest among the Aḍiyārs Sambandar and Appar, two of the three most celebrated among the Aḍiyārs, were undoubtedly contemporaries of Narasimha I. Thus we see the schools of Bhakti, the early features of which we already find reference to in the Śangam literature, began their great development under the Pallavas and took the form that they have at present, in this period.

---

[1] Early History of Vaishnavism : Oxford University Press.

INFLUENCE OF THE GUPTA CULTURE.

How much of this development may be due to any direct Gupta influence we are not in a position to trace in detail yet. It is impossible that there should not have been that kind of influence, but the whole of the Pallava development in point of religion of the Bhakti school is explainable without this external stimulus. It certainly was the age for the south of a certain amount of reorganisation of the Brahmanical religion such as it was in the earlier time. The reorganisation seems to have taken the form of a great emphasis being laid on what is generally described as "theistic religion"—religion whose centre and heart-core is a personal God watchfully beneficent for the salvation of devotees. Such a movement was called for to remedy one of the vital defects of *Vaidic* Brahmanism, and the great success that attended the early efforts of Buddhistic teachers, and to a certain degree of the Jain as well, was due to the congregationalism of both these religious systems. It is the need therefore of a religion that would appeal to the masses that led to this great development in Brahmanism in the period of Brahmanical reorganization as against Buddhism and Jainism. The recognition of a personal God and of popular religion necessitates the form of worship associated with temples.

Temple Building in the South.

If this happens to be the age during which the great majority of temples in the south came into existence the explanation is here ready. It was an age when the people were anxious to bring themselves into touch with God and that could be done only by means of the cult of *Bhakti* which necessitated the embodying in a visible form of the all-beneficent personal God. It is possible to trace the history of many of these temples to this particular period and the work of temple-building, at least so far as Śiva temples are concerned, is closely associated with the early Chola Ko-Chengan. It is demonstrable that this great Chola built temples both to Śiva and to Vishṇu so that he could be described by the Śaivas as no less than an Aḍiyār (devotee) among the sixty-three. The Vaishṇava Ālvār Tirnmangai refers to him also as having constructed 70 temples to Śiva. It is thus clear that temple-building on a large scale was only the outward exhibition of the inward ferment that led to the great development of the *Bhakti* school of religion.

Clear Evidence of Hindu Expansion in the East.

It is to the earlier portion of this period that Dr. Vogel refers the sacrificial inscription discovered at Koetei in East Borneo. The language of the inscription is Sanskrit, the character is Pallava-grantha and the donations have relation to the various benefactions and gifts that followed the completion of a Brahmanical sacrifice by the ruler Mūlavarman. This document illustrates the prevalence of Brahmanism so far out as East Borneo in a form which made the celebration of a sacrifice of the greatest importance, and which proves beyond a doubt, the existence of a colony of holy Brahmans that could celebrate sacrifices in the distant east. Later, we have it on the authority of Fa-Hien that in Sumatra and the Malaya Peninsula there were large settlements of votaries of the Brahmanical religion, but as yet nothing that could be called a community of Buddhists. A later traveller of this age, I-Tsing found the prevalence of Sanskrit culture in Sumatra so great that all the wealth of manuscripts that he was able to acquire by years of travelling in northern India he could take over with him and translate, in the first instalment of 500 volumes that he despatched, in Sumatra as offering all the facilities that India itself could have offered for that kind of monumental work of devotion and learning.

CHAPTER XII.

Śaivism.

Among the two principal schools of *Bhakti* cult prevalent in South India, Śaivism comes in for a large clientele. Śaivism consists in the recoginition of Śiva as the supreme beneficent deity. Śiva is believed to exercise the functions of creation, protection, destruction, prevention from lapses in the enjoyment of the results of one's action, and beneficence. These functions he is said to discharge with a view to release struggling souls from the bondage resulting from their previous action, and to present unto them the knowledge of the nature of Śiva, so that they might ultimately attain to the much desired release. In order to discharge these self-imposed functions of his, Śiva assumes the position of Lord with the following six attributes: omniscience, limitless contentment, knowledge that does not spring out of experience, self-possession, undiminished power, and limitless power. It is the possession of these qualities, exhibiting themselves in extreme purity, in the capacity to destroy the bondage of action and to improve the power for good, that gives appropriateness to the name of Śiva.

It is under command of this Supreme Deity that souls assume forms, and struggle in the world. They work their way gradually through the six outer forms of religion, *viz.*, Lōkāyata, Bauddha, Ārhata (Jaina), Mīmāmsa, Māyāvāda (Advaita) and Pāncharātra by faithfully carrying out the various regulations for conduct laid down by them. In the course of this struggle Śiva assumes the forms of the various beings that guide these souls, and makes them attain to the respective benefits resulting from what they do. They pass from this to the methods of the inner religion (inner to Śaivism) such as Śaivism, Pāśupatam, Vāmam, Bhairavam, Mahāvṛtam and Kāḷāmukham.

Souls in their next stage of development enter the inner religions as a result of their good action in their pursuit of life in the outer religions. Then they follow the "path of the *Vēda*," or the regulations of the Smṛitis and adopt the life of the four castes and the four orders. As a result of good action in this method they go to heaven and enjoy a higher life, only to be born again on earth at the end of their course of enjoyment. As a result, however, of their good deeds while living in the path of the *Vēda* and by the grace of Śiva they get into the "path of Śiva," and understand the significance of *Charya* (conduct), *Kriya* (duty), and *Yoga* (contemplation by concentration). Adopting this course they attain to the position of being at sight of Śiva (*Sālōka*), or in proximity to him (*Sāmīpya*) or of attaining to a form like him (*Sārūpa*). Those among them who have weaned themselves of the notion of enjoyment cease to be born on earth and get rid of the cycle of existence as a result of the grace of Śiva. It will thus be clear that, according to Śaivism, salvation is attainable only by means of the *Śaiva Siddhānta*; the only way to attain salvation is by the knowledge of the nature of Śiva; the attainment of this knowledge is achieved by the adoption of the four methods, conduct, etc. The rights and ceremonies prescribed by the *Vēda* however, produce good fruit, but these latter are not eternal. The results of action in the path of the *Vēda* are no less productive of bondage than evil action, only these are something like golden fetters, while those may be likened to iron ones. These lead to the enjoyment of good, but bring on re-birth inevitably. It is only the right knowledge of Śiva that puts an end to this rebirth. Of these four, *Śariyai*, *Kiriyai*, *Yōgam* and *Gñānam*, the first two constitute what is understood by the term *Śiva-dharma*. This *Śiva-dharma* is pursued both by an easy path and by a difficult path. The mere adoption of the rule of conduct laid down in the *Śiva-dharma* constitutes the former; while, as a result of the adoption of this line of conduct, the affection for

Śiva has so thoroughly engrossed the whole soul, it shrinks from nothing in doing what it conceives to be pleasing to Śiva. This duty extends even to the killing of parents and children, and the pulling out of one's own eyes in the service that would please the supreme deity. Those that pursue their unswerving duty to Śiva in either of these ways constitute his Bhaktas. Those that pursue it by the former method might well be called Vīra Śaivas, though this name is reserved for a class of people who adopted a similar, but a somewhat modified creed. Some of the well-known Aḍiyārs of the Śaivas actually adopted, according to the traditional accounts, this method and such classification could not be regarded as actually exclusive, or really strictly correct. In the ultimate analysis Śaivism comes to be this. It recognises the supremacy of Śiva as the beneficent deity who makes it his function to save souls (*paśu*) from their bondage in the fetters of action (*pāśam*, the results of *karman* or action); he does this as the result of his own grace.

Early Traces in Tamil Literature.

We have already seen that the Śangam literature does give evidence of this supremacy of Śiva though not quite exclusively. In the passage already quoted from Narkīrar, Śiva figures first among the four world-ruling deities,

Krishna, Baladeva and Skanda taking rank with him. In the passage quoted from the Maduraik-kāñji, Rudran Kaṇṇan seems to go a step further, and indicate more clearly the supremacy of Śiva where he is distinctly placed as the first. It will thus be clear that the rudiments were already there in the earliest period to which Tamil literature can take us while in the age immediately following a further vast development becomes discernible.

The Nāyanmârs.

Among the *Śiva Bhaktas* a certain number stand out as pre-eminently the devotees of Śiva. They attained to this distinction by various kinds of service extending from the simplest to the most exacting. These are grouped into two classes by the Śaivas. The first class consists of sixty-three and stand, each one by oneself. Then follow nine who are taken altogether in one group, constituting on the whole seventy-two. These are the recognised Saints of the Śaivas. The Śaiva canonical literature of prime importance consists of one group called *Aruṭpā* as a group. This group consists of the Tēvāram of the three most prominent of the devotees: Sambandar, Appar, and Sundara. The next is Tiruvāśagam, Tiruviśaippā and Tiruppallāṇḍu, all of them the work of Māṇikkavāśagar. This is followed of course, by an outcrop of other literature dependent on these.

The chronology of these Aḍiyārs cannot yet be regarded as a settled matter, but a rough and ready classification of these is possible from internal evidence of their works alone. They might all be regarded as pertaining to the age of the Pallavas, and this group of devotees had all lived and passed away before the Pallava dominance in South India gave place to that of the Chola. Practically the last of them Sundara composed a poem of 11 stanzas in which he describes himself poetically as a servant of all the rest of them who devoted themselves to the service of Śiva, and the date of Sundara had been for various reasons allotted to the commencement of theninth century as that of his contemporary Śēramān Perumāḷ. Eearly ninth century therefore would be the downward limit of the sixty-three Nāyanmars. The upward limit is not as easily, or even with the same degree of confidence, fixable. One at least of the earliest lends himself to this kind of inquiry and that is the early Chola king, Kō-Chengan. Even the Śaiva hagiologists have but little of historical detail to give us regarding him. All that they vouchsafe to us is that a spider devoted itself to the service of Śiva at Tiruvānaikkāval by weaving its web over the *linga* every day to prevent leaves dropping on the image. Every morning, at the same time, a white elephant used to come for performing worship. The elephant used to sweep off the cob-web, pour over the *linga* the water that it had brought in its trunk, and offer a few flowers similarly brought with it. Wearied by this act of wanton destruction of his own efforts, the spider managed to get into the trunk of the elephant and worried him so much that unable any longer to bear the pain the elephant struck its trunk against the earth violently and died; the spider also died in its pious efforts to destroy the elephant which so regularly and wantonly molested him in his act of worship. For this act of devotion the spider was ordained by the grace of Śiva to be born a Chola prince. So he was born of the Chola king Śubha Dēva and his wife Kamalavatī. The only feature of this story that might be at all considered historical is, and that is almost practically the only detail given of his life, that he built the temple of Tiruvānaikkāval (Jambukēśvaram) across the river Kāveri from Trichinopoly. His special service of devotion to Śiva therefore consisted in the construction of temples to Śiva either by himself or through the agency of his officials. A later Vaishṇava Āḷvār Tirumangai, the last of them, speaking of the Vishṇu temple at Tirunaraiyūr goes out of his way to state in clear terms [1] that he built seventy temples to Śiva. We may therefore take it that he was a historical person who contributed

[1] Periya-Tirumoḷi: VI. vi. 8.

to the development of Śaivism by the particular service of constructing numbers of Śiva temples, and the mention of such by a Vaishṇava Aḻvār has its own peculiar, significance. Both Appar and Sambandar of whose age we have some precise knowledge, allude in several places to the transformation of the spider into the Chola king.[1] This would mean that by their time the miraculous transformation had got so much into vogue that neither they nor their audience had any difficulty in accepting it as true. That would make Ko-Chengan anterior to the age of the great Pallavas of Kānchī whose period of rule began about A.D. 600.

There is a Kō-Chengan who fought a battle against a Chera King whom he threw into prison after defeating him in battle. A poet by name Poygaiyār, who seems identifiable with the Vaishṇava Aḻvār Poygai, celebrated the battle of Kaḻumalam (generally taken to the Śiyāḻi) in the poem of 40 Stanzas known in Tamil literature *Kaḷvaḻi, forty*. This identification rests on literary and stylistic grounds alone so far. There are certain historical considerations that make him contemporary with the Toṇḍamān Iḷaṁ Tiraiyan of Kānchī.[2] This line of investigation therefore would take Kō-Chengan to a period

---

[1] Appar, Tirunaḷḷaṛu 5 ; Śambandar, Ariśilkaraipputtūer 7 ; Tiruvaikal,4 ; Ambar, 1. 2, 5 and 9.

[2] Early History of Vaishṇavism, pp. 73. at seg.

which may be the closing period of the so-called Śangam literature.

Of the three Tēvāram hymners, we have referred Sundara to the commencement of the ninth century. The other two were contemporaries according to tradition, and several historical circumstances connected with each of the two, bring them into contemporaneity likewise. Appar lived to be a very old man, was born a Śaiva, became a Jain, and at the latter end of his life returned to Śaivism and was instrumental in converting the great Pallava king Mahēndravarman. The other, Sambandar, was his younger, but the more distinguished contemporary, who visited another Śaiva devotee Śiruttonḍar in the course of his peregrinations at Tiruchengāṭṭangudi. This Śiruttonḍār was the general of Mahēndra's son Narasimha, and rendered valiant service to his master in the destruction of Vātāpi (Badami), the capital of the Western Chālukyas under Pulikēsin II. This battle was fought some time about A.D. 642, and therefore these two Sambandar and Śiruttonḍar must have lived about that time and a little later. Appar, as the older, was apparently the contemporary of the father and the son among the Pallava rulers, and probably lived to the middle of the seventh century. The Aḍiyārs who are referred to either directly or allusively in the works of these two, Sambandar and Appar, have to be classified as the early Aḍiyārs; Sambandar and Appar and their contemporaries as perhaps the middle ones; Sundara, Śēramān Perumāḷ and those that could be associated with them as the last ones. Kō-Chengan was probably one of the earliest of those that flourished from say about A.D. 200 to A.D. 600, that is among the early Aḍiyārs.

Kaṇṇappa Nāyanār.

We have already seen that the peculiar form of service rendered to Śiva by Kō-Chengaṉ consisted in the building of temples to him. There are others who devoted themselves to rendering some kind of bodily service-gardening for Śiva, sweeping Śiva temples, providing garlands for Śiva and various other sundry acts of service all of them rendered with absorbing devotion. These are the milder forms of service. Reference was made already to a more vigorous form of exhibition of this single-hearted devotion to Śiva. To illustrate this and along with this various other items of devotion that went to make up the teachings of this school of bhakti, the story of an ignorant hunter whose secular name was Tiṇṇan, is given below. He attained to the sacerdotal designation of Kaṇṇappa Nāyanār, by which name alone he is generally known. He is referred to specifically by both Sambandar and Appar, and therefore he was anterior to both of them. In fact he is among the earliest of the Śaiva devotees. Sankarāchārya refers to him in the Śivānanda Lahari.

Kaṇṇappa was the son of a hunter-chief by name Nāga and his wife Tattai. He was born in a village Uḍuppūr in what used to be known as Pottappināḍu (south Nellore District). The parents were long childless, and got this boy as a result of service to Skanda rendered by making over to his temple numbers of ordinary fowls and pea-fowls. The boy was naturally brought up to be a hunter and was given the responsibilities of the chieftainship while yet a young man, as the father had grown too old. On one occasion he went along with others, his companions, on a boar hunt. One of these beasts was so powerful that it sprang out of the net, tearing it away in the act, and ran into the forests. Tiṇṇan with two others Nāṇa and Kāḍa gave the animal the chase and overtook it after covering a great distance. Tiṇṇan who was the frontmost and near enough to the animal drew out his sword and cut it in two. The other two came up and all of them were very hungry. They wanted to roast the flesh and eat it to satisfy their hunger; but water was a prime necessity. Nāṇa said he knew there was water at some distance on the side of the hill. Carrying the beast they walked along towards the water, and came in sight of another hill in the distance. Tiṇṇan made the suggestion they might proceed to that hill before they sat down to make a meal of the quarry, when Nāṇa, his companion, made the casual remark that that hill contained the God '*Kuḍumittēvar*.' That was the seed of the hunter Tiṇṇan's devotion. The three friends walked along carrying the boar till they reached the river flowing at the foot of the hill. Leaving one of them behind to make the fire and roast the pork, Tiṇṇan and his friend Nāṇan went up the hill. At the sight of the *linga*, Tiṇṇan was so attracted to the deity that he began to exhibit the extraordinary affection of a mother who had been separated from a child for a long time. Overpowered with affection then he began to conduct himself like one beside himself. It was some time before he noticed that somebody had washed the *linga* with water and put flowers on the top of it. Saying that somebody had done ill to have so treated the God, he learnt from his companion that a Brahman was in the habit of performing this kind of worship. On hearing this he thought that kind of worship must be acceptable to God. So he began to perform worship similarly according to his light. He made it his business thereafter daily to go up the hill carrying roast meat strung together on an arrow, a mouthful of water from the Ponmukhari and a few flowers tucked on to his hair. On reaching the *linga*, he used to spit the water over it from his mouth, take the flowers from out of his hair and put it on the top of the *linga*, and place the roast meat chosen by taste before it, and thus perform his worship. This desecration, as the Brahman considered it, gave moral pain to him, and, in his extreme distress of mind, he appealed to Śiva himself as to who brought about this desecration and why Śiva should have suffered it. Śiva appeared to him in a dream and pointed out to him that, hunter as Tiṇṇan was, his devotion to Śiva was so whole-hearted and hence was more pleasing to him than even that of those who had offered him excellent prayers with a mind prepared by the long study of the *Vedas* and *vaidika-āgamas*. He directed the much distressed Brahman to remain in hiding and see for himself. When next the hunter appeared before the idol, blood was coming out of one of the eyes of the idol.

Tiṇṇan fainted away at the sight of it, and, when he came back to himself, he took his bow and arrows and looked about for those that might have done this harm. Not finding anybody within sight of the idol he set about thinking as to how exactly he should cure it. Do what he might the blood still continued flowing. Then it struck him that the best way to cure such a disease was to put in flesh for flesh, that is, removing the rotten flesh and putting a fresh piece—a form of cure hunters know very well. He pulled out with an arrow his own right eye and put it in place of the right eye of Śiva. He found that the bleeding stopped. He was so delighted with his performance that he danced in sheer joy. In order the better to exhibit his single-hearted devotion Śiva made his other eye bleed. When Tiṇṇan was about to pull out his other eye to substitute it for the bleeding one of Śiva, Śiva put forth his arms from the linga and took hold of his hands that were in the act of pulling out his other eye and cried out "eye friend eye" ("Kaṇṇappa, Kaṇṇappa") and this ejaculation of Śiva gave him the name "Kaṇṇappa." The Brahman who was witness to all this was surprised and delighted at the intensity of devotion of the hunter, rude, unmethodical and uncanonical as the form of devotion was. This is briefly the tale of Śiva's miracle in respect of this particular devotee Kaṇṇappa.

The story of Kaṇṇappa has become so famous and hallowed by tradition that it is familiar to everybody not only in the Tamil country but in the Telugu. The simple-hearted devotion of the hunter, and Śiva's special approval of it exhibited by the miracle regarding him, have struck the fancy of the people so much that one of the Telugu poets of the first rank, Śrīnātha by name, made it the theme of a poem called Haravilāsam. The devotion of Kaṇṇappa has also become the model of austere penance to the Śaivas of a somewhat later persuasion. I have given the story above as it is found detailed in the Periyapurāṇam of Śēkkiḷār who lived early in the twelfth century. As it is worked by the hagiologist, the story exhibits certain features which are worthy of special note. The object of the writer is here to bring into contrast the single-hearted but ill-considered and ill-formed performance of devotion to Śiva such as the hunter's, with the performance of similar devotion by the cultured and pious Brahman performing his prayer according to recognised form. The moral is the victory of single-minded devotion however crude in form and even objectionable from the point of view of recognised usage. As a result of this the story makes a few points clear. The hunter gets into an ecstasy of devotion on hearing the name of Śiva as a result of preparation in previous existences. At the sight of the *linga*, his affection for his God so overpowers him that he forgets himself, and in this self-forgetfulness nothing is shown except affection for the God and anxiety for his safe keeping. When at last the idea is brought home to him, that somebody else more respected of human beings and obviously more acceptable to Śiva himself, had performed an act of devotion, the idea goes into him at once and without further consideration he makes up his mind to do so also according to his lights and in the manner familiar to him. This goes so far in its singleness that the height is reached when the rude man and the crude worshipper does not hesitate to pull out his eye to put it in place of what he thought the ailing one of Śiva. It is immaterial whether all these were acts ascribable to the hunter historically. These were the ideas that underlay the notion of *bhakti* as it was understood in his time. These ideas almost in the same form are found scattered all through the work of Śaiva hagiologists and required to be organised and put into form for sectarian purposes later on as we shall see.

In the cult of *bhakti* the first feature to be taken note of is, unalloyed affection for God, and this affection springs from the notion that God looks after man with an affectionate interest superior even to that of himself, and therefore deserves the return of unqualified devotion.[1]

Such an affection when it does exist exhibits itself on all occasions whenever there should be the slightest stimulus as in the case of Kaṇṇapa at the mere mention of the name God, and afterwards at sight of Him. Unless devotion is exhibited to the fullest extent of singleheartedness it is hardly possible to expect Him to exhibit His grace to the suffering human beings. According to Appar it is impossible that God

[1] Compare Appar.

should exhibit himself unless one performs his devotion with a mind unalloyed with other feelings than that of affection and devotion. A similar idea is more forcibly expressed in the Tirumandiram of Tirumūlar. The offering of sacrifice of one's own flesh by cutting it from out of one's own body and throwing it into a fire lighted with one's own bones is not as efficacious to evoke His grace readily as devotion which melts away one's heart and mind.

This goes one step further when the notion gets to prevail that pilgrimage to holy places, the contemplation upon the supreme and the performance of prayer on the approved style are all of them of no use in comparison to the realising of oneself in the extremity of affection for God himself.

This extraordinary affection for God springs in a human being as a result of deeds in previous existences without regard to fruit thereof and as the result of Śiva's grace and that grace alone.

In the last resort the moment that one attains to this single-minded and unalloyed devotion, he attains to the condition of Śiva, as this affection for him is not separate from Śiva himself. Where this affection exists there Śiva is bound down to the offer of this devotion. Wherever there is this affection, there Śiva becomes visible.

The story of Kaṇṇappa is intended to illustrate this development in the course of *Śiva bhakti.* The extraordinary devotion that the uncultivated hunter exhibited is believed to be due to what he did in his previous incarnation as Arjuna with whom Śiva wrestled in the disguise of a hunter. It is the ripened effect of his good deeds that required merely the stimulus of the mention of the name of Śiva to make him lose control over himself altogether like a virtuous young wife whose affection overpowers her completely at the mention of the name of her beloved. Being an uncultivated rude man not knowing how exactly to exhibit his devotion at sight of God he could only show his affection in the manner he was accustomed to do, and exhibited it as a father or mother would at the sight of a long lost child. But the devotion that he felt for Śiva so overpowered him that he forgot altogether the animal requirements such as hunger, sleep, etc., for six days.

In regard to his performance of devotion, that is the result of the ignorance that goes along with the birth and bringing up of this hunter. What is acceptable to Śiva and what is not, requires a preceptor to teach. Such a preceptor he had not had. And having heard but imperfectly what another man has been doing by way of devotion, he just imitated, to the very best of his ability, what he thought was being done by that other person, who, he thought, ought to know. So he bathed the *linga*, cleaned the surroundings and provided the food in a manner that appealed to him. In spite of all this there was at the back of it all in the rude crude man a devotion which knew no limit and which shrank from nothing by way of sacrifice to do that which according to him pleased Śiva. It is this singleness of purpose in devotion that made even the objectionable form of worship acceptable to Śiva and this same idea is expressed in the *Tiruvāśakam* of Māṇikkavāśakar.

The crisis of this devotion is reached in regard to Kaṇṇappa when it comes to Śiva's bleeding eye. The hunter had absolutely no hesitation in pulling out his own eye to put in place of the ailing eye of Śiva as he thought, and when that is done, the ultimate limit of devotion is reached. Kaṇṇappa is ripe for the attainment of Śivahood and attained it as a result of the grace of Śiva which showed itself by look.

Thus then we see from the history of this devotee that *bhakti* as understood by the early Śaivas was not incompatible with other forms of propitiation of God, but gradually developed by adding on the teacher to make *bhakti* exclusively the method for the attainment of God's favour.

It was already pointed out that in its undeveloped form *bhakti* consisted merely in the exhibition of unalloyed affection for God by some form of service however simple or humble. Visiting places of holy reputation, or doing some act of personal or even menial service to God in some temple or elsewhere, was apparently considered enough provided the feeling within of unmixed devotion was swelling up as occasion afforded ; and where persons subject to this ebullition of emotion had the means to give vent to this feeling, there naturally came the outpouring of the heart in the shape of verses in prayer. The works of such Śaiva devotees as left their impress upon their contemporaries were collected some time after and put in form for being chanted, and constituted the canonical literature of the Śaivas in Tamil. These were naturally thrown in forms peculiar to the expression of the feelings evoked, and the very composition of these poems partook of the character of the modes of expression peculiar to Tamil literature, and defined by Tamil grammarians and rhetoricians. This peculiar method of exhibition of one's love to that particular form of God which appealed to his heart, gave the whole body of this literature a peculiarity all its own. These poems were in course of time set to music and were adapted to representation by the art of dancing. A class of people set up separately for the study and development of these features of the works, so that one set came to be known as specially expert in setting the tune and rendering the poems in music, and the other, generally, women, gave themselves up to the practice of the art of rendering it by dancing to the accompaniment of music. It is these developments that made the greatest appeal, and maintained the character of the melting strains of music, to the songs of these devotees, even to the present day. Practised within limits and under the control of the dominating passion of selfless devotion to God, it exercises an influence unique in character. But at the same time it is liable to abuse where the controlling feeling is feeble, and when pretenders set up for prophets. This feature of the devotional works seems to have attained full development at the time when the works were originally collected and put in form about the tenth century A. D. Though the Vaishṇava devotional works partake of this character to a great extent they did not combine the practice of the accessory arts in connection therewith in the same form as Śaiva devotional works. This special development seems to be what ultimately associated *bhakti* with the Tamil country peculiarly in works treating specially of the subject.

One other feature seems also to come into prominence in the course of development of this school. This feature is the emergence of the saving priest or preceptor who becomes essential to the attainment of salvation ; and unless one attains to what is called *dīkṣā* from a *guru* or preceptor of the proper kind Śiva's grace becomes impossible. As far as it is possible to trace this institution, we see that the preceptor does not figure prominently in the case of the early and less developed devotees, but with the later ones the preceptor becomes indispensable; and this feature of the preceptor has developed a prominence, which it has not since lost, in regard to Māṇikkavāśakar in whose case the preceptor proves an indispensable necessity. This feature attained to its own peculiar development and gave rise ultimately to the development of the sects as we shall see.

JAINISM IN THE SOUTH.

According to Jain tradition as preserved in the various Paṭṭāvalies there was a schism and the Jains divided into two sections. This split is said to have taken place in the reign of the Maurya Emperor Chandragupta. The leader of one of the sections is known by the name Badhrabāhu, and he was the recognised head of the section known as *Digambara* (that made the directions for their clothing, *i.e.*, unclad). He is supposed to have lived in Magadha. A twelve years' famine supervening, he had to leave the country and move across till he finally settled in Śravaṇa Belgola in Mysore. According to this story, Chandragupta is said to have abdicated in favour of his son, and, adopting the vow of a Jain mendicant, followed his master Badhrabāhu and lived and died in the region of Mysore. There are certain place-names and other circumstances which seem to lend support to this tradition. Whether Jainism came into the South along with Bhadrabāhu, and in this manner or not, we have evidence, in the Śangam literature, of considerable value for the existence of the Jains in the South. Among the systems controverted in the Maṇimekhalai the Jain system also figures as one, and the words Śamaṇ and Amaṇ are of frequent occurrence as also references to their *vihāras* so that from the earliest times reachable with our present means, Jainism apparently flourished in the Tamil country. Buddhism seems to have had a clientele of its own also, and it is these systems that the poem 116 of the Puṛanānūru already quoted refers to as religions though seeming true still undermined the authority of the *Vedas*. These flourished side by side and enjoyed a certain degree of patronage from the rulers generally, while it seems likely that at one time one sect and at another time another had the more influential lead, and was capable of throwing the others into the shade by its influence. It has however been pointed out that there is nothing whatsoever to justify the old classification that there was an age of the Jainas which preceded all others, followed by an age of the Buddhists, and that again by the Brahmanical or the Purāṇic age. No such clearly marked chronological division is discernible in the evidence at our disposal. These lived side by side, and the most that we are warranted in stating from the evidence at our disposal is, these waxed and waned in influence at different periods of their history, and this variation of influence was in many cases due to the acquisition of influence over the monarchs for the time being.

CHAPTER XIII

LITERATURE OF ŚAIVISM

Nāyanmārs in the Age of the Pallavas

It was already pointed out that practically all the sixty-three devotees must have lived in the period which for convenience may be called the age of the Pallavas, taking it in the broadest sense as extending from about A.D. 200 to 900. It was also pointed out that the earliest of them may reach back to quite the commencement of the age of the Pallavas and the latest of them cannot have been many generations after the practical abolition of the Pallava power in South India. The Chola Kō-Chengaṉ and the hunter Kaṇṇappa, and some others among these are referable to the early period of the age of the Pallavas. Sambandar, Appar and a certain number of others are referable, on what might be regarded certain evidence, to the seventh century A.D. Of these, Sambandar had a comparatively short life while Appar must have lived a man of ripe old age. The two are however generally referred together, and the younger is generally regarded as the more influential of the two, both in regard to his following and the importance of his teaching. Then follows the third section headed by Sundaramūrti. He had a friend in another of the sixty-three, a Śēramān Perumāḷ. These had been referred, the one as providing the occasion for the founding of the Kollam era and the other as having celebrated in a poem the other sixty-two devotees, to the early part of the ninth century A.D. Of these, Sambandar, Appar and Sundaramūrti constitute the three recognised leaders of the school of *bhakti* as represented by the sixty-three Aḍiyārs or Nāyanmārs, and the works of the three constitute the first seven sections of the Śaiva literature of this school. The oldest among these Appar was born a Śaiva, became a convert to Jainism and leader of the Jain settlement at Pāṭali (now the new town of Cuddalore) and became a Śaiva again as the result of a miracle, by means of which Śiva cured him of what seemed an incurable disease. Śaiva tradition has it that it was through his influence that the Pallava King Mahēndra Varman was converted to Śaivism from Jainism. There is a burlesque "*Matta Vilāsā Prahasana*" ascribed to this Pallava Mahēndra Varman where he brings into a somewhat ludicrous colloquy a Pāśupata, a Kāpālika and his wife, and a Bauddha, and no Jain however is brought into this religious squabble. This may support the contention that he was a Jain to begin with. His monuments however seem alike devoted to the Brahmanical trinity though this is no bar to his having been a Śaiva.

According to the story as embodied in the Periyapurāṇam of the life of Sambandar the Pāṇḍya contemporary had adopted the faith of the Jains while his wife, a Chola Princess was a devoted Śaiva. So also was his chief minister. Through the influence of these latter two, Sambandar obtained the opportunity to convert this Pāṇḍya to Śaivism. Both the queen and the minister are counted among the sixty-three canonical devotees. The miracle that brought about the conversion of the king was that after a successful disputation with the Jainas, Sambandar made the hunch-backed king stand erect and gave him the name "*Ninraśir Nedumārar*" which can be interpreted the great Pāṇḍya of enduring prosperity, or the great Pāṇḍya who had stood erect. It is on this occasion that at the instigation of Sambandar the whole body of Jains in Madura are said to have been impaled. This story of persecution has in it features which seem the common features of similar stories. Such stories are told of a Jain king of Kānchī who gave to Buddhists similar treatment, and of the Vaishṇava apostle Rāmānuja having treated the Jainas similarly by instigating the Hoysala king Vishṇu Vardhana against them. In such cases these stories seem to have been concocted by the later hagiologists to enhance the glories of their own particular form of religion. In each one of these cases it can be proved conclusively that there is no evidence of a general act of persecution, such as is described, as these religions flourished in undiminished influence even after the period to which these persecutions are ascribed.

MĀṆIKKAVĀŚAKAR.

The eighth of the twelve sections of the Śaiva canonical collection consists of Māṇikkavāśakar's Tiruvāśakam and Tirukkōvaiyār. Māṇikkavāśakar was, like Sambandar and Sundaramūrti before, a Brahman by birth, and enjoyed the title and the responsibility of the ministry to a Pāṇḍya king, apparently the Pāṇḍya king Varaguṇa referred to in the Tirukkōvaiyār. The story of his life briefly is that he was deputed by his sovereign to go and make large purchases of horses for his cavalry. Going on this mission with the requisite amount of treasure, he came on the way to a place called Perumturai where under the shade of a *kurunda* tree he saw a priest at the head of a body of Śaiva disciples. Feeling the call and seeing the opportunity presenting itself in this fashion, he stopped there, received the teaching and *dīkṣa* (ordination) from this devoted preceptor, and spent away the money that he carried with him for purchasing horses in devotional works and charity. For this act of sheer neglect of his duty to his sovereign and state, he was subjected to various acts of bodily punishment from which Śiva saved him by the performance of miracles. Of these one took the form of converting the jackals of the forests into horses and leading them into the Pāndyan stables. He obtained the release of Māṇikkavāśakar by working as a labourer in Madura and showing himself to the Pāndyan king. Mānikkavāśakar thereafter was allowed to follow the bent of his mind, and having visited various Śaiva shrines of importance, he stayed for some considerable time in Chidambaram having overcome a large body of Buddhists from Ceylon in controversy, and attained to Śivahood. He has been ascribed by various scholars to a very early period, but the weight of scholarly opinion seems to support the order in the arrangement of Śaiva canonical literature which groups his works in the eighth of the twelve canonical sections.

Māṇikkavāśakar's works partake of the character of the Tēvāram hymners before him. They exhibit however a more intense kind of devotion, if that were possible, and a literary form which is perhaps more directly in accordance with the canons of criticism. His second work in particular is supposed to provide the model, for that special section of rhetoric which we have labelled for convenience, erotic. We have stated before that the modes of expression characteristic of Tamil literature gave that peculiar character to *bhakti* in the Tamil country which raises it from the region of mere abstraction to that of actual realisation in life even by the imperfect human being. While all considerable writers of this school have more or less contributed towards this end by their mode of composition, the matter itself appeals straight to the heart. Māṇikavāśakar excels all of them both in form and in feeling.

The ninth section of this canonical literature is composed of the works of nine others including in it the Tirupallāṇḍu of Śēndan. The tenth is composed entirely of the Tirumandiram of Tirumūlar. The eleventh is composed of a miscellaneous collection including in it the works of Paṭṭinattaḍikal, a devotee of considerable influence, and those of Nambi Āṇḍār Nambi who is given the credit of having compiled the whole collection. This collection is composed of about 40 poems of these various authors. Nambi Āṇḍār Nambi lived in the eleventh century and is regarded by the Śaiva Tamils to have done for Śaivism what Vyāsa is believed to have done for *Vēdic* Brahmanism. These eleven sections of what the Tamils call *Tirumurai*, together with the lives of these saints written by Śēkkiḻār constitute the complete set of Śaiva canonical literature which in the estimation of the Śaivas corresponds to the *Vēdic* literature of the Brahmans. Śēkkiḷār lived in the twelfth century, and by his time the whole body of Śaiva canonical works were collected and thrown in form so that he could take upon himself to write a classical poem on the lives of these saints. The whole body of these works including the Periyapurāṇam of Śēkkiḷār have this character in common. They are all works of devotion, and each work or each set of verses could be regarded as some form of prayer addressed to Śiva in various modes as occasion demanded. Hence the whole set is compared to the *mantras* of the *Vēda*. This comparison acquires a certain degree of validity when there grew up in the age immediately following an outcrop of literature, the purpose of which was designedly to give logical form and philosophical shape to Śaiva Siddhānta as a religious system.

The Śāstras of the Śaivas.

The Śaivas claim fourteen treatises which are named either after the author or from some characteristic of the work itself.

All of these were composed in the age immediately following that of Śēkkiḷār. The two authors however, called respectively Tiru-Undiyār and Tirukkaḷiṟṟuppaḍiyār, called so from the circumstance that he presented his work to God

Naṭarāja at Chidambaram from the steps supported by elephants on both sides, form a sort of transition between the twelve books of prayer we have dealt with before and the other twelve books of science that constitute the *Śaiva Śāstras* proper. The most important of the *śāstraic* section of Śaiva canonical literature is the work of Meykaṇḍadēva entitled Śivagñānabodham. This is a work composed of twelve Sūtras framed in Sanskrit forming part of Raurava Āgamam. He not only wrote the *Sūtras* but also provided a *Vārtika*, prose passages in explanation. He is said to have provided the work with a *chūrnika* in addition. This work which constitutes the basis of the āgamic or śāstraic portion of the Śaiva Siddhānta was somewhat elaborately expounded in the work of an elder contemporary scholar who became the disciple of Meykaṇḍa. His name is Aruḷnandi Śivāchārya, and the work is known by the name Śivagñāna Siddhiyār. This work is composed of two sections. The first part is called *parapakshaṁ*, and examines the various other systems in vogue such as Lōkāyata Bauddha, Śamaṇa (Jain), Bhaṭṭāchārya, Prabhākara, Śabdabrahmavādi, Māyāvādi (Advaita), Bhāskara, Nirīśvara Sānkhya and Pāncharātram, and condemns them all as not meeting the religious needs of humanity. The second part is called *svapaksham* in which he deals with the *Śaiva Siddhānta*, and establishes the truth of it as against the former. The last among this group of śāstraic works is what is called *Sankalpa-nirākaraṇam* which like *Śivagñana Siddhi* was composed to convert votaries of other systems by a member of the Brahman community of "the three thousand" of Chidambaram by name Umāpati Śivāchārya. He was also an author of several other works bearing on the same subject. These three together with the preceptor of the last by name Maraigñāna Sambandar constitute the four pontiffs who are called by the Tamils *Santāna Kuravar* (succession of pontiffs). This nomenclature for these four is in contrast to the four *Samaya Kuravar*, preceptors of religion, a name collectively applied to the four devotees Sambandar, Appar, Sundarar, the three Tēvāram hymners, and Māṇikkavāśakar, the author of *Tiruvāśakam*. The former founded the system of religion, or at least expounded it, and thus provided the philosophy indispensable to the successful maintenance of it as against controversialists of other creeds.

CHAPTER XIV.

Vīra Śaivism.

The course of development of what might for convenience be called orthodox Śaivism of the Tamil land was described in the last two chapters. Along with this there were other forms of Śaiva worship prevalent in the Tamil country, and these come in for reference in the course of some of the works accepted by the orthodox Śaivas. We have referred already to the five divisions of what is called outer Śaivism, that is, Śaivism outside the circle of orthodox acceptance. These are Pāśupatam, Vāmam, Bhairavam, Mahāvṛatam and Kāḷāmukham. Several of these had at various times attained to considerable influence and patronage in Southern India. They do not differ much in the essentials of their teaching and differ mainly in the rigour with which they carry out single-minded devotion to the form or aspect of Śiva to which they devote themselves. It is this characteristic that generally groups them together under the designation of Vīraśaivism. We already referred to the prevalence of both Pāśupatam and Kāḷāmukham under the Pallava King, Mahēndravarman. It is those apparently that are referred to as prevalent in north-western India, the Frontier-Province, in the accounts of the early Chinese travellers. Notwithstanding the prevalence of Śaivism of these rigorous types in the North-West, Bāṇa, the biographer of Harsha, makes Bhairavāchārya come from the South to the Court of Harsha's ancestor Pushpabhuti.[1] Strangely enough a form of Bhairava is the presiding deity in a temple in the Tanjore District hallowed by the tradition connected with the Pallava general Śiruttoṇḍar who with the assistance of his dutiful spouse cooked up their boy son to satisfy Śiva appearing in the form of a Śaiva Sannyāsi of one of these sects: and this form of Śiva is called Uttarāpatha Nāyaka clearly indicating his northern filiation. We have reference to a colony of Śiva-worshippers from Bengal, who were imported and settled by the great Chola Rājēndra I[2] in places like Kānchī and the Chola country hallowed by the Śaiva holy places. This region has from the earliest times been associated, though not quite exclusively, with the worship of Śiva. Thus, it is clear that even the more vigorous and aggressive forms of Śaivism were prevalent in the Tamil country ever since the beginning of historical times, reinforced, time and again, by the infusion of Northern

---

[1] Bāṇa's Harsacharitam, p. 111, Nirnaya Sāgar edition.

[2] A. S. D, 1911-12, p. 176.

teaching and by influx of Northern votaries. It was left however to the Kākatīya country of Telingana and for the twelfth century to inaugurate a new movement of this form of aggressive Śaivism which is generally known by the term Vīra-Śaivism in modern times. What exactly was the exciting cause of this movement, we are not able to see quite clearly, unless it be the settlement of the Śaiva Brahmans from Bengal by the Great Rājendra already referred to, and a later influence from Bundalkhand in the reign of Kākatīya Rudra I.[3] The movement seems to have received a special impetus from a certain zeal for social reform by the abolition of caste and by otherwise removing some of those social restrictions, against which there has generally been much feeling among social reformers down to this day. This movement falls into two sections of which one may be described as conservative and the other radical. The conservative movement seems to be a Brahman movement essentially, and is confined to a class who claimed to have been Brahmans before and after the separation of this Vīraśaiva sect. The common feature of these are a considerable subordination of *Vēdic* rights and rituals, and a proportionate raising into importance of personal devotion or *bhakti*. While attaching all importance to *bhakti* and

---

[3] Ep. Rep. 1917. Secs. 30-37.

according acceptance even to the self-surrender which is a characteristic of Vīra Śaiva teaching, this particular section of them base their teachings in great part on *Vēdic* philosophy and are believers in the principles, even of *Vēdic* religions. These go by the name of *Ārādhyas* and are found as a distinct class largely in the Telugu country and in some number in the Kanarese country as well. The more extreme form of these Vīra Śaivas, Lingayats as they are called, hold these beliefs in comparatively little esteem and follow the teachings of Basava, himself a Brahman and the founder of their sect.

According to tradition embodied in the Basava Purāna, Basava was a Brahman born in a village in the Bijapur district of the Southern Maharatta country, who attracted the attention of the chief minister of the Kalachūrya usurper, Bijjala. Bijjala was a Jain and usurped the throne of the descendants of the great Chāḷukya Vikramāditya VI in the year A.D. 1156, and ruled for a period of about ten years, when he abdicated in favour of his sons, four of whom ruled in succession for a short period of less than ten years. Basava rapidly advanced in his official career and became one of the Ministers of state. He made use of the position for the advancement of his particular sect. His followers growing in numbers and influence consequently came into conflict with the Jains of the capital. Bijjala had to intercede and in spite of the miracles which Basava is said to have worked in favour of his new cult in the capital, Bijjala's influence could be got rid of only by assassination, according to the Purāṇa. It states circumstantially that Basava found his position untenable in the capital and had to flee for safety. He instigated two of his faithful followers to assassinate Bijjala, himself proceeding to a place called Kūdali Sangamēśvara, where he was absorbed into Śiva. The mantle of leadership fell upon Channa Basava, the son of his sister by favour of Śiva. He had however to keep out of headquarters with his followers and pursue his religion beyond the reach of the royal arms. Such in tradition is the story of the two founders of this form of Vīra Śaivism according to their canonical literature.

It will thus be clear that the course of development of this particular section of the school of *bhakti* which for the Aryan or the northern part of it might reach back to the Śvētāśvatara and Atharvasiras Upanishads and may even be anterior, is found if somewhat in a rudimentary form in the South in the earliest extant literature of the classical Tamils where Śiva is regarded as the dominating deity and may even be regarded with something of personal attributes. Therefrom the development takes on the form of devotion and personal service to the personal god Śiva by human individuals with a view to the attainment of salvation which to the Śaivas is nothing less than absorption into Śiva. Throughout the age of the Pallavas, roughly from about A.D. 200 to 900, this development takes on the peculiarly emotional form of out-pouring of these devotees' love to God, and the whole body of literature may be characterised as emotional. Each particular poem might be regarded as thrown in form to illustrate the various modes of expression of emotion in current use in the literature of the Tamils to which some similarity could be discovered in the Gātha Saptaśati of Hāla. It is this sensuous character of the emotion, which has drawn particularly from human analogies and human experience, that gives the peculiar character to this class of literature and associates with this somewhat realistic form of *bhakti*, this peculiar characteristic of the Dravidian country. While therefore the analogy which the Tamil Śaivas acknowledge between the *Vēdic Mantras* and the pious songs of the sixty-three devotees and their immediate followers, is not without justification, there is this peculiarity to be noted that this attempt at devotion is realistic to a degree that appeals straight to the heart of human beings and justifies itself by the experience of each individual. This realism may be carried too far and may be liable to abuse, and such abuse is not altogether without illustration in later developments. The establishment of the ascendancy of the Cholas at the commencement of the tenth century introduces a new factor. The Cholas were many of them Śaivas themselves, and it is the Śaivism of the ruling sovereigns that is the real factor in its further development. The period seems to be an age of renaissance, and there is a renascent spirit in the general attempt that one notices at the rehabilitating of the works of all worth having for civilised life. It is as part of this general movement that the schools of *bhakti*, both Śaiva and Vaishṇava, attempt to provide themselves with a philosophical system intended. chiefly for purpose of controversy, and therefore providing the very essentials of sectarian religion. In this re-modelling Sanskritic culture from the North perhaps bears the main part. It was not that there was no Sanskrit influence before, but now it is not a question of influence. It is a question of copying the actual model as it were of the post-Vedic Sanskrit works. This is clearly traceable in the attempt to provide the school of *Śiva-bhakti* with the characteristic *śastric* literature of its own. This character is discernible in Southern India throughout the whole period extending from A.D. 900 to almost 1700. Hence every scholar of eminence of this particular age is primarily a controversialist, and everything else afterwards. This is also the age of the special school of Sanskrit commentators, and controversialists especially, and the same character is visible even in the vernacular works of the time. The age therefore may be likened to the so-called age of the Sūtras in the north.

Comment and controversy lead on to reform, and reformers become the normal product of the age. The history of the two reformers of the Vīra Śaiva sect is wrapped in considerable obscurity in spite of the fact that there is a Basava Purāṇa and a Channa Basava Purāṇa, dealing professedly with the legendary history of these two respectively. The former of the two constitutes the first of the three canonical works of the Lingāyats, and is a work composed in the thirteenth cemtury, whereas the other one Channa Basava Purāṇa is a work belonging to the end of the sixteenth and the beginning of the seventeenth century. Basava's death according to the latter is ascribed to a year corresponding to A.D. 785 which is impossible from the known dates of Bijjala with whom Basava is connected in all accounts. The Channa Basava Purāṇa was composed by the Poet Virūpāksha in the year Śālivahana 1507, corresponaing to A.D. 1585. The historical value of these works therefore seems comparatively little as several misstatements of main incidents, such as the death of Bijjala, make it clear.[1]

The Bijjala Rāya Charitam which is the Jain version of the story of Bijjala differs in very many particulars from the purāṇas of the Lingāyats. Bijjala is there said to have been poisoned at the instance of Basava, and had time enough to warn his son who is called Immaḍi Bijjala that it was Basava who was responsible for the deed.

The fact of Basava's death is mis-stated here and the dating even is wrong as Bijjala's death is ascribed to a date 12 years before Bijjala's abdication in favour of his son in A.D. 1167 and even before 1156, when Bijjala established himself upon the throne. The actual date given in the Jain peom, Kaliyuga 4255 expired would correspond to Saka 1077 or A.D. 1154-55.[2] In spite of these discrepancies, there is enough in the circumstantial accounts for assuming that Basava and Channa Basava did live and were reformers of the Śaiva religion as it was practised, one result of the reforms being an aggressive assertion of the

[1] For a summary account of these two Purāṇas in English see J. Bom. A.S., Vol. VIII, pp. 65-221.

[2] This actual date was taken by Sir Walter Elliot apparently from a work which he calls Bijjala Kāvya. The late Dr. Fleet does not find the authority for the statement however. Mad. J. of Lit. and Science, VII, pp. 213-14. Bom. Gaz., Vol. I, Part ii, p. 481, Note 3.

superiority of this particular Śaiva sect as against Jainism which seems to have been the religion of Bijjala.

Ekāntada Rāmayya.

Early epigraphical records however seem to lend support to another tradition which ascribes the origin of this form of Vīra Śaivism to a certain Brahman called Ekāntada Rāmayya, and this story is found recorded in an inscription in the temple of Somanātha at Ablūr in the Dharwar district, pertaining to the time of Mahāmanḍalēśwara Kāmadēva of the family of Kadambas of Hangal (A.D. about 1181-1203). According to this version of the story, Rāmayya was the son of Purshottama Bhaṭṭa and his wife by favour of Śiva, chiefly with a view to putting an end to the prevalence of Jainism. The child was called Rāma and he grew up so intensely devoted to Śiva that he came to be known as Ekāntada Rāmayya[1] ("Single-minded" Rāmayya).

When he had completed his period of preparation, he set himself up at Ablūr as an ascetic ready to controvert any votary of a hostile religion. It would appear one day the Jains led by the village headman chanted the praise of Jina within the hearing of Rāmayya in the temple

[1] In the technical religious sense this term stands for "the right of private *entree* to the Divine presence"

of Brahmēśvara of the locality. Rāmayya accepted their challenge to controvert them by cutting off his head and getting it restored to him. The Jains on their side agreed that if he should successfully perform this miracle, they would destroy their Jain temples and become Śaivas. Rāmayya sang the praise of Śiva and cut off his head, which came back to him on the 7th day after the mutilation. As the Jains did not carry out their part of the promise, Rāmayya was supposed to have carried out a wide and systematic persecution against the Jains, and built at Ablūr the temple of Somanātha under the name of Vīra Somanātha. The suffering Jains carried the news to Bijjala. Rāmayya produced the written agreement of the Jains and offered to repeat the miracle, letting the Jains even burn the head detached from his body promising to recover it as before, if the Jains would stake their 700 temples as wager therefor. The Jains would not accept the challenge. Bijjala ordered the issue of a *Jaya Patra*, "a certificate of Victory," to Rāmayya. Bijjala so far appreciated the single-minded devotion of Rāmayya that he performed the acts of veneration due to ascetic votaries of all Indian religions, and granted to Rāmayya's temple of Vīra Somanātha a village. The miracle performed by Rāmayya was repeated to Chāḷukya Someśvara IV, the last of the dynasty, in a public assembly and he similarly showed his respect to Rāmayya by the grant of another village to the same temple. A similar grant was made after a similar interview with Rāmayya by Kāmadēva, and it is this chieftain who is responsible for the inscription. The story of Ekāntada Rāmayya is found mentioned in the Channa Basava Purāṇa with variation in details of minor consequence, but Rāmayya's story as described in the inscription seems to favour the inference that he was the founder of the Lingāyat Sect rather than the two Basavas, uncle and nephew. It is just possible that Rāmayya preceded the two Basavas by a short period as Bijjala is referred to in the record not as a ruler, but as only a governor (Mahāmanḍalēśvara). There is a lithic representation in the temple of Brahmēśvara at Ablūr of Rāmayya's performance. Although it would be unwarranted to infer therefrom that the actual performance was quite an historical event, Rāmayya's name figures among the four sages of the Lingāyats who are taken to be the predecessors of the two Basavas. It is a common feature of both the Lingāyats and the Ārādhyas on all solemn occasions to set up four vases of water in the name of the four Ārādhyas (worshipful ones). These four are Rēvaṇa, Maruḷa, Eko-Rāma, and Panḍita Ārādhya. The third of these apparently stands for Ekāntada

Rāmayya. If such is the case, Rāmayya has to be counted among the predecessors of Basava uniformly regarded as the founder of the religion of the Jangam or Lingāyats. It is likely therefore that Rāmayya was responsible for really originating this sect, the teachings of which had been organised and carried into actual practice by Basava.

The sacred literature of the Lingāyats consists of the *Basava Purāṇa*, the *Prabhu Linga Līla* and *Paṇḍitārādhya-charita*. These are briefly known to them as the *Purāṇa*, the *Līla* and the *Charita*. There is a superficial resemblance in this triplicate classification to the Buddhist Tripiṭaka, but the resemblance is only superficial. These three are apparently formed on the earlier Śaiva creed which might for convenience be described in their later modification as Śaiva Siddhāntam. These Siddhāntins have their literature which can also be classified into a *purāṇa* part, a *līla* part and a *charitra* part. An instance in point is Māṇikkavāśakar's life described in the Vāduvūrar Purāṇam, which describes a certain number of *līlas* (playful acts) that Śiva performed in favour of Māṇikkavāśakar, the other parts of the work being of the character of a life-history of Māṇikkavāśakar himself. The three works referred to therefore constitute the canonical literature of the rigorous Lingāyats. The Arādhya still exhibits attachment to the

Brahmanical lore of the *Vedas* and the literature springing therefrom. Of these, Prabhulinga Līla is a work found in Telugu, Kanarese and Tamil. The Tamil version which seems to be the latest of them all, is referable to about A.D. 1620, and is ascribed to the Śaiva ascetic Śiva-prakāśa. This was apparently founded on the Kanarese version. Whether the original was written in Telugu remains an open question.

The Paṇḍitārādhya Charitra is the legendary and miraculous history of Paṇḍitārādhya one of the four sages already referred to. This work seems to have been first written in Telugu by an author who goes by the name Pālkuriki Soma or Somanātha, an Arādhya Brahman who is said to be a contemporary of the Kākatīya Rudra. There are two kings of the name Rudra among the members of the Kākatīya dynasty. It is probable that Soma was a contemporary of the first Rudra, in which case he might have to be assigned to the commencement of the thirteenth century. If however it should turn out that the Rudra referred to is the second of the name, he would have to be assigned to the commencement of the fourteenth century. In either case, it falls within the age when this form of Śaivism was in the ascendancy in the Telugu country, the Kākatīyas of Telingana being special patrons of the Śaivas to begin with, the Hoyasalas and other dynasties of the Southern Maharatta country later extending their patronage to this particular form of the creed.

During the age of Vijayanagar the Lingāyats certainly existed and flourished. We know of contemporaries of Vidyāraṇya belonging to this sect occupying high positions in the service of the state. Several sovereigns of the first dynasty of Vijayanagar seem to have patronised this particular creed. But it does not appear to have been exactly what might be called the state religion, as in fact it would be misleading to speak of state religions in regard to Hindu sovereigns. From what has been said, it would have become clear that Śaivism like Vaishṇavism began in the South during the historical period as not a systematised religion or creed, but merely as the convictions of individual men who could give expression to their own convictions in felicitous language full of overflowing emotion.

The early part of *bhakti* literature is in a sense emotional, resting upon faith and appealing to the hearts of those who came under its influence. Naturally therefore, that literature must be somewhat unsystematic and unconnected by any logical arrangement of sequence. That was the condition of both the religions in the centuries from A.D. 200 to about A.D. 1000 roughly.

With the Great Cholas, there comes a free infusion from the North of Brahmanism chiefly from Bengal. About the time of the Great Chola Rājendra I, the forest regions of Kosala became hallowed by Brahman colonies who fled for protection from the land of Aryāvarta which received then the repeated onslaughts of the iconoclastic Mahmud of Gazni. Rājēndra's invasion of this locality has to be ascribed to A.D. 1024-25, and that was the year of the last invasion of Mahmud.

The foundation of Goḷaki Maṭha in the Telugu country was due to the incoming of a colony of Śaiva Brahmans from Dāhala, the region of Bundelkhand.[1] These influxes of Northern Brahmans gave a stimulus to the systematisation of the teachings of the votaries of Śiva and that is the period to which we have to ascribe at any rate the so-called Śāstraic literature of the Śaivas. The first work belonging to this school is in Sanskrit Sūtras and is based on one of the Āgamas, the Raurava Agama, as was indicated already.

[1] See note at foot of p. 247 above.

CHAPTER XV.

VAISHṆAVISM IN SOUTH INDIA.

We have already shown under the section *bhakti* that the rudiments of Vaishṇavism in the ordinary form and in the *āgamaic* are traceable in the classical literature of Tamil. This form of *bhakti* had a course of development on much the same lines as Śaivism in the Tamil country. In general outline, this would involve the substitution of Vishṇu for Śiva as "the soul-saving supreme being" whose grace is of paramount importance to the attainment of salvation by an individual. We have already pointed out that the most popular form in which Vishṇu figures in early Tamil literature is that of several of his *avatāras* of the *paurāṇic* character. It would be easy to quote references from the early classics to the *avatāras* (descents of God) Rāma and Krishṇa even in secular literature. Along with this, simultaneously, we find indubitable references to the *āgamaic* four *Vyūhas*. But the idea of Vishṇu is of course indicated by the general name Tirumāl for the god. We thus find that, almost at the beginning of the Christian era, the features of northern Vaishṇavism in all its variety were prevalent in the south. It is the course of further development of Vaishṇavism that lends character to the movement and makes it a distinct feature of South Indian history.

Vaishṇava Literature.

The literature pertaining to this school falls into two classes also, similar in character to that of the Śaivas of the *Siddhānta* school. The Vaishṇavas have their saints and their teachers. They count twelve of the former and give them the general name Āḷvārs. The latter go by the name Āchāryas, and constitute a continuing series differing for each group and in some cases even for smaller groups of families, as the list proceeds to nearer modern generations. The twelve Āḷvārs composed hymns in praise of Vishṇu in the various forms in which his representation is worshipped in the various temples of South India. These partake generally of the character of the *paurāṇic* pantheon of the Hindus. The most popular of these, of course, are Rāma and Krishṇa; but references are traceable in their works to the most recondite manifestations of Vishṇu referable to the Purāṇas. The twelve Āḷvārs fall into three groups: the early, the middle and the later ones. The first of them consists of four names, of whom three are undoubtedly contemporaries and the fourth is certainly so regarded by the Vaisṇavas.

These four are Poygaiāḻvār, Bhūdattāḻvār, Pēyāḻvār and Tirumaḻiśaiāḻvār. In the middle group come Nām Āḻvar and Madhuraakavi, followed rather closely by Kulaśēkhara, Periyāḻvār or Vishṇuchitta and the daughter of the last, Godā or Āṇḍāḷ. The last group is composed of Bhaktāngrirēṇu or Toṇḍaraḍippoḍi, Yōgivāha or Tirup-Pān Āḻvār and Tirumangaiāḻvār, the last of them all. The works of these Āḻvārs and their poems of devotion are admittedly renderings of the teachings of the Vēda and Vēdic literature to a far greater degree than even the literature of the Śaiva Aḍiyārs. On a historical examination of this orthodox order of the Āḻvārs and their grouping according to chronology, it has been pointed out elsewhere [1] that there is sufficient historical evidence available to make the accepted order more or less correct, and that the range of time during which this particular group flourished corresponds to the age of the Pallavas, as in fact the age of the Śaiva Aḍiyārs was already pointed out to be. If the age of the Pallavas was characterised by the infusion of northern culture into the distant land of the south, this provides an excellent and unmistakable illustration of the position.

---

[1] See my Early History of Vaishnavism in South India (Oxford University Press).

THE AGE OF THE ĀḺVĀRS.

The first of this group of saints, Poygaiāḻvār has for good reasons been connected with the early Tonḍamān chieftain of Kānchi by the name Tonḍamān Iḷaṁ-Tiraiyan who must have lived in the same generation coming very late in it as the great Chola Karikāla. His work included in the Prabandham collection comes in for reference by later commentators, and they invariably group it along with very early classical poems. This Āḻvār is invariably associated with the two others that follow him immediately in the lists and rather indirectly with the fourth. All of them are associated with Kānchi and the part of the country dependent on it, that is, Tonḍamanḍalam. Each one of the first three is the author of one hundred stanzas (a śataka) in praise of Vishṇu and these form part of the fourth section of the Vaishṇava "Prabandham, Four Thousand." Bhaktisāra, the fourth has similarly one hundred stanzas included in this group. He has also a poem of 120 stanzas included in the first "Thousand" of the same collection. This one among the four gives unmistakable evidence of acquaintance with all that was best in the Sanskrit literature of the time. It is possible also to trace in his works references to the Vaishṇava āgamas.[1] A fugitive

[1] Tiruviruttam, Stanza 17.

stanza is generally ascribed to him which states "we have learnt the religion of the Śākya, that of the Śramaṇas and examined the āgama work composed by Śankara (Śiva). But by our own good fortune, we have put our faith in the "Black one with red-eye" (Vishṇu) and got rid of all that is evil. There is nothing that is beyond us hereafter." Whether he was actually the author of this verse or no, the same idea repeats in a modified form in one of his own verses, where he puts it in a somewhat modified form as follows:

"The Śramaṇas do not understand; the Bauddhas are in a delusion, and those that worship Śiva are unknowing innocents. Those that do not worship Vishṇu are of low intelligence indeed." In another place he sums up his conviction by saying that "the God that exists as the Dēvas, and the arrangement by which he shows himself as "The Three" (Brahma, Vishṇu and Śiva) among the Dēvas, and his showing himself in other forms besides, all this is the manifestation of Vishṇu. To those that do not know this truth, all that they learn is of no value." This shows that very early in the course of this movement the essence and the teaching of the orthodox school of *bhakti* had assumed the form of an interpretation merely, though a liberalised interpretation, of the orthodox creed of the North. So little that is historical is known about the life of these early saints that it is difficult to postulate anything definite about their position in society. The feature of their teaching however seems to be that the way of salvation was attainable even to the uninitiated according to the orthodox standards. It is this element and its teaching by these saints that gave them the ultimate ascendency among the people even as against the rival creeds of Buddhism, Jainism and to a certain extent even of the āgamaic Śaivism. It was said in the poem translated in an earlier part of this work that even the Vedic Brahmans of South India had to organise themselves for purposes of controversy to expose the hollowness of the teachings of seemingly *Vēdic* religions. It would therefore be reasonable to infer that this movement, represented by the Vaishṇava Saints, was a continuation of the orthodox development of the Brahmanism in the south liberalised in the manner already indicated. Among these twelve saints of the Vaishṇavas as among the sixty-three of the Śaivas, were men and women, women being perhaps not unnaturally the fewer. There were also people of all castes. The greatest among these twelve goes by the sacerdotal name, Nam-Āḻvār, and he was a Śūdra. What is more he does not show in the very least that his having been of this particular caste was anyway matter for regret to him. One of them at any rate belonged to the class even of Paraiya. He goes by the name Yōgivāha, as according to the traditional life of this Saint, a Brahman *Yōgi* carried him on his shoulders into the sanctum of Ranganātha. The story briefly is this. Being a Paraiya he could not get into the temple. He used to come none the less every morning, have his bath in the Kaveri altogether aside of the bathing ghats of the higher classes, and used to offer his devotions to Ranganātha therefrom. The god was so delighted with the single-minded devotion of this man that he directed a Brahman ascetic Bhārgava who was in his hermitage not far of, to carry him to the temple on his own shoulders, as the Paraiya kept out of the holy spot lest he should contaminate the holy ground by his unholy tread. His own name was Tiruppāṇ Ālvār. The word Pāṇ indicated a caste akin to the class of the Paraiyas whose usual profession was that of the wandering ministrel. That is the really liberalising part of this movement. This consisted in an effort, and an organised effort too, at uplifting those who must necessarily have been outside the circle of those admissible to divine grace, so long as that grace was attainable in the exact performance of an exceedingly difficult and elaborate series of ceremonial rites. The simplification of the process for the attainment of the divine grace was in response to the needs of the time, and one might even say was so recognised as very often one comes upon the statement that for the Kaliyuga more elaborate courses were impossible of adoption.

The Vaishṇava hagiologists do not give any more information about Yōgivāha, and it is only a work of 10 stanzas ascribed to him that is included in the Vaishṇava collection. There is nothing by which to fix his age and the probabilities are that he was one of the later saints, when class or caste distinction needed to be smoothed, and a recognised compromise between the opposing principles of religion seemed called for. Following perhaps close upon the first four, who have all been ascribed to the earliest period of the Pallavas comes in Nam-Āḻvār by common consent, the greatest of the Āḻvārs. He is pre-eminently the Vaishṇava Saint and stands out of the group both by the eminent quality of his teaching and by the very volume of his work—Tirumangai Āḻvār's contribution to this collection is slightly in excess of that of Nam-Āḻvār. He is known among those that followed him in the field of literature as the one pre-eminently who rendered *Vēdic* lore in Tamil. They even go the length of dividing his works and classifying them according as they relate to the one *Vēda* or another of the recognised four Vēdas. Of the details of his life we know very little and if the hagiologists could be given full credit for their statements, his life was absolutely an uneventful, and withal a comparatively short one. He was born of Kāri and his wife. Kāri was the Adhikāri (officer) of the village Kuruhūr and belonged to the Śūdra caste as was already stated. The child from the moment of its birth declined to take any nourishment and conducted itself in a peculiar way without weeping, or otherwise having food, as babies do. The parents in their perplexity consigned the baby to the God in the local temple, and found it seated in what is generally described in the *Yōga n udra* pose (in the pose of one rapt in contemplation) for a period of sixteen years under the sacred tamarind tree in the temple. At the end of this period he received divine inspiration and began his teaching. Such as he was, an agent was required, through whom he could give publicity to his teaching. The one found was a scholarly Brahman, somewhat miraculously directed on this mission. This saint goes by the name Madhurakavi, probably a title. He was a Brahman of the top-knot community belonging to the Tinnevelly District and of the *Sama Vēda* section. After finishing his schooling, he went on his pilgrimage, and was in Ayodhya (Oudh) at

[1] Stanzas 8 and 9 of the poem ascribed to Madhurakavi.

the time. Thinking of his own native country one evening, he looked in the direction of his native place and found to his surprise a huge column of light. Somewhat taken aback by this apparition, he set forward in the direction indicated by the light to investigate what it was, till he ultimately reached the temple and the tamarind tree under which Nam-Āḷvār was seated. When he set forward from there he found the light in the opposite direction and thus discovered that the place indicated to him was the temple where Nam-Āḷvār was in contemplation. After making an enquiry and obtaining an answer which satisfied him, he adopted the Āḷvār as his Guru (preceptor in religion) and put himself in the position of a disciple. He then took down all that was given out by the Āḷvār; and what was thus given out and recorded constitutes the principal work of this Vaishṇava Saint. This is called by the Vaishṇavas, Tiruvāymoḷi, which can be rendered literally as "the word of the mouth." But the expression Tiruvāymoḷi has another significance for which there is classical literary authority and that is *the Vēda.*, for the good reason that it emanated originally by word of mouth from Vishṇu, and Brahma received the inspiration. The Tamils of the classical age made the distinction between *Vāymoḷi* and *Maṛai*, the first standing for the *Vēda* and the second standing for the *Upanishads*, which lie hidden in the *Vēda*. It is this distinction that seems embodied in the name given to Nam-Āḻvār's work, Tiruvāymoḻi.

It was already pointed out that to the Vaishṇavas Nam-Āḻvār is the type of Āḷvārs and stands pre-eminently as the representative of the whole group and their teachings, so much so, that in the daily recital of the Vaishṇava creed, Nam-Āḷvār alone is counted among the section of "Holy Preceptors," proceeding from the actual preceptor of the individual backwards to Vishṇu himself, among the Āḷvārs. This acknowledged pre-eminence is owing entirely to the character of Nam-Āḷvār's works as it is acknowledged to embody the whole essence of *Vēdic* teaching. So much is clearly stated to be the case by Madhurakavi.

One other point that comes out clearly from what little we know of the life and work of Nam-Āḷvār is the emergence of a preceptor (guru) as essential to the attainment of salvation by the individual. The whole burden of the teaching of Madhurakavi in the short poem ascribed to him amounts to this and no more. Madurakavi states clearly that having found the preceptor in the Āḻvār, his salvation was as good as guaranteed to him. This notion of the essential need of the preceptor comes out in another poem included in the Prabandham 4000, where a disciple of Rāmānuja's chief follower Kūrattāḻvān, by name Amudan of Śrīrangam, makes a confession of his faith in this creed of his own salvation being the responsibility of his preceptor so long as he had taken the pains to discover the suitable one and put his faith in him. The idea of the need of a preceptor could not be said to have been non-existent at any stage of this kind of development of the teaching of the bhakti school, whether Śaiva and Vaishṇava; only at this particular stage in the history of Vaishṇavism it emerged into greater prominence as it does in regard to Śaivism in the case of Mānikkavāśagar. The importance of this development consists in this that bhakti or devotion as the means to attain salvation develops certain prescribed methods for prosecuting this work of devotion to God which become essential. The approved method begins at first to be simple, but as various influences come to bear upon this personal devotion to God it gets modified in the attempt at effecting a compromise with other lines of thought. A methodised and formal system of worship emerges as the result of the compromise, the adoption of which in the rough and tumble of ordinary life becomes impossible to a great many people. At this stage it becomes necessary that a class of people take up the actual and unerring performance of these acts of worship, and leave the bulk of the people to proceed in the simple style of the earlier and the more primitive form of personal devotion. This naturally develops into each man or woman finding a suitable preceptor whose duty it will be to direct the individual in his daily life and take the responsibility for the attainment of his salvation. From out of this ultimately develops the doctrine of self-surrender that one puts his faith in God, and places the burden of his salvation upon Him through one of His instruments on earth in the character of a worthy and accredited preceptor. This emergence of the *Guru* and the doctrine of self-surrender, which is implied in the idea of the preceptor, becomes an essential portion of the creed hereafter and develops more fully as we advance from the age of the Āḻvars into that of the so-called Āchāryas of the Vaishṇavas.

Nam-Āḻvār was followed in the course of centuries by the six others of whom Kulaśēkhara, a king of Travancore, is a representative of unalloyed devotion. There is one śloka of his Sanskrit work Mukundamāla which summarises his unlimited devotion and faith in the saving character of God. As a free rendering, 'he has no ambition either for the acquisition of merit (Dharma) or for wealth ; nor for the enjoyments of this world or other. He would let things take their course shaped by his previous deeds. He would only make one prayer and that is that, whatever may be the number of his births to come, in all of them his devotion to the feet of God may remain unchanged and firm'.

Periyāḻvār and his daughter Āndāl, each one shows this devotion with a peculiarity all their own, and the last of them Tirumangai Āḻvār brings this group to an end chronologically. He was, according to the traditional account, an official of some importance in the Chola kingdom, and had his place of birth and office in the Tanjore District. He got his inspiration in a very peculiar way in the act of committing robbery upon a Vaishṇava bridal party said to have been composed of no other than Vishṇu himself and his followers, and thereafter he gave up secular life and devoted himself entirely to works of service to Vishṇu and the Vaishṇavas. This aspect of his life is indicated in the arrangement of his works which begin with 10 stanzas, each one of which ends in the refrain where he breaks out into the declaration that he had discovered the saving truth in the name Nārāyaṇa. His works constitute the largest portion of the *Prabandham*, and count more than 1,300 stanzas out of the 4,000 of the total. They are far more elaborate in their mode and matter, and are considered by the orthodox to be more or less an elaborate commentary upon the teachings of Nam-Āḻvār in particular. If tradition preserved by the Vaishṇavas could be relied on, he organised the teaching of Nam-Āḻvār to the extent of celebrating annually a festival in honour of this Saint, where Nam-Āḻvār's works were recited *in extenso.* This is what continues to be done to-day, though after a break between Tirumangai Āḻvār and the first Āchārya Nāthamuni in the so-called *Adhyayana Utsavam* in Śrīrangam in the month of December-January. There are references in his works to some contemporary kings among the dynasty of the great Pallavas which enables the inference that he was probably a contemporary of the great Pallava Nandivarman I, who was himself a Vaishṇava probably, and that gives us the age of this Āḻvār to be the latter half of the ninth century. It will thus be seen that the age of the Vaishṇava development represented by the Āḻvars and their works could be brought into the six centuries extending from A. D. 200 to A. D. 800 approximately, by tradition alone which happened in this particular case to be confirmed by various other items of circumstantial evidence. The teachings of the Āḻvārs must have been of the same character as the teaching of the Śaiva Āḍiyārs, and required to be organised for the effective creation of a school of that teaching to come into existence. What was said about the effort of Tirumangai Āḻvār to set up an annual festival and get people to recite the works of Nam-Āḻvār in Śrīrangam indicates that the need for organising it had already begun to be felt, but the organisation thus created seems to have fallen early into desuetude and remained for sometime so, so that when the first Āchārya started active work the whole of Nam-Āḻvār's works had so far got into neglect as to have been forgotten. It is by a revival of the teachings of Nam-Āḻvār and by a provision against a similar neglect afterwards that the succession of Āchāryas came into being. This "Āchārya Paramparā" of the Vaishṇavas begins with Nāthamuni, and continues in an unending series down to the present time, each section of the Vaishṇavas having its own list; but all the Vaishṇavas however have a certain number of names in common and they cover the first eight or ten generations of these preceptors.

The Āchāryas of the Vaishṇavas—Nāthmuni.

Nāthamuni was the fifth ancestor of Rāmānuja and from the known age of Rāmānuja calculating backwards, Nāthamuni ought to have flourished in the first half of the tenth century A.D. According to the traditional account of Nāthamuni's life, he lived in a village called Vīranārāyaṇapuram, and was following the life of an ordinary Vaishṇava of those days. He heard a certain number of Vaishṇavas in the course of their pilgrimage recite, in the temple of his village, a particular verse from the works of Nam-Āḻvār.

The verse appealed to Nāthamuni as embodying in the happiest phraseology, the sentiments of devotion, which must have infused the author. Making enquiries as to whose work it was, they were only able to recite to him the particular ten of which the verse under reference was one; but beyond that they were not able to recite any more of Nam-Āḻvār's works. As these *ten* related to God enshrined in the temple at Kumbhakonam, Nāthamuni was referred to that locality. He proceeded there and found the people knew no more than the ten. Therefore he proceeded to the birthplace of Nam-Āḻvār, in the hope that perchance he might recover the whole there from somebody; but it had been so far forgotten that one among the Vaishṇava inhabitants of the locality who bore the name Parānkuśadāsa (Parānkuśa being a name of Madhurakavi) stated that they had heard of the name Tiruvāymoḻi, but knew nothing more of it. He could however recite the eleven stanzas ascribed to Madhurakavi in praise of Nam-Āḻvār. Nāthamuni received these eleven stanzas ascribed to Madhurakavi, and is said to have recited these repeatedly till both Nam-Āḻvār and Madhurakavi appeared to him and gave him not merely the Tiruvāymoḻi, but also various others of the works, Sanskrit and Tamil, that went to constitute the basal authorities of Vaishṇava teaching. The story goes on to say in so many words that Nāthamuni had to remain practising single-minded contemplation upon Nam-Āḻvār (*yōgic* practice) for full 340 years before the two Āḻvārs appeared to him in the manner indicated above. This is only the hagiologist's way of stating something like a gap of 340 years, or roughly three and a half centuries between Nāthamuni, it may be, and Nam-Āḻvār, or at the very best Tirumangai Āḻvār. The works were apparently in existence according to this tradition in the age of Tirumangai Āḻvār, and the traditional teaching of these had been broken since his time. Counting five generations backwards from Rāmānuja and taking three centuries more for this interval, gives us the approximate age of Tirumangai Āḻvār or, at any rate, the latter end of the age of the Āḻvārs. Other lines of investigation confirm this chronology more or less. What we are concerned with here is that the work of Nāthamuni, the first Āchārya consisted in the revival of the teachings of the Āḻvārs and the organisation of that teaching by providing for its unfailing continuance. This last object was attained by the creation of a pontificate not of an official character like the Christian pontificate, but of a more or less popular character.

One other feature of Nāthamuni's work that deserves attention is the setting of the tune and the prescribing of the form of recital of the works of Nam-Āḻvār. This arrangement would necessitate a class of people whose contribution practically it would be, to recite the work in the truly orthodox style, and even accompany the recitation with action of a suitable character.

A class of people known by the name *Araiyar* at Śrīrangam recite even to-day and perform in this style on the occasions of festivals in the temple. The adoption of the tunes and the singing was not confined to this class of men alone. A class of women whose profession had come to be music and dancing also adopted this as part of the temple order which continues, in certain places at any rate, up to the present time. All this seems to have formed part of the arrangement by which Nāthamuni first made the collection of Nam-Āḷvār's works. And this was confirmed by the final arrangement made by Rāmānuja who collected not merely the works of Nam-Āḷvār but even went forward to collect the works of the other Aḷvārs and arrange them in the form in which the Prabandham 4000 is accessible to us at present. A similar arrangement, it was already pointed out, was made in regard to the works of the Śaiva Aḍiyārs by Nambi Āṇḍār Nambi under the patronage of a Chola ruler who is called Rāja Rāja Abhaya Kulaśēkhara, in all probability Rāja Rāja the Great. It was on that occasion that the Śaiva works also got set to tune and there is a reference under the later Cholas to a class of dancing women, who rendered these poems in the esoteric mode [1] (*ahamārgam*). It may be pointed out again that it is not likely that either Nāthamuni or Nambi Āṇḍār Nambi originated this mode. We have stated already that even from the classical age, there was a class of people who set devotional poems to tune, and that this arrangement is exemplified in the early classic Paripāḍal. All that this means is that the two classes of works got set to music for purposes of devotional recital by these two teachers respectively.

Though the Vaishṇavas count the succession of *Gurus* in the line of descent from preceptor to disciple, the more prominently recognised apostolic succession of Vaishṇavism passed from Nāthamuni to his grandson Yāmunāchārya, whose sacerdotal name is Aḷvandār. He received the teachings of Nāthamuni from two of his disciples, who may be taken to be in their turn preceptor and disciple.

Yāmunāchārya or Āḷavandār.

The mantle of the leadership of the Vaishṇavas fell by common consent upon the shoulders of this teacher, who was a married man and led the life of a householder. He lived in the age of the early great Cholas and the

[1] Ins. of Rāja Rāja III, at Tiruvoṛṛiyūr, Ep. Rep., 1912, No. 211.

age was one of great religious ferment, the outward exhibition of which in India took the form of controversial activity. Yāmunāchārya comes into prominence as the result of a successful controversy that he held against a Śaiva. He was a great dialectician and indisputably secured success by a clever stroke. His opponent seems rather too foolishly to have undertaken to establish the contrary of whatever Yāmuna would state categorically. The Vaishṇava turned the tables upon him by making three statements. (1) "The king who was presiding over the controversy was a Sārvabhauma, (2) the queen who was seated by him was unquestionably chaste, and (3) the mother that gave birth to him (the Śaiva champion) was certainly not a barren woman." The establishment of the categorical negative of these statements was obviously impossible. But the story has it that he controverted him successfully, even on questions of philosophy and religion, and established his position at the court. As the wager of the controversy he obtained the means to live in comfort, and even in some affluence, and that put him beyond the need of earning a livelihood. He lived to a ripe old age and obtained as the bequest of his grand-father all that was worth learning of the Vaishṇava philosophy and religion from the successors of Nāthamuni. The one thing that remained uncompleted at the latter end of his life was the provision of a successor to continue the Vaishṇava teaching and organisation. He looked about and found a suitable young man in a great-grandson of his who was undergoing education at Kānchī. While still under his teacher the young man had made such an impression, that his reputation had already reached the ears of the saintly old Āchārya in Śrīrangam. The venerable old man undertook a journey to Conjeevaram to see if reputation spoke true of the achievements of Rāmānuja, and the story has it that he caught sight of the young man in the company of his fellow disciples and the great teacher Yādavaprakāśa in the enclosure of the great Vishṇu temple at Kānchī. The site at which Āḷavandār caught the first glimpse of his successor is yet pointed out by the old residents of the town.

Rāmānuja.

Rāmānuja was the son of a grand-daughter of Āḷavandār. One of the grandsons of Āḷavandār obtained his permission to go and live at Tirupati, and took along with him his father and two sisters, who were in course of time married by him to two eligible young men. The elder of these had married a Kēśava Sōmayāji belonging to Perumbūdūr. In course of time Rāmānuja was born of this marriage. After undergoing the recognised early education in his own native village, he went to Conjeevaram to complete it by a course of instruction in philosophy under the famous "*Vēdānta*" teacher Yādavaprakāśa in Kānchī. It was while under this professor that Āḷavandār caught a glimpse of the young man and was impressed with his appearance as a fit person for ultimate succession to his position. In course of time Āḷavandār was drawing near his end, and sent people to fetch Rāmānuja from Conjeevaram. Before Rāmānuja could reach Śrīrangam, however, Āḷavandār had breathed his last. It was miraculously indicated however to Rāmānuja that Āḷavandār had left three things undone, and designed Rāmānuja as the chosen one to discharge the responsibility of fulfilling these cherished wishes. These were, a commentary, according to the Vaishṇava teaching, on the Brahmasūtras, a similar commentary upon the Sahasranāma by one bearing the name Parāśara, and a similar commentary upon the Tiruvāymoḻi of Nam-Āḻvār. This was the mission to which Rāmānuja had become heir on the death of Āḷvandār. He had ultimately to settle down in Śrīrangam to fulfil this mission and all that was involved in it by way of getting the Vaishṇavas together, providing them an organisation with sufficient vitality to continue, overcome controversies and meet the needs of the times by putting the teachings of this form of religion in shape to continue from generation to generation unimpaired. Rāmānuja himself performed the first, commissioned the son of his chief disciple Kūrattaḻvan to do the second, and got his uncle's son, who was adopted by him as his successor, to write out the commentary on the Tiruvāymoḻi. After a varied life, he succeeded ultimately in making Śrīrangam the headquarters of the Vaishṇavas, and providing for the permanent continuance of the teachings of these commentaries and various other works. He also provided for the propagation of this teaching by the recognition of seventy-four persons as "occupants of the apostolic throne" of the teachers of Vaishṇavism. He had to carry on controversies with the *advaitins*, generally called Māyāvādins, with the Jains, and with others even including the Śaivas. He succeeded in his mission so far as to put Vaishṇavism on a permanent footing.

As it came to Rāmānuja, several problems of religio-secular character confronted him. Of these, two features deserve special mention. It was already pointed out that the teaching of the Āḻvārs might be regarded as an adaptation merely of *Paurānic* Hinduism; there was a rival popular creed in the *āgamaic* form of worship, of which two sections at least, Pāncharātra and Vaikhānasa Āgama, are recognised as Vaishnavaic. The former of these two seems the more important, from the point of view of the community as a whole. This Pāncharātra was regarded as *unvēdic* by Kumarila Bhaṭṭa.[1]

It is similarly regarded to be outside of the fold of the *Vēdic* religion by Śankara in his commentary on the 2nd of the Brahmasūtras. Even the Śaiva works on their Siddhānta, view Pāncharātra as a separate religion, and controvert it in the recognised text-book Sivajñāna Siddhi. The Vaishṇavas of the Rāmānuja Sect, at least the great bulk of them now-a-days, are Pāncharātrins. The establishment of the teaching of the Pāncharātra as *Vēdic* in character and as one form of Vaishṇavism was one of the achievements of Rāmānuja.

The next item has reference to the needs of the community composed of classes of varying grades of intelligence and mental outlook. It was one of the items of Rāmānuja's teaching, which in this particular case, happened to be merely laying an additional emphasis upon the teachings of the Āḻvārs generally, that salvation was attainable alike by all, whatever their earthly position. Here again Rāmānuja effected a compromise as in the case of the Pāncharātra. Rāmānuja's position amounts to this. Whatever be the position of a man or woman in society, one stood as near to God as anyone else, provided one kept to the high requirements of

[1] Tantravārttika, translation by Ganganath Jha, p. 165. Also Mr. Rama Prasad Chanda's Indo-Aryan Race, p. 99.

godly life. What this amounts to, as a measure of social reform, has since become a moot point and there has been considerable division of opinion on the question.

Rāmānuja lived in the age of the great Cholas having been a contemporary of the great Chola Kulottunga. It was already stated that the period of the Chola ascendency began about the end of the ninth century and lasted till about the middle of the thirteenth century. During this age, it was already pointed out Śaivism came in for a cosiderable amount of patronage under some of the Cholas, of whom Rājēndra, the Gangaigonḍachola, stands out prominent. It was under the first of these that the Śaiva works of the Aḍiyārs were collected and put in the form in which they have come down to us. It was also the age when Śēkkiḻār wrote the lives of the Śaiva saints in his great work Periyapurāṇam; and Śēkkiḻār lived either as a contemporary of Rāmānuja or slightly later. The four later teachers of the Śaivas also belonged to this age and the various Mutts (relgious houses) of the Śaivas were founded at this period. Similarly though the Vaishṇava organisation began with Nāthamuni practically at the commencement of this age of the Chola ascendency, it received full shape and final form of its teaching under Rāmānuja early in the twelfth century. From

Rāmānuja onwards, as in fact from Nāthamuni, the succession of *gurus* continued unbroken, and the Vaishṇava temples became the attractive centres of propagation of this teaching. Among these Śrīrangam and Conjeevaram constituted the two principal centres. The religious literature of this age both of the Śaivas and Vaishṇavas are thrown into a controversial form clearly indicating that it was an age of great controversy in matters religious. The religious ferment of which religious controversy is merely the outward expression, became a prominent feature, as soon as the Chola ascendency gave to the country the requisite degree of peace.

The great temples of South India, which came into existence, at any rate the great majority of them, in the age of the Pallavas beginning from the time of the early Chola Ko-Chengaṇ, received considerable additions by way of patronage under the Cholas. These naturally constituted active centres for the propagation of the teachings both of the Śaivas and of the Vaishṇavas. The chief opponents they had in view in all their controversies seem to be the Jains. This is but natural, as Jainism was just emerging full-grown owing to the active support and patronage of the Rāshṭrakūṭas who seemed several of them to have been of that persuasion. The active controversy against the Jains began with the Śaivas of the days of

Sambandar and Appar under the great Pallava Mahēndravarman and his contemporary Pāndya Sundara. These religious controversies seemed to have attained to a considerable degree of bitterness that a series of general persecutions of the Jains have become the common feature of the lives of these saints, Śaiva and Vaishṇava, compiled in a later period. The most prominent instances of these are a persecution set up at the instance of Sambandar by his Pāṇḍya contemporary Neḍumāran, otherwise Kūn Pāndya and Sundara, who was at first a Jain and was converted to Śaivism by Sambandar. The story has it that the whole body of Jains were impaled by order of the monarch at the instigation of the Saint. The late Dr. Vincent Smith has so far gone in accepting this story as embodying a historical incident that he regards it as one of the genuine though exceptional instances of persecution for religion. He relies principally upon the evidence of a painting of this incident on the walls of the great temple at Madura. It is not only on the walls of the temple of Madura, but in all the bigger Śiva temples of the south the representation of this story is found. The historicity of this incident will have to depend upon the particular date at which the painting or even a stone representation of this incident, was set where it is. When once the hagiologists set the fashion by giving currency to these stories, it is not difficult to understand that they passed into popular currency, and in the representation of various *līlas* of Śiva or Vishṇu (performance of miracles in sport) or any other God, these would naturally figure. This position is most clearly illustrated in the renovation of temples carried out by the class of Nattukottai Chettis at the present time. Whether pictures of these already existed or no, such representations, as constituted one of the *līlas* of Siva, are made by them without sacerdotal impropriety. It does not require much interval of time even, as we have already stated, that a lithic representation of the performance of Ekāntada Rāmayya is found built in a temple constructed at a period following close upon the age of this Rāmayya. It need hardly be said that it is impossible for history to believe that Rāmayya actually cut off his head and got it back after it was turned to ashes. The stories of such persecution occurred time and again in the accounts of the hagiologists (Śaiva, Vaishṇava, Jaina, or Bauddha), and these stories have always a family likeness in the details regarding the incidents, thereby stamping them as pious fabrications of latter-day hagiologists.

The Jains are said to have conducted a wholesale persecution of the Bauddhas under a king by name Himasītala at the instance of a Jain Āchārya Akaḷanka. A similar story is told of

Rāmānuja of having persecuted the Jains by getting them ground in oil-mills. Vishṇuvardhana, the Hoysala, who adopted Vaishṇavism, is said to have perpetrated this atrocity. We have pointed out elsewhere[1] that the chief queen of Vishṇuvardhana died a Jain. His loyal and faithful commander-in-chief of all of his forces lived and died a Jain under him, and his son succeeded in the same persuasion. When late in life, a son was born to the king, the tutor for the son was a most respected Jain Āchārya. It need hardly be added therefore that these stories of persecution as they are found current could hardly be regarded as historical, and one ought to look for satisfactory evidence in each separate case before accepting the historicity of any of these incidents of persecution, or even for postulating that no persecution took place. This does not necessarily involve the assumption that religious riots and excesses by parties of people were always non-existent. The Rāshṭrakūṭas, as already pointed out, were great patrons of the Jains and in the best days of Rāshṭrakūṭa Empire it was that Jainism did its best work in literature in the Southern Maharatta country and Mysore. These are the portions of South India that happen to be the great Jain centres even now, and in that region Jainism flourished even in the age of the great Cholas. One of the

[1] Ancient India, Chapter IX.

constant complaints of the destructive operations of the war carried on by the Cholas against the latter was that the Cholas destroyed these Jain monasteries and temples, without showing the usual consideration due to these holy places. Jainism continued to flourish under the Chāḷukyas and under the Hoysalas at a later time and even in the age of Vijayanagar.

The Śaiva Aḍiyārs and Vaishṇava Āḷvārs, both of them had to carry on an active propaganda against Buddhism and Jainism, and there are many indications in their works that the aim of their teaching was to overcome these two religions which apparently had a large popular clientele. Both Kumarila Bhaṭṭa and Śankarācharya's works give clear indication that they set to themselves the serious task of controverting the Jains and Buddhists, also incidentally of various other forms of teaching outside the sphere of the *Vēda*. It was this need for a controversy that gave the turn to the literature both of the Śaivas and the Vaishṇavas, and as we advance in this history, we find the tendency is in this body of literature to develop a controversial character.

This work so far as the Vaishṇavas were concerned was carried on for three generations both in Śrīrangam and in Kānchī, when the Mahammadan invasions broke in upon South India.

CHAPTER XVI.

MAHAMMADAN INVASIONS.

It is well-known that the Mahammadan irruption this side of the Vindhyas commenced in the last years of the thirteenth century, under the Khilji ruler Alau-d-din, and that it began as a mere raid for purposes of plunder. Once Alaud-din obtained a considerable amount of wealth that served him the useful purpose of paving the way to the throne. He often had occasion to look out to this source of revenue to fill his treasury even when he had placed himself firmly upon the throne. Alau-d-din's needs were great as the main purpose of his reign was to keep the Moghals out of the North-Western frontier. If the Mahammadan historian Wassaf speaks the truth, and there is nothing to doubt his veracity in this particular, Alau-d-din had to maintain a standing army of 475,000 at a cost of 180 dinars a month each man, and 230 for each horse; he even allowed a spare horse to a soldier, and to those who maintained a second animal he gave an additional allowance of this amount. One could understand therefore that the demands of the military department of Alau-d-din's reign were more than the ordinary revenues could meet. He therefore adopted the prudent policy in respect of South India by making an impression upon the Hindu rulers of his own great power and putting these Hindu rulers under heavy tribute. Such in fact were the instructions that he actually gave to the generals he deputed on these several invasions, as recorded by Amir Khusru.

In the carrying out of these instructions the generals had a great deal left to their own discretion, and these invasions generally meant a considerable volume of destructive work. The first object of these generals was to take possession of what was termed "royal wealth." This consisted in what in modern parlance would be called materials of war, not necessarily contraband of war, and included elephants as the first item, horses, gold and jewels, and other commodities of value that could be carried off easily. The royal treasuries were one source; and the generals soon found the temple treasuries equally fruitful as a source of revenue. The armies sent out could not be very large having regard to the distance, which in the language of the Mahammadan historians were six months' journey and twelve months' journey. They consisted merely of picked cavalry, and had, as a military necessity, to carry on the war on a more destructive method than would otherwise have been necessary. Hence to the South Indian, Mahammadan invasions meant destruction of all the cherished wealth of the people. One specific instance of such destruction recorded by the Mahammadan historians is the destruction of fruitful trees, which sometimes were cut down by the thirty thousand, to the great horror of the Hindus. Naturally therefore these invasions of the Mahammadans extending over a period of about thirty years struck the Hindus of the south with consternation and terror to such an extent that they felt it necessary very early to organise themselves for fighting for their existence. This organisation found its leader in the Hoysala ruler of Mysore at the time, Vīra Baḷḷāḷa III.

Almost after the first raid upon his capital by Malik-Kafur, he understood what the Mahammadan invasions meant and as a consequence he adopted a temporising policy. Till his contemporaries should be of a temper to act together as against this common enemy, he entered into terms of treaty with Alau-d-din, and kept up to the terms of the treaty as long as he found it necessary to do so. But fortunately for him, the death of Alau-d-din created such a series of disturbances in Delhi, and, thanks to the exertion of Alau-d-din, the Moghal troubles ceased to be imminent. The Hoysala had found time to organise his forces and put himself in a position of readiness for eventualities. He slowly set about reorganising his own resources and leaving his neighbours to do what they thought best in the circumstances for themselves; so much so, that, when Mubarak organised a South Indian Province for the Mahammadans with Deogir as its capital the Hoysala showed no activity outside of his frontier even when garrisons of Mahammadans were planted quite on his northern frontier. It is when Mahammad-bin-Tughlak placed himself upon the throne and undertook his invasion of the South, that the time had come for a Hindu organisation of the South Indian rulers, and that was brought about by the Hoysalas with the co-operation of the contemporary Kākatīya ruler.

In the meanwhile the Mahammadan garrisons left by Malik-Kafur had been dislodged from the Tamil country by the Kēraḷa ruler, Ravivarman Kulaśīklara, who broke out of his mountain frontier and carried his armies successfully as far as Poonamallee, perhaps only to retire, when the Kākatīya general advanced against him. The Tamil powers having become powerless or practically extinct, it was left to the Kākatīyas and the Hoysalas to do the work of organising a successful resistance. This was made the more necessary, when Mahammad undertook another invasion to re-assert his authority in South India and locate a permanent garrison in Madura. This was done successfully, and the South was held in the interests of Mahammad for a period of about seven years by the successive governors sent out to Madura. A rebellion set up early in the reign by his cousin Bahau-d-din at Sagar gave the signal for other rebellions, and the establishment of a Mahammadan sultanate at Madura by Mahammad's own governor provoked the Hoysala and the Kākatīya rulers to join their resources and make a stand for themselves. A too early rising would have put them between two fires, Mahammad's province of Deogir in the north and the Mahammadan Sultanate in the South. But Mahammad, with his wonted imprudence, involved himself in a sea of trouble nearer his headquarters, and that engaged him fully. The two high powers of the south were left to watch the northern frontiers and carry on a campaign to destroy the Mahammadan garrisons in the South including that at Madura. The latter portion of the work fell upon Vīra Baḷḷāḷa himself who since A.D. 1328, the year of Mahammad's last invasion of the south made Tiruvaṇṇāmalai his capital, and was carrying on a systematic campaign against the Sultanate at Madura. The northern frontier was left in charge of a number of generals of whom three happened to be brothers. They held the frontiers successfully against the Mahammadans, and this frontier extended from the west coast, somewhere a little north of Goa, right across to the mouth of the river Krishna. The flank of the Mahammadan province of Deogir was watched by the Kākatīyas, nominally under tribute to Mahammad. The Hoysala was therefore able to carry on war in the south unmolested by any action of Mahammad. He fell in the fight however about the end of the year 1342, and his son followed after a short rule of about two to three years.

In the meanwhile Mahammad involved himself inextricably and died in the course of the next five or six years. His death was the signal for the generals of the Hoysalas to carry out the policy of their late master to a successful termination, and it is to a son of one of the brothers who held the northern frontier to whom is due the credit of having destroyed the Mahammadan Sultanate of Madura.

This war takes on the character of a patriotic struggle by the Hindus for mere existence and for the preservation of all that was cherished as sacred from the point of view of religion, and all that was worth having by way of secular resources. This aspect of the movement it was, that gave it its peculiar character and culminated in the foundation of Vijayanagar. Vijayanagar stood forth as the visible embodiment of the national resistance to save this enclave for the Hindus and keep it free from being over-run by the Mahammadans.

CHAPTER XVII.

The Character and Significance of the Vijayanagar Empire.

Coming into existence from out of the ashes of the last powerful Southern kingdom, that of the Hoysalas, Vijayanagar stood out for all that was worth preserving in Hindu religion and culture. As a necessary concomitant therefor, it pitted itself on the south bank of the river Tungabadra in a position of advantage wherefrom it satisfactorily kept the Muslim tide from advancing farther south, and thus saved South India as the home for the undisturbed further development of Hinduism, such as it had come to be under the great Cholas of the South. The movement was national, a nationalism which was infused through and through with the sentiments of religion. In the actual circumstances of the origin and growth of Vijayanagar anything like an attachment to a particular form of Hinduism was out of the question. The object of Vijayanagar, and those that were responsible for it was to preserve all that was Hindu, irrespective of the multifarious minor differences that went to constitute the Hinduism of those days as they do that of these days. It was a comprehensive movement and adopted a policy of comprehension, so as to take into its fold all forms of the Hindu faith, including in it to a great extent even the prevalent form of Jainism of the locality. The one object was the preservation of Hindu independence in South India, with all the multiplicity of its religions, Hindu and Jain, perhaps even to a very slight extent Buddhist, and providing, for the further development of these on peaceful lines, a home in the country, south of the river Krishna. The whole organisation of the forces of Vijayanagar had this object in view.

Social and Political Reconstruction.

When the first struggles for the dislodgment of the Mahammadan garrisons from the south were over and the hostile Mahammadans from the north had been successfully driven out from their strongholds in South India, chiefly Madura and Trichinopoly (actually Kaṇṇanūr, 8 miles from Trichinopoly), those that were responsible for it set about organising social and political life with a view to the dominant needs of the new imperial foundation. The first need was a political organisation, which would place in the hands of the Government the necessary resources, material and men, to keep the aggressive Mahammadan efforts confined to the northern side of the Krishna. This involved the organisation of an administration and the development of the military resources, that would assure a successful resistance against the repeated attacks of the Mahammadans to break through the barrier set up by the new Empire. The Empire was organised into great Viceroyalties called Mahārājyas of which there were as many as three along the northern frontier. The first from the west coast took into it two Governments, those of the Malērājya and Tuḷurājya. The former took into it the whole of what is now the Malnad territory of Mysore and the whole of what might be called Karnātic Dakhan, almost as far north as Kolhapur. It went by the name of its capital, the great Viceroyalty of Araga, now a village in the Shimoga district of Mysore. This was probably under the overlordship of Haribare I whose capital must have been at Bankapur or Goa. Next to that, came the headquarters Viceroyalty having for its capitals in the early stages, Dvārasamudra (Haḷebīḍ in Mysore) and Vijayanagar itself, alternately. Later on the latter became the chief capital and the former suffered comparative neglect. Military necessity however called for other places coming into importance. This region was therefore dominated by the fortified cities of Vijayanagar and Adoni, at the two vulnerable spots along the northern river frontier. At the back of these two and almost midway between, lay the hill fortress of Penukoṇḍa which later on became the capital of the empire of Vijayanagar itself. The last of the three viceroyalties was the Mahārājya of Udayagiri with its capitals, Nellore and Udayagiri. The three elder of the five brothers were Viceroys of these to begin with. Behind this front line lay another Mahārājya with its Viceregal head-quarters, at Muḷbāgal in Mysore, and taking into it the territory of the Gangas, the Bāṇas and the whole of what used to be known as Tonḍamanḍalam, or the Drāviḍa country. Later on another Viceroyalty was constituted with Madura for its headquarters and the charge "the Lordship, of the Southern Ocean" attached to it. Within this great province the administration was organised on the lines on which it had existed from time immemorial in the country. The civil administration was so organised over this vast region that the people carried on the administration themselves more or less completely subject to the supervision and control of the great officers of state, who constituted a comparatively small hierarchy touring the country to set matters right, wherever their attention should be called for. This kind of an organisation left the Imperial revenues almost exclusively for the purposes of organising the military resources for the defence of the northern frontier. It was necessary on this frontier to adopt the policy of avoiding war by being ever the most ready for it. Such a policy involved a military expenditure which would have exhausted the resources of any ordinary Empire.

This organisation implied a considerable amount of social reorganisation also, and this took on naturally the form of hardening and more clearly demarcating the rights and duties of the various castes of which Hindu society was then composed. The system was there with an organisation of its own, being the only organisation on which society rested ; that had to be made use of even for administrative purposes, perhaps more largely than heretofore. This necessity coupled with the ever present danger of the Mahammadan irruptions from the north, gave this organisation a hardening, some of the worst features of which remain even yet, though several of the best features have gone out of it by desuetude. Such an organisation of society had this advantage that society looked after itself and the civil administration had but comparatively little to do except when called upon to interfere in matters of serious dispute between communities, territorial or social. The imperial resources might then be concentrated upon the organisation for the predominant purpose of defence, and, if occasion called for it,of offence as well, against the northern neighbour who was perpetually on the look-out for regaining lost hold. There was complete devolution of the civil administration except for a certain degree of control exercised by the officers of the Government; the central Government, divested of the ordinary civil power to a very large extent, devoted itself entirely to the needs of defence.

That this was the idea that dominated the rulers of Vijayanagar is clearly in evidence in the policy adopted by successive rulers of which we gain glimpses here and there with the imperfect resources for their history at our disposal.

The greatest monarch of the first dynasty, Dēvarāya II, who crowned a series of efforts by completing the fortifications of Vijayanagar so as to include in it a bit of country measuring diagonally 13 by 8 miles, providing facilities for irrigation and cultivation to an extent, that the capital city might have food resources to fall back upon within its walls for a considerable period of time. He also adopted, on the advice of the most responsible officers of the State, measures for improving his military resources by removing a vital defect. It was brought to his notice that the Hindu arms proved inferior to those of the Mahammadan in cavalry and archery, and that the Turkish soldiers employed for this purpose in the Mahammadan armies were found to be very efficient. Dēvarāya at once ordered the enlistment of two thousand of the Mahammadan soldiers; gave them a separate quarter of the city consulted their religious feeling to the extent of providing them with a mosque and a slaughter-house in their own quarter and got by their means about 60,000 of his soldiers trained in this branch of the art of war. It was not the Mahammadan as Mahammadan that they hated; much rather, it was the destructive work of the first Mahammadan invaders that left an indelible impression of hatred in them. This re-organisation was carried out actually by the Brahman Viceroy of Madura, who was called from his Viceregal headquarters obviously for this purpose at a critical period in the history of Vijayanagar.

The first usurper Sāḷuva Narasimha fully realised what exactly were the needs of the Empire, and his usurpation was with a view to meeting these needs which as it appeared to him, had not received at the hands of his predecessor the attention that they deserved. His last testament which the Portuguese chroniclers record indicate his policy clearly. He had repaired the damages suffered by the Empire during the weak rule of his two predecessors, but had failed to attain to the fulfilment of his wishes, as he had not had the time to take back from the enemies of the empire the fortresses of Muḍkal, Raichūr and Udayagiri.

Udayagiri happened to be in the hands of the Gajapatis of Kaṭak. Raichūr and Muḍkal were in the hands of the Bahmani Sultan. His successor Krishna, the great Krishnadēva Rāya of Vijayanagar, made it his life-work to fulfil this desideratum of his great predecessor. He could however take up this work only after quelling the internal rebellions which had occurred in the short reign of his elder brother, whom he succeeded. Having taken the fortress of Śivasamudram and destroyed the chief rebel of Ummattūr, he set himself seriously to the task of regaining these three fortresses after he had carefully provided himself against a flank attack by entering into a treaty with the Portuguese at Goa. He then undertook a war first against the ruler of Orissa, who was in occupation of Udayagiri. He beat Orissa garrisons from out of all the fortresses beginning with Udayagiri right up to the frontiers of the Ganjam District. Having gone so far, he deliberately adopted the policy of not driving the powerful enemy to desperation; but entered into a definitive treaty with him restoring to him all his conquests up to the river Krishna. He was then able to turn his attention to the recovery of the other two fortresses of Muḍkal and Raichūr, confident of having secured both his flanks. He succeeded wherever his great predecessor failed and brought under the Empire the two fortresses, the possession of which was to the Mahammadans a source of vital weakness to the Empire.

As he returned from his campaign against the ruler of Kalinga, while he was still on the banks of the Krishna and the region of Bezwada he made a grant of 10,000 gold pieces to the temples of South India and set about the work of restoration and repair to all the temples that had suffered any damage during the Mahammadan invasions. There is one other act of his which exhibits even more clearly than this, the policy that underlay his operations. He made an effort during his reign to provide temples in Vijayanagar to all the gods that had suffered at the hands of the Mahammadans. The great Viṭṭalasvāmi temple in Vijayanagar, which in many features exhibits Vijayanagar architecture at its best, was projected with a view to providing accommodation at the head-quarters to God Viṭṭala of Pāndārpur, whose temples had suffered at the hands of the Mahammadans. It is with a view to similar reparation that the great temple of Anantaśayana on the road from Hospet to Vijayanagar was also projected. His work as a whole indicates clearly the character of the movement that culminated in Vijayanagar and the policy adopted by the Empire when it had established itself permanently is shewn in its efforts to realise this ideal in practice.

Religion under Vijayanagar.

The Sanskrit epic poem Kamparāya Charitam of Ganga Dēvi, wife of Kumāra Kampana, who conquered, for his father, both Toṇḍamaṇḍalam and the Madura country from the Sultans of Madura makes the goddess of the South appear to the Prince in a dream. She is made to recount to him all her sufferings, material and moral, as a result of the irruption of the Mahammadans in the south. At the end of this doleful tale, she assured him that he was no less than an *avatār* of God for the purpose of repairing injuries that she had suffered, and encouraged him to proceed on the expedition of conquest on which he had already proceeded some way to carry it to completion. In token of her goodwill she presented him a sword with which he was to overcome in single combat the Mahammadan Sultan of Madura. Notwithstanding the epic treatment, it is clear that the poetess wishes to convey to the readers that the invasion of the south by Kumāra Kampana of Vijayanagar had in it something of the crusading spirit.

He went on his campaign dislodging the Mahammadan garrisons from the various centres and completed it by killing one Sultan of Madura and abolished the Sultanate finally by further campaigns round Madura itself. When the hostile Mahammadan garrisons were dislodged from the south and when they felt quite clear that the death of the Sultan Mahammad Tughlak and the succession of his nephew

Feroze did not produce any change of policy in the Imperial head-quarters in regard to the distant south, they signalised the re-establishment of Hindu dominion in South India by carrying out a complete restoration of Śrīrangam, and the re-establishment of God Ranganātha there. This rehabilitation of the Vaishṇava "holy of holies" is symbolical of the policy that started the movement, and exercised a strong influence throughout the history of the Empire of Vijayanagar. The restoration of temples and rehabilitation of gods merely did not complete the religious policy of these rulers.

The first ruler of Vijayanagar who assumed imperial titles was Harihara II, son of Bukka, the third of the five brothers, who were responsible for the foundation of the Empire. The five brothers and their friends and officers did yeomen service in this national effort. In spite of it all, Bukka, to whom more than to any other, the credit of this enterprise must be given, did not feel that the time had come for the assumption of imperial titles all the time that he lived. He died sometime in A.D. 1378 and his eldest son succeeded as Harihara II. It is he that assumed imperial titles sometime about A.D. 1380 almost about the end of the reign of Feroze Tughlak and when the first two well-known kings of the Bahmani kingdom had ruled and passed away. Among the titles assumed by

Haribara occur the following that call for reference here: "The establisher of the four castes and orders; the publisher of the commentaries on the *Vēdas*, the master in establishing ordinances prescribed by the *Vēdas*; he who has provided the Adhvaryu (priests) with employment, the auspicious ornament of Kings." These titles clearly indicate the ideas underlying the movement, and the duties that the founders of this Empire prescribed to themselves.

In this great work of Hindu rehabilitation in South India a number of great men played a very prominent part, each according to his opportunity. With the foundation of Vijayanagar is associated the name of the two Brahman brothers, Mādhava Vidyāraṇya and his brother Śāyaṇa, two Vēdic scholars of high rank. Another Mādhava generally called Mādhava Mantri, is generally described as "Upanishaṇ mārga-pratisṭhāpanāchārya," he that established the path of the Upanishad to distinguish him from the other Mādhava who takes the attribute "Vēda-mārga-pratishṭhāpanāchārya," the title by which learned Brahmans are addressed even now. This Mādhava belonged to the orthodox school, while the other was a disciple of Kāśi Vilāsa Kriyāśakti Paṇḍita, a Śaiva Āchārya.

The brothers Mādhava and Śāyaṇa were both of them scholars and statesmen. The elder brother is said to have occupied the position of chief adviser to Bukka at the court of Vijayanagar, while Śāyaṇa was associated with the Viceroyalty of Udayagiri and was the guide, philosopher and friend in a literal sense of the elder Kampana, while he was alive. At the death of Kampana, while his son Sangama was yet a child, Śāyaṇa assumed the responsibilities of the regency, conducted the administration for the boy, educated him as his teacher, fought a battle for him when his Viceroyalty was attacked, and thus discharged his debt to his sovereign. But the names of these brothers are not so widely known for their achievements as statesmen, but are handed down to us as Vēdic scholars.

Śāyana was grammarian and commentator, commented on the Vēdas, and did all the work under the inspiration of his brother, called some of them by Mādhava's name, such as Mādhavīya Dhātu Vṛitti. Mādhava seems to have been a sort of venerable president of an academy of scholars assembled from various parts, and these were set to work to comment upon and to commit to writing various Vēdic works which were dangerously near to being lost. These brothers and their companions discharged their duty to the community to which they belonged, which community had already, for thousands of years, discharged the duty of preserving learning. The spirit underlying this work of Vidyāraṇya is best illustrated by a story in connection with a life of his great Vaishṇava contemporary Vēdānta Dēśika.

After the second sack of the temple of Śrīrangam in 1328, Vēdānta Dēśika had to retire to the southern border of the Mysore plateau, and was there leading the life of a teacher which was the Brahman's birthright. For the sake of maintenance, because he lived as a married man and we know he had a son, he used to go out asking for alms in the shape of raw rice. The moment he had collected enough for the day he returned to the duties of the scholar. Vidyāraṇya who had known him and his worth, sent an invitation on behalf of himself and his sovereign inviting Vēdānta Dēśika to court, as in fact, he seems to have taken pains to collect all the scholars about him for the great purpose that he had in view. Vēdānta Dēśika politely declined the invitation on the ground that, having undertaken to serve God, the Great King of Kings, he found it impossible to accept services under an earthly monarch. Notwithstanding this refusal Vidyāraṇya continued to maintain a high regard for his scholarship and set about his work and completed it with the aid of a number of other scholars.

Vēdānta Dēśika pursued his life quietly and unostentatiously, and gave in many respects the final shape to the Vaishṇavism of South India following closely the teachings of Rāmānuja, explaining and supplementing it wherever it was necessary. He was the author of about 120 works, of which about one-fourth of the number was in Tamil, the rest of them in Sanskrit including a few which he composed in Prakrit. The Madhva Mutt at Udipi under the third Āchārya in the succession seems to have received a certain amount of patronage under Vijayangar. Two Śaiva centres flourished, one in the Malnad country of Mysore and another in Śri Śailam, not to mention various other localities of Vira Śaivism. The Jains were a flourishing community in the Tuḷunāḍ, the country between the Western Ghauts and the Sea, and one of the most trusted generals of Harihara II was Irugappa, the Jain, at whose instance the lexicographical work Nānārtharatnamālā was composed, and to whom is given the credit of having erected in Vijayanagar itself, the Jain temple which goes by the popular name Gaṇigiti Temple (the Oil-woman's temple). Without going into too much detail, it may safely be said that for good and for evil, the present-day Hindusim of South India retains the form that it received under Vijayanagar which ought to be given the credit of having preserved Hinduism such as it is. When at one time in the life of Sivāji he set up a claim to Hindu Empire in the south and wished to stand forth as the champion of Hinduism as against the Puritanic great Mughal Aurangazeb, it was not as a mere bombast or bathos that he did so. It was hardly a few years since that the widow of the last king of Vijayanagar appealed to Śivāji in behalf of her children for maintenance. Śivāji made a grant of two villages and got the grant[1] indited, with a sense of delicacy all his own, on silver plates which have recently been discovered. He could well feel, in the position to which he had elevated himself at the time, that he stood in the position of the sovereign, to whose widow and children he made this grant. That such a notion was entertained by him is indicated by the coinage of Śivāji. Mr. R. D. Banerji, the Superintendent of Archæology, Western Circle, notices a coin of Śivāji carrying the effigy of a pagoda on it and containing the inscriptions characteristic of Vijayanagar. It will thus be seen that in South India Hinduism has had a history of peaceful development culminating in the efforts of Vijayanagar to give it the final form in which it has come down to us to modern times.

Cataclysmal irruptions of foreigners causing revolutionary changes in doctrines and practice there were none. Into South India, the

[1] The date of the grant has since been found to be irregular and this casts a suspicion upon its character for genuineness. It seems quite likely a grant was made in the circumstances, having regard to other known facts of history and to the coin referred to.

immigrant Brahmans brought with them the pristine religion of the *Vēda* which produced protestant movements like Jainism and Buddhism in the north. They found a congenial home in the south and went on developing peacefully without being subjected to aggressive influences, like that of Buddhism under Asoka. Other influences there were, and these evoked responses by way of modifications and readjustments, but beyond these there was nothing of a radical character by way of change. Buddhism and Jainism flourished, but flourished side by side with Brahmanism, and with it controversies there might have been, but these controversies apparently were under the control of the civil authorities for the time being. When the religion of *bhakti* came in, probably in two ways, one in a somewhat developed form from the north, and perhaps another by a process of natural evolution from the popular culture of the time, a series of influences came into rivalry with the *Vēdic* religion of the Brahmans. One could see a serious effort at the reconciliation of the one with the other, and the result for South India is a compromise which exhibits a school of *bhakti* which on the one side countenances *Vedic* ritual and preserves it to a considerable extent ; and on the other adopted some, even perhaps of the non-Vedic practices and gave them a place in the religious system of the Hindus of to-day.

The works of the early saints give clear indication of this effort at synthesis, and the teaching of the earlier Achāryas give considerable evidence of the effort at a logical compromise. The effort at giving to this religious compromise a logical character naturally develops schools of thought which in the progress of society hardens into sects. The feature therefore of South Indian development from the second or third to the tenth century A.D. is the slow evolution of that compromise, and the further course beyond the tenth century is characterised by the evolution of the sects. The invasion of the Mahammadans gave the necessary corrective to the rancour and animosity which were creeping into the relation of these sects and the resulting foundation of Vijayanagar had its best to do in introducing civil order so that each sect by itself might live at peace with the others and achieve each its destiny unmolested by the others. This position is very clearly illustrated by what Bukka did, according to the so-called Rāmānuja inscription. The Vaishṇava holy place Tirunārāyaṇapuram was known among the Jains as Vardhamānapura. The Vaishṇavas apparently took to ill-treating the Jains, who carried a complaint to the headquarters. Bukka conducted an enquiry and, as it is said in the inscription, committed the charge of seeing that the Jains were not molested by the Vaishṇavas to one of the Vaishṇava Āchāryas at court belonging to the family of the Tatāchāryas of Conjeevaram. That spirit of compromise and insistance upon peaceful living by the various sects was adopted as the religious policy of the civil authorities by the sovereigns of Vijayanagar, who each had his own particular persuasion.

It is the reflex action of this *bhakti* school of thought that one could trace in Vaishṇavism as it is prevalent in northern India. In some cases the somewhat sensuous feature that was imported into the literature of *bhakti* in the south is carried beyond the limits imposed under the recognised canons of Tamil literature. This excessive zeal leads to a corruption of the faith where the effort is made to translate a mental realisation into the physical. That is a result, and an evil result at that, of transplantation. On the whole this undesirable development has not shown itself in southern India, at any rate to any noticeable degree. The contribution therefore of South India in this particular sphere is to have a genuine school of *bhakti*, and it is small wonder that the later *purāṇas* accord to Southern India the monopoly of it, as the Bhāgavata and the Padma Purāṇa would make one believe. Outside the sphere of Āryāvarta as it is, it could claim to be the land where *Vēdic* Brahmanism could be found to-day in the form which is the product of actual evolution from the Brahmanism of the *Vedic* age.

The Brahman has been able, thanks to the goodwill of the communities amidst which he cast his own lot, to carry his Brahmanical life unimpaired and even encouraged by the communities on whom he exercised his influence in the direction of elevating them to a higher plane of life. So much so was this the case that an European writer making a study of Indian women gives it as the characteristic of southern Indian women-folk as a whole, that their ideals in this life are other-worldly. The Brahman has on the whole discharged his responsibility as the teacher of the community by preserving the ancient learning of the Hindus; he has made an honest effort, according to his lights, at preparing the people to lead a good life here, and to go to a better life hereafter; and had through the ages maintained the ideal of uplifiting, however short he may have fallen in actually achieving this ideal.

CHAPTER XVIII.

Greater India: Expansion of India beyond the Seas.

Overland Communication of Northern India.

India falls geographically into two divisions in respect of her communication with the outside world. In spite of the mountain barriers on the north, north-west and north-east, there is a volume of evidence, though of an indirect character, of considerable communication with the rest of Asia, with the portions of China and Indo-Chinese peninsula on the east, with Tibet and the western portion of China in the middle, and Central Asia stretching westwards as far as Asia Minor itself and the Mediterranean Sea on the the west. In respect of these overland communications with the west, we have comparatively speaking few glimpses by way of evidence. The discovery of the Bogaz-Keui inscription referring to the Vedic deities, Mitra, Varuṇa, Indra and Nāsatya, and the Aryan character of the people of Mittani have led to the possibility of the inference that one section of the Āryans moved into that region. The irruptions of the Kassites who over-ran Babylonia about three centuries previous to this, also implies the existence of a powerful community of Aryan speaking people so far out. The question wherefrom they came is involved in the general problem of the Aryan home which is still a matter for discussion. The representation of apes, Indian elephants and Baktrian camels on an obelisk of Shalmanesser III in B. C. 860 gives the first clear indication of a communication between India and Assyria. It is the expansion of the Empire under Cyrus and his successor Darius that brings the Persian Empire directly into touch with India, and opens the way for the establishment of regular communication with western Asia. Similarly, on the eastern side, there is evidence of considerable early communication with the east ; much of the continental civilisation of the Indo-Chinese Peninsula seems derivable from northern India of the Buddhistic age, some of which may possibly be referable to times earlier. This communication of northern India with the outside world is not what concerns us directly.

Overseas Communication of South India.

Such communication as South India had with the rest of the world, must of necessity have been across the ocean. The early navigators of the Indian Ocean seem to have been many, and the history of this subject is only very partially worked for the satisfactory reason that the material that exists for such work is at the very best, scanty. The Egyptian efforts under the Pharaohs have reference only to the coasts of Arabia and of Africa, certainly as far down as Somaliland, and it may be much farther down towards Zanzibar. The expedition to Punt under the eleventh dynasty and before then, had for their object various articles of value to the Egyptians.[1] The most famous of this enterprise under the Pharaohs is the great expedition sent out by the great Queen Hatsheput. It had for its object the bringing of quantities of gold, incense and other articles, much prized in Egypt. They are all of them represented on her monument at Der al-Bahri.[2] It is possible to refer some of these articles to India; but most of them are obtainable in the region of the Somali coast. It is the enterprise of Alexander which found its visible embodiment in the founding of Alexandria, that gave an additional stimulus to this navigation of the Indian Ocean. Patrocles, an officer of Seleucus I and his son, sailed the Indian Seas, and under the Ptolemies, great efforts were made to open the Red Sea trade with the East. It is put down to

[1] H. R. Hall; the Ancient History of the East, p. 147.

[2] Breasted, History of Egypt, pp. 274-5.

the credit of Ptolemy-Philadelphus that he cut out a canal connecting the Nile with the Red Sea either newly or by opening out an old channel. As a necessary corollary to this, he founded a number of ports on the Red Sea. Among these foundations, Arsinoe of Ptolemy near the Suez and Berenice, lower down on the Red Sea coast, appear most prominent. Almost up to the time of the Roman conquest however, trade seems to have been carried on even in Indian commodities from the great exchange marts of Arabia Felix or, as the Greeks called it, Eudæmon, that is, the coast district round Aden. The discovery of blue cloth wrapped round the mummies, recently excavated,[1] and the further discovery that they were all dyed blue with Indian indigo is clear evidence of Indian trade, but not necessarily of communication with India. With the Roman conquest of Egypt, a new impetus is given to this eastern trade and we come upon a new era of nautical enterprise on this side of Egypt.

Indian Trade with Western Asia.

In respect of Indian trade with western Asia, the matter seems to rest on a somewhat better footing. The earliest definite reference that we can get is a commercial expedition sent out by

[1] India and the Western World.

Soloman with the assistance of Hiram of Tyre. According to Josephus, Soloman gave the command to the pilots of the expedition, "that they should go along with his stewards to the land that of old was called, Ophir, but now Aurea Chersonesus which belongs to India, to fetch gold." The expedition left Ezion-Gebeir (Akaba at the head of the Gulf of Suez), and was three years on its voyage. It brought with it 420 talents of gold, almug wood, ivory, apes, and peacocks. According to the statement of Josephus, the objective of the expedition should have been the Malay peninsula, the "golden Chersonese" of Milton. Several scholars take it to mean the Malay peninsula and Sumatra, both of which produced enormous quantities of gold, and came to be known to the inhabitants of India by the name Suvarṇa Bhūmi. But the variant of the name in the Septuagint is Sophir. Sophir and Ophir can be considered equivalent if the word with "S" passed through Persia. Sophir is the proper form or the form nearest to the Indian equivalent. Thus the country under reference may be taken to be Sauvīra which might have been one of the stages, or the final stage, which the mercantile fleet of India left as the last part of a coasting voyage. The only difficulty that scholars appeared to have felt against this identification seems to be, the 420 talents of gold. That this region Sauvīra between the mouths of the Indus and Broach produced gold is in evidence in the name of one of the rivers being "golden sands" (Suvarṇa-sikatā). This name is found recorded in the Junaghād inscription of the famous Ksatrapa king, Rudradāman of A.D. 150. Of about the same time, we have another reference to a region lower down the west coast of India, which contained gold mines. The territory of north and south Kanara under the Tamil chief Nannan is said to have contained hills showing gold-veins. What is more telling as a piece of evidence is a story connected with this chieftain, who had been branded with ignominy as woman-killer, as a result thereof. He is said to have had a fruit garden producing specially delicious fruits. A girl who went to a canal for water, picked up a fruit floating down the canal which happened to be flowing through the royal garden. She took the fruit and ate it without a thought; and for this great crime against His Majesty, the king ordered the girl to be killed. Her parents and relatives offered to ransom her by giving to the king a life-size statue of the girl in solid gold or whatever else the king might require by way of ransom. The story concludes by saying that the king refused the offer, and handed himself down to evil fame as woman-killer. The river Kaveri is known to classical Tamil literature by the name *Ponni*, and the name is said to have been given to it as it carried gold in her sands. Hence the difficulty on the score of gold ceases to be of force in regard to this identification.

Indian Names of Imported Articles.

Taking the other articles, almug wood is no other than sandal. It occurs in Greek as *santalān*, and could have come from Tamil *śandana* or Sanskrit *chandana*, the pure Tamil word for it is *āram*. This is a peculiar product of the Malaya Hills, the southern portion of the Western Ghats. Apes are known in Hebrew as *koph*. In Egyptian, the word takes the form *kafu*, and these are derived from the Sanskrit word *kapi*. *Satin* (cotton cloth) becomes *sadain* in Hebrew and *sinthon* in Greek, probably from Sanskrit *Sindhu*. These are all traceable to a part of India where the prevailing language might be Sanskrit. There are two words however for two articles imported from India which cannot be traced to Sanskrit, and these are peacock and rice. *Peacock* occurs in Hebrew in the from of *tukim*. In Persia, it occurs as *tavis*; in Greek as *tofos*. All of them seem derivable from the original *togai* which is unmistakably Tamil, at the worst Tamil-Malayalam. Rice occurs in Aramaic in the form *aruz*; Greek, *oruza*; Latin *oryza*, and Spanish *arros*, all apparently from the Tamil *ariśi*. The last two words must be held decisive, and must have reference to their origin in the Tamil country. This is confirmed by the discovery of a beam of teak in the excavations at Ur in Chaldea ascribed to the king Ur-Bagas, the first ruler of united Babylonia circa B.C. 3000 according to Sayce and Hewit. A similar teak beam was found by Rassan in the same locality in a building which was known to have been constructed by Nabonidus to the Moon-God in the middle of the sixth century B.C. Another beam of Indian cedar was found in the palace of Nebuchadnezzar at Birs-Nimrud. It is impossible that the teak wood could have gone to these places from anywhere other than the Malabar coast or from Burma. Rice and peacock were known in Athens in their names of Indian derivation in 430 B.C. Thus for about 500 years from the 5th century B.C. backwards, direct communication with India seems provable. That this was across the sea directly from India, and not overland through Persia may be established by the word for muslin being *sinthon* without the change of "S" into "H" as the Persians invariably change the "S" of Sanskrit into "H." This assumption of direct communication receives some confirmation from the fact that the South Indians, particularly of the classical Tamil literature, knew the western people by the designation *Yavana*, not by the northern designation of

Yona, even after the days of Asoka, showing thereby that communication between the Yavana region and South India belonged to an age when the Greek digamma had not dropped out of the word. The Bavēru-Jātaka, the Suppāraka-Jātaka, and the Mohosada-Jātaka, all of them would be confirmatory equally, though these might well refer to communication between northern India and Babylon. The explicit statement of Berosus, that the Babylonian market exhibited crowds of all nationalities, may be held to include some Indian nationalities as well. That it was so will acquire greater probability from the following extract from Mr. Hornell's work already quoted :—"This sea-trade with Babylon, carried on in Indian vessels, cannot be less ancient than the sixth century B. C. and is probably a good deal older. Its centinuance in Achæmenid times is rendered probable by the discovery of Indian articles in the ruins of Susa, these consisting of libation cups, bangles and ornaments made from the shell of the conch fished even yet in quantities in the Kathiawar coast.[1] The age of these ruins brings Indian trade with this region down into the fifth century, but some of the ornaments, one bangle especially, obtained from a lower stratum belong to a much older date, as Susa was a capital of the

[1] Hornell, J. : Marine Zoology of Okhamandal, Pt. II.

Elamites long before the Achæmenid occupation of the site. I have also identified chank ornaments from Tello (the site of ancient Lagash) in the Louvre Museum, Paris.[1]

The Situatio of Ophir.

In respect of the question as to the situation of Ophir, whether it was somewhere in southern Arabia or whether we should look for it on the continent of India or the Malay peninsula, the decisive factor would be the three years' navigation from Akaba to the region of Ophir and back, which would mean a voyage of more or less 18 months up and 18 months down. An eighteen months' voyage being regarded as the fact, it must have been generally a coasting voyage so far as the westerners were concerned : it would seem to indicate the coast of India as answering to Ophir, though Malay peninsula may be possible. A station on the south coast of Arabia would hardly answer this indication satisfactorily. All this would have reference however, only indirectly to the Indians having sailed across even the Arabian Sea. Direct evidence of Indian navigation is however not wanting. Even the Rig Veda knew of hundred-oared ships, although these have reference more to eastern navigation than to western. The Bavēru-Jātaka

---

1. Hornell. *op. cit.*, p. 208.

however is certain evidence of western navigation, by the Indians as also the Suppāraka Jātaka. But behind this period lies the far older one of possible communication between the Persian Gulf ports and the west coast of the Indian peninsula. Some antiquarians incline to the opinion that the early Sumerian civilisation, the mother of Babylonian, may after all be Indian.[1]

Early Indian Voyage to Babylonia and the West.

Whatever might be the ultimate verdict of scholars in regard to this question, there could be no doubt even on the indirect evidence available to us of early communication between Babylon and India. There is considerable reason for the opinion, if it is not yet put beyond doubt, that the Indians borrowed the week-days, from the Babylonians, rather than from the Greeks, leaving the possibility open that they might themselves have originated it. We have already urged reasons[2] and are pleased to find ourselves supported in this position by Dr. Vogel in an article published in the "East and West," January, 1912. We have direct evidence of the westward navigations of the Hindus in two references. The first is that Q. Metellus Celer received from the King of the Suevi, some

---

[1] H. R. Hall, Ancient History of the Far East. pp. 173-174.

[2] *Vide* Beginnings of South Indian History, pp. 304 ff.

Hindus who had been driven by storm into Germany in the course of a voyage of commerce according to Cornelius Nepos.[1] The other is contained in the visit of an Indian named Sophon (Subhanu) to which reference is made in a Greek inscription[2] found in the ruins of a shrine between the Red sea port of Berenice and Edfu near the banks of the Nile. The few sentences of Kanarese found by Dr. Hultzsch embodied in a Greek Farce contained in the Papyrus of Oxyrhynchus[3] and the same learned Doctor's find of a silver coin of Ptolemy Soter in the bazaars of Bangalore would only be evidence of communication and not of the Indians' voyaging westwards.

With the beginning of the Christian era and with the discovery of the south-west monsoon by Harpalos, voyages of communication became more regular and we have even reports of Indian embassies to the Emperor Augustus, one of which is said to have reached him at Terragona in Spain and another in Cyprus. The westward navigation and communication had become so great that there are constant references to Yavana ships coming to the west coast bringing gold in their well-rigged ships to pay in

[1] Macrindle's Ancient India, p. 110.

[2] The inscription is quoted in H. G. Rawlinson's India and the Western World, p. 99; J. R. A. S., 1904, p. 402.

[3] J. R. A. S., 1905, pp. 399,

exchange for the spices that they carried from that coast of the Indian Peninsula.[1] What is perhaps a more important point from the Indian side is that these Yavanas had at one time suffered defeat at sea at the hands of the Chēra ruler of the west-coast who is said to have punished them by tying their hands behind their back, pouring ghee or oil on their heads, and holding them up to ransom after this punishment.[2] There are other references to Yavanas. Yavana women are referred to as immediate servants of South Indian monarchs, particularly the Pāṇḍya king, and Yavanas are said to have constituted his body-guard. One of these references is to Yavana women handing him western wine in golden cups for the delectation of their royal master.[3] The other is much more interesting as it exhibits these Yavanas constituted as a body-guard of cavalry men. The Pāṇḍya king is described as being in camp in solitary bed overnight, and his tent constituted the centre of the camp which was surrounded by tents of womenguards enclosed by partitions of cloths; and then came the tents of men-guards, yavana and mlēccha and their camp of occupation. The whole camp was enclosed within a stockade of wooden palisades, sometimes even of the steel javelins that

---

[1] Aham 148, Beginnings of South Indian History, p 12.

[2] Padiṟṟuppattu, pp. 22-3, Mah. Svaminath Aiyar's edition.

[3] Narkīrar in Puram 56; also Neḍunalvāḍai ll. 101-2 and Silappadhikāran, XIV, 122-33.

the soldiers carried.[1] The question arises whether these could all be Greek and whether the Indian king could have obtained so many Greek men that could hire themselves out for service of this character. The dress and other details of the description seem to lead to the inference that these might have been people other than Greek. It seems far more likely that they were Arabians who hired themselves out for service like this in this fashion. That the ancient Arabs were known by the designation Yavana is warranted by the term Ethiopian applied to the inhabitants of Abyssinia. The term is derived from |*Atyab*—meaning incense, and *Yavan*—the Yavana collectors of incense in the region of the Somali country.[2] Those that constituted the original inhabitants of this locality are regarded by scholars, to be colonists from Arabia. If that is so the term Yavana must be the ordinary designation for an Arabian at any rate, as much as for a Greek. However it is an open question whether the carpenters from Yavana [3] who are said to have worked with a number of other foreign workmen from various divisions of India in the building of Kaveripatam were Greek

---

[1] Mullaippāṭṭu, 41–46.

pp. 214-18; Silappadhikāram V. pp. 9 12. The term Yavana is rendered Sonagar by the earlier and mlēccha by the later Commentator.

[2] Schoff's Periplus, p. 62.

[3] Maṇimekhalai, Canto XIX, pp. 107-10; *cf.* also passage from Perum Kada (Tam Bṛhatkathā) quoted thereunder.

Yavana or Arabian. It may even be Chinese Yavanas. It would be hazardous to attempt to be precise in the face of the statement contained in the Paṭṭinappālai,[1] that one quarter of Kaveripatam close to the sea was set apart as the quarters of the sea-going inhabitants of various countries who had come in for residence in the course of their voyages and who spoke a multitude of tongues, almost in the samestyle as Berosus speaks of a multitude of people of all nationalities collecting in the Babylonian market. The picture that we can form of this branch of Indian enterprise from the classical geographers would only confirm this indirectly.

The Evidence of Classical Geographers.

The classical geographers, the author of the Periplus and Ptolemy the geographer, that date respectively about A. D. 80 and A. D, 150, exhibit knowledge of a division of the country that we derive from the Tamil classical literature. The author of the Periplus[2] begins his account of the west of India with the Indus (Sinthus). He says that the river had seven mouths, shallow and marshy, and therefore not navigable. On the shore of the central channel was the sea-port Barbaricum

---

[1] Ll. 214-15; also Śilappadhikāram ll. 9-12. The term Gavanar is rendered Śonagar by the earlier and mlēcchar by the latter of the two commentators.

[2] The Periplus of the Erythræan Sea, translated and edited by W. H. Schoff, Secs. 42 to 66.

with a capital in the interior of the Scythians called Minnagara (the city of the Min, Scythians); the port Barbaricum has not satisfactorily been identified. It seems to be the Sanskrit Barbaraka (belonging to the country of the Barbara, perhaps the same as the Gk. barbarian). Passing down from there, the Periplus comes down the Surāshṭra coast (Syrastrene), and the Rann of Cutch (Eirinon); sailing across what is the Gulf of Kambay, he takes us to Barygaza (Sans. Bṛgukachcha, Mod. Broach). With this is supposed to begin Ariaca "which is the beginning of the kingdom of Nambanus and of all India." In regard to the divisions of that part of the country both Ptolemy and the Periplus agree except for the omission of some in the latter. The southern limit of the coast of Ariaca is Tindis according to both. The corresponding portion of the country inland is described in the Periplus as Ābhīra, the coast portion being Surāshṭra, as was already stated. This part is described as a fertile country producing wheat, rice, sesame oil and clarified butter; cotton and coarser sorts of cloth made thereform. Pasturing of cattle seems an important occupation and the people are described as of great stature and dark in colour.[1] The chief point to note here in

[1] Note the tradition that Agastya took with him a large colony of people from here in his southward migration above.

connection with this statement of the Periplus is that the coast under reference is described as the beginning "of the kingdom of Nambanus and *of all India.*" The latter expression indicates clearly that whoever Nambanus was, he was, at the time that the author of the Periplus got his information, known to the outside world as the king of India. In other words, it seems to have been the days of the Āndhra empire of Magadha. The name Nambanus itself is a correction of the text which has Mambarus. This latter might well be the Lambodara of the paurāṇic list of the Śātavāhanas or the Āndhras of the Dakhan. The chronology of the early rulers of these Śātavāhanas cannot yet be regarded as being definitely settled, and at any rate the expression in the text seems of very doubtful application to identify Nambanus with Nahapana, the Kṣaharāta ruler. After describing the difficulties of navigating up to the port of Broach and the arrangement made by the ruler for piloting the vessels safely into the port, the Periplus proceeds to give the countries inland set over against that coast between Barbaricum, at the mouth of the Indus obviously, and Broach. He notes among them the Āraṭṭas of the Punjab, the Arachosii of Southern Afghanistan, the Gandaraei (Sanskrit, Gāndhāra), and the people of Pocalais (Sans. Pushkalāvatī) both in the region between the Kabul and the

Indus in Northern Afghanistan including also the Northern portions of the Punjab where was also the city of Alexandria which Bucephalus located very near the Jhelum. Beyond these he says were the warlike Bactrians. He gives an interesting fact that in his day coins bearing Greek inscriptions or Greek legends were circulating in the country round Broach, and they contained, according to the Periplus, the devices of the Greek rulers, among them, Apollodotus and Menander. Coming further east from these countries he speaks of Ozene (Ujjain), and refers to it as the former royal capital. Passing over all that he says about the trade of Broach which is not to our present purpose, we come, in Sec. 50, to another statement which is of immediate interest to us. He says "beyond Barigaza the adjoining coast extends in a straight line from north to south and so this region is called Dachinabades, for Dachan in the language of the natives means 'south.' The inland country back from the coast towards the east comprises many desert regions and great mountains; and all kinds of wild beasts, leopards, tigers, elephants; enormous serpents, hyenas, and baboons of many sorts, and many populous nations as far as the Ganges." This clearly indicates that he describes the whole of the region known as the Dakshiṇāpatha or the Dakhan, and the Daṇḍakāraṇyam of the Sanskrit writers; the central region of India corresponding to our modern division of the Dakhan. He then describes the interior marts of Paitan and Tagara, and of the sea-ports along the coast till he reached Naura and Tindis, the first marts of Damirica as he calls them (Sanskrit Dramiḍaca, the correct equivalent of the Greek), and the Tamiḻakam of the Tamil classics. Damirica, sometimes written by error Lymirica, is the Sanskrit Dramiḍaka which the author must have heard in contradistinction to Aryaka. It is perhaps a little far-fetched to see in it Tamiḻakam except through the Sanskritised Dramiḍaka. With Tindis began according to both Ptolemy and the Periplus, the kingdom of Cherabothra (Cheraputra or Keraḷaputra). The next port of importance we come to, is 50 miles from Tindis again at the mouth of a river; the port called Muziris (Muyiri or Muśiri of the Tamils, the modern Cranganore). Fifty miles further south was the sea-port of Nelcynda which the late Mr. Kanakasabhai Pillai correctly identified with Nīrkuṉṟam in the country of the Pāṇḍyas. This place was situated about ten or twelve miles in the interior with an out-port at the mouth of the river, the village Bakare, Vaikkarai as we know it now. The kings of both these market towns, the Periplus says "live in the interior." The imports into Muziris are given "as a great quantity of coin; topaz, thin clothing not much, figured linens, antimony, coral, crude glass, copper, tin, lead, wine not much but as much as at Barigaza; realgar and orpiment, and wheat only for the sailors, for this is not dealt in by the merchants there." The exports from this place are the "pepper" coming from "Kottanora" (Kuṭṭa Nāḍu in the interior) "great quantities of fine pearls," ivory, silk cloth, spikenard from the Ganges, malabathrum from the interior, transparent stones of all kinds, diamonds and sapphires and tortoise-shell, "that from the Chryse (golden) island and that taken from among the islands along the coast of Damirica." One may so far compare this statement with the following two extracts from Tamil Literature:—

(1) The Kuṭṭuvan king of the beautiful garland dropping honey like water, gives away in head-loads, to those that go to him, the sandal from the hill and the pearl from the sea, along with the gold brought in payment by ships, and carried by canal boats into his port of Muśiri of the noisy beach—Paraṇar in Puram, 343.

(2) The prosperous Muśiri to which come the well-rigged ships of the Yavanas tearing up the foaming great river Śuḷḷi of the Cheras, carrying gold to pay for the cargo of pepper with which they returned usually—Kāṭṭūr Tāyaṁ Kaṇṇan in Aham 148.

Beyond Vaikkarai, the Periplus refers to the dark-red mountains and of the district (stretching along the coast towards the south) "Paralia" generally taken as equivalent to Pural or Coast; the first port in this coast region is what he calls Balita, identified with Varkkali or Janārdanam, which in those days had a fine harbour and a village by the sea shore. Then comes Kumāri with a cape and a harbour. It is also referred to as a holy bathing place, and the coast region is then described as extending eastwards till it reaches Korkai " where the pearl fisheries are," and the Periplus offers the interesting piece of information, " that they are worked by condemned criminals." Then follows another coast region with a region inland called according to the Periplus Argaru,[1] taken to be the equivalent of Uraiyūr. These two regions of the coast country are somewhat differently named in Ptolemy. He calls the region between Nīrkuṅṛam and Camorin as in the country of Aioi. (Tamil Āay). Then follows the region which he calls Káreoi (Tamil Karai or Karaiyar, a class of fisherfolk), and the coast country extending from Korkai upwards is spoken of by Ptolemy in two divisions. The country of the Batoi (Tamil Vōṭṭuvar) and Poralia in the country of the Toringoi (error for Soringoi, Cholas). The exports from this region according to the Periplus

[1] Is this not more correctly Uragapura (Hālāsya or Madura), the capital of the Pandyas? Uraiyūr the Chola capital and the country dependent thereon must have begun far north of this region—somewhere about Tondi in the Ramnad District now.

are the pearls[1] collected from part of what was gathered each season in the appointed pearl-fields, and a kind of fine muslin called Argaritic. The next important ports mentioned in this region by the Periplus are three, Camara (identified with Kaveripaṭṭaṇam), Poduca (may be a Puduvai) and it is doubtful whether it stands for Pondicherry or a place in the vicinity. Then Sopatma (Tamil Śopaṭṭinam or fortified-port). There come ships from what he calls Damirica

[1] Pliny says (Macrindle's Ancient India, Chap. IX, pp. 54-58):—

"Our ladies glory in having pearls suspended from their fingers, or two or three of them dangling from their ears, delighted even with the rattling of the pearls as they knock against each other; and now, at the present day, the poorer classes are even affecting them, as people are in the habit of saying, that "a pearl worn by a woman in public is as good as a lictor walking before her." Nay, even more than this, they put them on their feet, and that, not only on the laces of their sandals but all over the shoes; it is not enough to wear pearls, but they must tread upon them and walk with them under foot as well.

"I once saw Lollia Paulina, the wife of the Emperor Caius—it was not at any public festival, or any solemn ceremonial, but only at an ordinary betrothal entertainment—covered with emeralds and pearls, which shone in alternate layers upon her head, in her hair, in her wreaths, in her ears, upon her neck, in her bracelets, and on her fingers, and the value of which amounted in all to 40,000,000 sesterces; indeed she was prepared at once to prove the fact by showing the receipts and acquittances. Nor were these any presents made by a prodigal potentate, but treasures which had descended to her from her grand-father, and obtained by the spoliation of the provinces. Such are the fruits of plunder and extortion. It was for this reason that M. Lollius was held so infamous all over the East for the presents which he extorted from the kings; the result of which was, that he was denied the friendship of Caius Caesar, and took poison; and all this was done, I say, that his grand-daughter might be seen, by the glare of the lamps, covered all over with jewels to the amount of forty millions of sesterces!"

and from the north for the exchange of commodities. Here the Periplus has an important statement to make in respect of the capacity for navigation of the Tamils. In these ports that he mentions, he says were ships of two kinds, those intended for coasting voyages as far as Damirica as he calls it ; these were small and large, and are called by him Sangara (Tam, Śangāḍam). Those intended however, for the voyages to Chryse and to the Ganges were called, according to him, Colandia, and are described as very large. The term Chryse which in Greek is the equivalent of Gold, seems to refer to Suvarṇabhūmi in Sanskrit, and has been identified with the Malaya Peninsula, spoken of by the Periplus in another place as an island. That it indicates the region about the Malaya Peninsula is clear from what he says in regard to the direction of the land ; "just opposite this (river Ganges) there is an island in the ocean the last port of the inhabited world to the east under the rising sun itself ; it is called Chryse and it has the best tortoise-shell of all the places in the Erythræan sea." There are said to be imported into these ports everything that is made in Damirica "the greatest part of what is got from Egypt." Then he proceeds to mention Palaesimundu, "called by the ancients Taprobane." Further north from this, according to him, was the region Masalia, and further north of this Dosarene

(Sans. Daśārṇa). Ptolemy however interpolates between the Chola coast and Maisalia (Masalia of the Periplus) the country of the Aruvarṇoi or Arvarnoi (the Aruvāḷar of the Tamils) whose country was known to the Tamils in two divisions Aruvānāḍu and Aruvā Vaḍa-talai (northern Aruvā) which would take us more or less close to the mouth of the Krishna river, the Maisalos of Ptolemy.

Of the trade of this coast, the most important ports are the three referred to already, and the imports of trade are set down as "everything made in Damirica and the greatest part of what is brought at any time from Egypt comes here together with most kinds of all the things that are brought from Damirica and of those that are carried through Paralia."

We have similar reference to the imports at Kaveripatam in the Tamil work Paṭṭinappālai: "horses were brought from distant lands beyond the seas, pepper was brought in ships, gold and precious stones came from the northern mountains, sandal, akir (aromatic aloe wood) came from the mountains towards the west, pearls from the southern seas and coral from the eastern seas; the produce of the regions watered by the Ganges; all that is grown on the banks of the Kaveri; articles of food from Īḻam or Ceylon, and the manufactures of Kāḻakam in Sumatra."[1] This

[1] Paṭṭinappālai, II, 127 ff.

looks like a restatement in a somewhat expanded form of what is found briefly stated in the Periplus.

Tamil Knowledge of the Eastern Archipelago.

It was already pointed out in a previous section that the Malabar coast got into touch with the western world, Egypt, Western Asia, and across as far as the western extremity of Europe. The Hebrew references to various articles of Indian, particularly South Indian, production, the Bavēru Jātaka [1] which apparently relates to Babylon, the Suppāraka[2] Jātaka and a story in the Kathāsaritsāgara relative to the westward voyage from the port of Patri, and the Sanskrit origin of the name of the island Sokotra, all these might be cited as evidence of westward trade, at any rate, as arguing familiarity with navigation on that side. That Indians did take part in these distant voyages is directly stated in the reference in Tacitus to a Hindu sailor having been stranded in the region of the North Sea, and that in Eudoxus, to the famished Hindu-sailor who piloted the Greeks across the Arabian Sea to the Malabar Coast.[3] There is further evidence of

---

[1] The Jātakas, Trans. by Cowell, etc., No. 339, III, p. 83.

[2] No. 463, IV, 86-90. Trans. by Cowell and Rouse.

[3] Macrindle's Ancient India, p. 110.

a reference in an Egyptian inscription to a Sophon-Indos (Subhanu the Indian)[1] in the heart of Egypt, apparently along the road from the chief Red Sea port to Alexandria. The busy and the profitable character of the western trade and the part that the Roman empire took in it in the early centuries of the Christian era have already been indicated. The question in these circumstances would naturally arise whether the Tamils had any knowledge of the Eastern Archipelago and whether they ever came into direct touch with it.

Evidence from Tamil Literature.

The Eastern Archipelago was a region with which the Tamils were much more familiar apparently, and their commercial efforts seem to have gone on as far as the comparatively distant coast even of China.[2] We have direct evidence on the Tamil side of not merely knowledge of the islands near the eastern shore of the Bay of Bengal, but also of regular commercial voyages and even settlements of people. During the period with which we are concerned people in the south, particularly the coast of the Chola country, kept up a busy trade over-sea.

[1] H. G. Rawlinson's India and the Western World, p. 99, where the Greek Ins. is quoted.

[2] In the excavations at Chandravalli, Mr. R. Narasimha Chariar says a coin of the Chinese Han. Emperor Wu-ti of the 2nd century B.C. was found as also a denarius of Augustus.

The principal ports from which these fleets of commerce started and of which we have any reference are two in the Chola country, namely, Kaveripatam at the mouth of the Kaveri, and Toṇḍi farther south on the coast of Rammad set over against Jaffna. Puhār which is the Tamil name for the port at the mouth of the Kaveri is spoken of as a great port where a crowd of merchant shipping brought horses from across the waters, spices, particularly pepper, gold and precious gems from the northern mountains (Himalayas). Sandal and aloe-wood (akil) from the western hills, pearls from the southern sea, *coral from the eastern sea*, various kinds of commodities from the Ganges, other commodities coming down the Kaveri, food articles from Ceylon and *the wealth produced in Kāḷaham*, other rare articles (such as camphor, rose water, etc.) *from China and other places.*[1] This catalogue of articles coming from various places in the east into Puhār is confirmed by various references in the Śilappadhikāram which state specifically sugar-candy from the western region of the Yavanas, black aloe from the east, stones for rubbing sandal from the northern mountains[2] and sandal from the southern hills. There is a further reference in the same work

---

[1] Paṭṭinappālai, ll. 185-192.

[2] Canto IV, ll. 35-38. This is also referred in the Neḍunalvāḍai and Perum Kurinchi.

to the special quarter of the town near the port occupied by the Yavanas (rendered by the commentator Mlēchchas)[1] and people from various countries whose profession it was to go oversea and trade.

Referring to the port of Toṇḍi[2] which in those days was considered a port in the Chola country, the fleet of ships arriving there brought the following commodities; aromatic aloe (akil), silk, sandal, fragrant articles and camphor. The commentary explains elaborately the varieties of these articles that came in indicating also the sources from which they came. In regard to the first *akil*, four varieties are mentioned, of which two seem to take their name undoubtedly from the localities of production. They are respectively named *takkōli* (product of Takola) and *kiḍaravan* (the product of Kiḍāram). Under camphor, there are two varieties that are named respectively *vārāśan* and *varōśu* both of which seem the Tamil name of Barus or Barusai of Ptolemy, and another variety which is specially called China camphor. Apart from Barus there stand out the names Takkola and Kaḍāram. Takkola, or as it is sometimes written Takkōlam in Tamil, is the famous port in the Malay peninsula near the mouth of the Takopa

[1] Canto V, ll. 9-12.

[2] Canto XIV, ll. 106-111.

river which gives the name to one of the aromatic plants, the fruit of which is called *takkolam.* The port of Takkola is mentioned as a prominent mart of the east shore of the Bay of Bengal by Ptolemy. Kaḍāram that is referred to there is apparently the Kadāram that is found associated with one of the titles of Rājēndra Chola, and which figures in the records of both Rājēndra Chola and his father Rāja Rāja. These records refer to the same place in Sanskrit as well in the form Kaṭāha. Hence we are justified in taking it that the Sanskrit Kaṭāha is the Tamil Kaḍāram. Is it the same as the Tamil Kāḻaham? Kāḻaham used to be identified hitherto with Burma by antiquarians. Kaḻāham is equated with Kaḍāram by the commentator Nachchinārkkiniyar[1]; and the articles of import therefrom referred to by the commentator as "articles of enjoyment," seem similar to the articles that the embassy from San-fo-Chi carried to China in the tenth and eleventh centuries of the Christian era. We seem therefore justified in taking Kaḻāham, Kaḍāram and Kaṭāha all of them to be one place, and that place as being the island or group of islands dominated by Sumatra, the Śāvakam of the Tamils, the Yavadvīpa of Sanskrit, and Sabadiu of Ptolemy. The classic Maṇimēkhalai has much so say in its own legendary fashion of Śāvakam, and a

[1] The Nighaṇṭu Pingalandai gives the equation also.

mythical king of the island by name Puṇyarāja. The work refers to a famine for the relief of which a man possessed of a miraculous bowl which supplied food without its being ever exhausted, agreed to go. The information of the famine was given to him in one of the ports of the Pāṇḍya country by a body of people who came from over-sea. He started with the next commercial fleet that sailed forward towards the east. Being overtaken by a storm the fleet had to go for shelter to one of the islets round Ceylon. When the fleet set sail again they sailed away in the belief that he was on board.[1] In another connection the same work refers to an island which the work calls the island of the "naked Nāgas" apparently Nakkavāram, the modern Nicobars, then inhabited by naked cannibals. The particular point to notice in this connection is that the individual concerned was born a rich man and had squandered away all his wealth in evil company. Disgusted with himself he set forward on a new life and got into the company of a body of merchants trading overseas. In the course of the voyage the fleet of ships got tempest-tossed and several of them destroyed. He took hold of a broken piece of mast and reached the island. The story goes on to say that he was threatened with death having been sighted by the cannibals.

---

[1] Canto XIV.

He managed however, to satisfy the cannibals that what they were doing was wrong, and so far persuaded them into friendship to him that they were quite prepared to send him away with whatever he cared to take from the accumulated wealth of the previous ship-wrecks near the shore. They brought him quantities of all kinds of articles of wealth and let him take whatever he liked of them and as much as he pleased. When the next regular fleet of ships touched that port under the lead of the merchant chief Chandradatta he got on board ship and sailed across to the Tamil coast. The story indicates regular caravans of ships going backwards and forwards across the sea, and the number of incidental references that we get to various matters connected with overseas navigation in this class of works goes to confirm the conclusion that they were familiar with the islands on the eastern shore of the Bay of Bengal. This is confirmed by the specific statement of the author of the Periplus in reference to the eastern ports of the Tamil country that "there are ships of the country coasting along the shore as far as Damirica,[1] large vessels made of single logs bound together called Sangara; *but those which make the voyage to Chryse*[2] *and to*

---

[1] Meaning appa rently to the end of the Tamil country on the west coast.

[2] Gold country, Suvarṇabhūmi, the Malay peninsula generally.

the Ganges are called Colandia and are very large."[1]

Other Confirmatory Evidence.

There are various pieces of evidence of a somewhat indefinite character which would lead to the inference that there were a large number of settlements of the Tamils in this region and that the southern culture had spread so far out as the Eastern Archipelago itself. This is made clear in the voyage of Fa-hien on his return journey from Ceylon to China. He set sail from Ceylon and was caught in a storm, and after a difficult and dangerous voyage arrived at Javadvīpa (the Tamil Śāvakam) where he found "various forms of error and *Brahmanism flourishing*"; while he found, much to his regret, that the Buddhists in the locality were not worth speaking of. This character of the Indian emigrants in the Eastern Archipelago is in a way put beyond a doubt altogether by the so-called Yūpa inscriptions of a king Mūlavarman found in East Borneo (edited formerly by Dr. Kern) and of which an excellent new edition is given us by Dr. J. Ph. Vogel. These inscriptions are four in number and refer to a colony of Brahmans who celebrated a *yagā* in the true orthodox Vedic style giving at

[1] Schoff's Periplus, p. 46, Sec. 60.

the end of the ceremony various gifts including even the *kalpavṛkshadāna*.[1]

These are put on the *yūpa stambhas* (sacrificial posts) by the Brahmans who officiated in the sacrifice. Unfortunately the inscriptions are not dated, but they are of the "Pallava-Grantha" character which Dr. Burnell called "Vengi-alphabet," a misnomer which is now no more accepted. Here are the words of the learned doctor who gives us the revised version: "among the epigraphical records of southern India we cannot point to any specimen which exhibits exactly the same style of writing as is found in the earliest inscriptions of the Archipelago. But among the southern alphabets, it is undoubtedly the archaic type of the ancient *grantha* character (to retain Bühler's terminology) used by the early Pallava rulers of the Coromandel coast, which appears to be most closely related to the character of the Koetei epigraphs." Arguing on paleographical grounds alone and admitting the defective state of our knowledge of the palæography of this particular period Dr. Vogel would ascribe this inscription to the middle of the 4th century A.D. This indicates that in that early period there were colonies of

[1] The expression *sakalpavṛkshadānam* (gift of a gold wish-giving tree of the same form, leaves and all, as in nature) in the inscription is badly rendered.

Brahmans apparently from South India so far east as East Borneo celebrating a sacrifice there and handing down the fact of such celebration by putting up inscriptions on the very sacrificial posts in the unmistakably south Indian characters of the fourth century of the Christian era. The question would arise whether these colonies maintained any connection with India which could be regarded as of a political character and whether such colonisation would warrant any assumption of a greater India are questions—answers to which we cannot attempt yet with the material available for this period.

The Character of this Period of South Indian History.

The period with which we are concerned in this portion of South Indian History is coeval with the position of the dominance of the Āndhras in the Dakhan and over the empire of the Mauryas. The question would naturally arise whether these Āndhras had anything to do with South India. As far as the material available to us goes they do not appear to have been brought into direct connection unless we could interpret the hostile Aryas who figure in the history of many of the Tamil rulers as indicating the contemporary Āndhra sovereigns of the north; as in the case of the Chēra who defeated the Aryas, and the elder, Pāndya, the hero of the Śilappadhikāram who claims to have defeated the Aryas as well. There is a more precise reference to the *Kannar* in the Tamil classic *Śilappadhikāram.* This term could be rendered *Karṇas* and they are clearly stated to be "the hundred Karṇas." Whatever the significance of the hundred may be by itself, it is doubtful if we could regard it as the equivalent, even by mistake, of the Śātakani or Śātakanis of the Dakhan.

These last, however, have left us a few inscriptions among the earliest of which is a Prakrit inscription of the second century A. D. This is in a pillar at Maḷavalli in the Shikārpūr[1] taluk of the Shimoga district, recording a grant by Hārītīputra-Śātakarni for the god *Īśvara* of the village. The next inscription comes from the same taluk[2] and is on a pillar standing in front of the Praṇavēśvara temple. This record states that the God Pranavēśvara had been worshipped by Śātakarni and other kings. Near the town of Chittaldroog itself some recent excavations unearthed several lead coins of the Āndhras and their Viceroys. The Prakrit inscription on the Maḷavalli pillar is followed by an inscription of the early Kadamba king, Kakutsthavarma dated by the late Prof. Kielhorn,

---

[1] Shikārpūr, 263, Ep. Car., Vol. VII.

[2] *Ibid*, 176.

about the middle of the sixth century. The inscription (Shikārpūr 176) known as the Tāḷgunda pillar inscription contains the further reference to this Kakutsthavarman and gives him credit for the construction of the tank in front of the temple. This Kakutsthavarman was a contemporary of the Guptas and seems to have entered into a matrimonial alliance[1] with them. During this period therefore the Āndhra power stretched southwards as far as northern Mysore. Their frontier extended southwards on the eastern side as far as the south Pennār at one time as their ship coins found in that region would enable us to infer. Generally speaking however the Āndhra power came into touch with the Tamils on the northern frontier marked by Tirupati and Pulikat. The wild people called Vaḍukar by the Tamils must have interposed between the Tamils and the Āndhras. It was probably to keep guard over this somewhat dangerous frontier, one capital of the Āndhras was located at Dhanakaṭaka near Amarāvati in the Guntur district. This would mean that the Krishna in this region constituted

[1] Mr. Rice would date the record in the third apparently on the ground that Kakutsthavarman claims to have entered into marriage alliances with the Guptas, that is, according to him Samudragupta, who came as far south as Kānchi in his southern conquest. This is hardly necessary; but the boast would be pointless if we date the record at a period when the Gupta power was on the decline. The fifth century would be a better date.

the normal southern frontier of the Āndhras. This position of the Āndhras and the interposition of the tribes of Vaḍukar between them and the Tamils, raises the question whether the Āndhras of to-day, the Telugu-speaking peoples, can lay claim to any affinity with the imperial Āndhras of the two centuries on either side of the beginning of the Christian era. The evidence available to us at present does not seem to warrant a categorical answer one way or the other. The Āndhras are described as Āryan people who had given up the Āryan customs and practices in religion, in other words mlēcchas or even Vrātyas. In the Mahābhārata the region of wild tribes is said to have intervened between the Āndhras and the Tamil country which constitutes at the present time the heart of the Āndhra country. It is a well-known phenomenon in history that people still in tribal organisation keep moving forward from place to place and give their name to the districts that they may occupy for the time being. Their name certainly attaches itself to the locality where they effect something like a permanent settlement. Even other people that come and settle in that locality afterwards take their name from the district rather than give their name to the district. The present-day Āndhras are undoubtedly Āndhras in the sense that they occupy the Āndhra country, but whether they are the legitimate successors of the Āndhras by race is more than can be postulated on the evidence available to us so far. Unless the reference to the Āryas in Tamil literature be to the Āndhras of the Dakhan[1] (or the imperial Āndhras if they ever rose to that dignity), it may be safely stated that the Āndhras as such do not find mention in Tamil literature. There is a chieftain known by the name Aay-Anḍiran. The second word of this name is rendered Āndhra by some. It is just possible that it is the Tamilised form of the word Āndhra.[2] It would be unsafe, however, to assert that the Āndhras as such came and settled in the south. This position is made still more difficult by the reference to the Vaḍukar, which term occurs very often in the literature of this period. Vaḍukar is the present-day vernacular name for the Telugu-speaking people in the Tamil country, but they are described in this body of literature

[1] There is some ground for this equation Ārya-Āndhra, as the Tamil Lexicon Divākaram gives among the synonyms of the term Ārya, the word mlēchchar. This last cannot mean here the foreign barbarian in the face of the statement these were Kṣatriya Vrātyas. The term is here used in the sense indicated in the Śatapatha Brāhmana as those who changer into l in pronunciation. This phonetic peculiarity is a feature of the Āndhra country, as is exemplified in the Asoka Inscriptions.

[2] If the term Anḍar used to designate shepherds, comes from the Sans. Andhaka (a Tamil derivation seems impossible) there is justification for this interpretation. The term Anḍiran is used in the compound in contradistinction to the term Eyinan in Āay-Eyinan, undoubtedly denoting the caste or tribe from which he came. The two names would stand Āay, the shepherd and Āay, the hunter.

as still in the savage stage of frontier tribes living as marauders. They are located in the region immediately to the north of the Tamil frontier of Pulikat and Tirupati. This would seem to preclude the equation that the Tamils regarded the Vaḍukar and the Āndhras as one. Hence for the time the question has to remain open whether the Telugus of the present day as a body should be traced to the Vaḍukar or to the Āndhras.

It thus seems clear that the Tamil country remained a compact territory with a well-defined frontier in the north inhabited by wild tribes, who were kept under control, separating the Tamil country from the territory of the Āndhras. This Tamil country remained the asylum of the orthodox Brahmanical religion, which was able to hold its own as against the sister religions of Jainism and Buddhism within its own territory. During the four or five centuries of its history from the period of Asoka onwards the Tamils seem to have set themselves up in opposition to the systematic propagation of Buddhism under the imperial influence of Asoka himself. This apparently it was that caused the perpetual hostility between the Buddhist Ceylon and the Tamil country set over against it particularly the Chola country. This attitude of hostility would naturally have continued when the Āndhras succeeded to the empire of Asoka and his successors in the south. So the Āndhras were kept out of the Tamil country on the northern frontier. The Tamil country therefore remained the land of freedom in point of religion, and Brahmanism seems to have received the countenance, if not the active support, of the rulers and the body of the people as a whole. Hence the development of Brahmanism here was on the more natural orthodox lines which do not exhibit the ever-recurring reorganisation necessitated by the impact of foreign invaders and hostile religions. In the course of this evolution of Brahmanism there appears to have been a stage of orthodoxy when sea-voyage was not held to make a Brahman fall from his high estate—Manu's objection seems to have had but a restricted applicability; but the Koetei epigraphs seem to make even the restriction of feeble force, as a prohibition of sea-voyage for the Brahman. That the emigrants apparently started from the Pallava country and not the Tamil country proper may be significant of the fact that these were followers of Baudhāyana and not of Āpastamba.

The Industrial Arts of South India.

Passing on from the political to the industrial condition of India, we have already described the principal sea-ports, both on the western and eastern seaboard. If, as has been pointed out, there were so many thriving ports and, if foreign merchants sought these for trade at considerable risk of pirates, and if there was so much enterprise in sea-going among the inhabitants of the country itself, the conclusion is irresistible that the country had a prosperous industry, and so, on examination, it appears certainly to have been. Apart from the complaints of Petronius that fashionable Roman ladies exposed their charms much too immodestly by clothing themselves in the "webs of woven wind," as he called the muslins imported from India, Pliny says that India drained the Roman Empire annually to the extent of 55,000,000 sesterces, equal to £486,979 [1] sending in return goods which sold at a hundred times their value in India. He also remarks in another place, "this is the price we pay for our luxuries and our women."

That the industrial arts had received attention and cultivation in early times in India is in evidence to the satisfaction of the most sceptical mind. The early Tamils divided arts into six groups:—ploughing (meaning thereby agriculture), handicrafts, painting, commerce and trade, the learned arts and lastly the fine arts. Of these agriculture and commerce were regarded as of the first

[1] Mommsen gives the total £11,000,000, £6,000,000 for Arabia, £5,000,000 for India.

importance. Flourishing trade pre-supposes a volume of industry, the principal of which was weaving then, as it also has been until recently. Cotton, silk and wool seem to have been the material that were wrought into cloths. Among the woollens we find mention of manufactures from "the wool of rats"[1] which was regarded as particularly warm. There are thirty varieties of silks mentioned, each with a distinctive appellation of its own, as distinguished from the imported silks of China which had a separate name. The character of the cotton stuffs that were manufactured is indicated by the comparisons instituted between them and, 'sloughs of serpents,' or 'vapour from milk,' and the general description of these as "those fine textures the thread of which could not be followed even by the eye."

Exports and Imports.

The chief exports from the country, as the author of the Periplus says, were these; "the produce of the soil like pepper, great quantities of the best pearl are likewise purchased here, ivory, silk in the web, spikenard from the Ganges, malabathrum from the countries further to the east, transparent stones of all sorts,

[1] This seems a technical expression meaning the kind of wool which lent itself to weaving.

diamonds, rubies and tortoise shell from the golden Chersonese or from the islands off the coast of Damirke. This is all from the port of Muziris on the west coast. He goes on to say, "there is a great resort of shipping to this port for pepper and malabathrum; the merchants bring out a large quantity of spice and their other imports are topazes, stibium, coral., flint, glass, brass and lead, a small quantity of wine as profitable as at Barugaza, cinnabar, fine cloth, arsenic and wheat, not for sale but for the use of the crew." That Pliny's complaint about the drain was neither imaginary nor hypersensitive is in evidence in a passage descriptive of Muziris in one of the ancient classics of Tamil literature [1] 'Musiri to which come the well-rigged ships of the Yavanas [2] bringing gold and taking away spices in exchange.'

Regarding the trade of the east coast, here follows the imports into Puhār, "horses were brought from distant lands beyond the seas, pepper was brought in ships, gold and precious stones came from the northern mountains towards the west [3]; pearls from the southern seas, and

[1] See Aham 148, quoted above.

[2] Yavanas in this connection stand undoubtedly for the foreign Greeks and Romans. Other foreigners also were known and these were called Mlēchchas. Mullaippāṭṭu, ll. 61-65, Maha., Svāminatha Aiyar's Edn. of Pattupāṭṭu.

[3] The Western Ghats in Konkan and Tulu seem to have produced gold. See Aham, 70

coral from eastern seas. The produce of the region watered by the Ganges; all that is grown on the banks of the Kaveri, articles of food from Īḷam (Ceylon) and the manufactures of Kāḷaham (Sumatra)[1] were brought there for sale as was stated already. The products of particular importance received in the port of Toṇḍi (east or Chola Toṇḍi in the Rāmnad Dt.) are akir (a kind black aromatic wood), fine silk, camphor, silk stuff (from China), candy, sàndal, scents, and these articles and salt were carried into the interior by means of waggons drawn by teams of oxen or buffaloes slowly trudging along through town and village, effecting exchanges with commodities for export. Tolls were paid on the way and the journey from the coast up the plateau and back again occupied many months. A brisk and thriving commerce with the corresponding volume of internal trade argues peace, and the period to which the above description will apply must have been a period of general peace in the Peninsula. They did not forget in those days to maintain a regular customs establishment, the officials of which piled up the grain and stored up the things that could not immediately be measured and appraised, leaving them in the dockyards

[1] Paṭṭinappālai, 127 ff.

carefully sealed with the tiger signet of the king.[1] The Tamils built their own ships, and in the other crafts of the skilled artisan they seem to have attained some proficiency, though they availed themselves of experts from distant places. In the building of the royal palace at Puhār, skilled artisans from Magadha, mechanics from Marādam (Mahratta), smiths from Avanti (Malva) carpenters from Yavana worked[2] together. There is mention of a temple of the most beautiful workmanship in the same city, built of Gurjjara[3] workship. In the building of forts and in the providing of them with weapons and missiles, both for offence and defence, the Tamils had attained to something like perfection. Twenty-four such weapons are mentioned among the defences of Madura.[4]

Sources of Information.

I now proceed to consider the sources of the information which are the classical writers, Indian literature, Tamil and Sanskrit, and the

---

[1] Paṭṭinappalai, 134-6, Śilappadhikāram, Canto. VI, ll 2-39.

[2] Maṇimēkhalai, Canto XIX, l. 107 ff.

[3] *Ibid*, XVII, l. 145. This has reference to the small temple of Champapāti the Guardian-deity of Jambudvīpa. The Tamil *kuchchara* can have a number of equivalents in Sanskrit and Prakrit one of which of course is Gurjjara. If it is proved that the Gurjjaras were unknown in India before the end of the fifth century A. D. this equation with Gurjjara will have to be given up. Apart from this it is possible we get a more satisfactory equivalent. Either way this cannot be held to be a decisive test of chronology.

[4] Śilappadhikāram, Canto XV, ll. 207-17.

Ceylonese chronicle. Of the first group, Strabo wrote in the reigns of Augustus and Tiberius; Pliny published his geography in A. D. 77; the Periplus of the Erythræan Sea was written in the first century A. D., probably A. D. 60; Ptolemy wrote his geography about A. D. 150; the Peutingerian Tables were composed in A. D. 232. There were other writers who wrote later, but we are not concerned with them directly. I would draw attention to three points, taken from the works of classical writers. Pliny remarks: At the present day voyages are made to India every year, and companies of archers are carried on board, because the Indian seas are infested by pirates. Later on he says: It (Muziris) is not a desirable place of call, pirates being in the neighbourhood, who occupy a place called Nitrias, and besides it is not well supplied with wares for traffic. This was before A. D. 77. Ptolemy regarded this port Muziris as an emporium, and places the country of Aioi south of Bakarai. Though Ptolemy does mark the division of the Konkan coast extending northwards of Nitra (Nitrias of Pliny) and up to the port of Mandagara which is identified with some place not yet definitely accepted in the southern Maharatta country north of Goa, as Ariake Andron Peiration, meaning the Ariake of the pirates in his time, says no more of pirates at all, meaning there was no piracy at the time to which his work relates, a period not far from him. The Periplus on the contrary does make mention of the piratic character of this coast and gives a straightforward account of its active prevalence at the time in regard to the ports in the neighbourhood. The bearing of this we shall see presently.[1]

---

[1] The following account from Marco Polo of this coast is worth noting :—There go forth every year more than a hundred corsair vessels on cruise. These pirates take with them their wives and children and stay out the whole summer. Their method is to join in fleets cf 20 or 30 of these pirate vessels together, and then they form what they call a sea cordon, that is they drop off till there is an interval of 5 or 6 miles between ship and ship, so that they cover something like a hndred miles of sea, and no merchant ship can escape them. For when any one corsair sights a vessel a signal is made by fire or smoke and then the whole of them make for this and seize the merchants and plunder them. After they have plundered them they let them go saying go along with you and get more gain, and that may-hap will fall to us also.

He also notes in respect of the kingdom of Eli the following :—

If any ship enters their estuary and anchors there having been bound for some other port, they seize her and plunder the cargo. For they say, you were bound for somewhere else, and it is God has sent you hither to us, so we have a right to all your goods. And they think it is no sin to act thus. And this naughty custom prevails all over the provinces of India, to wit, that if a ship is driven by stress of weather into some other port than that to which it was bound, it was sure to be plundered. But if a ship came bound originally to the place they receive it with all honour and give it due protection.

It would be interesting to note, as Yule remarks, that it was in this neighbourhood that Ibn Batuta fell into the hands of pirates and was stripped to the very drawers." That region continued to be piratical up to the days of Clive and Watson as we know. In the days of Sivaji it continued to be piratical also, as he is said to have replied to an English embassy protesting against this piracy that "it was

The *Peutinger an Tables* state clearly that two Roman Cohorts were maintained in the same town for the protection of Roman commerce.

Mr. Sewell who has made an elaborate study of the Roman coins found in India, considers that an examination of the coin finds leads to the following conclusions[1]:—

1. There was hardly any commerce between Rome and India during the Consulate.

2. With Augustus began an intercourse which enabling the Romans to obtain oriental luxuries during the early days of the empire, culminated about the time of Nero, who died A.D. 68.

3. From this time forward the trade declined till the death of Caracalla, A.D. 217.

4. From the death of Caracalla it almost entirely ceased.

5. It revived again, though slightly, under the Byzantine emperors.

He also infers that the trade under the early emperors was in luxuries; under the later ones in industrial products, and under the Byzantines

---

against the laws of Conchon, to restore any ship or goods that were driven ashore." The Central Asian Ambassador Abd-er-Razzak has something to say of pirates near the Calicut coast. Marco-Polo, Yule and Cordier. (3rd Edn.) III Chap. XXIV and XXV, pp. 385-392.

[1] J. R. A. S. 1904, p. 591.

the commerce was with the south-west coast only, and not with the interior. He differs from those who find an explanation of this fluctuation in the political and social condition of India itself, and the facilities or their absence for navigating the seas; and considers that the cause is to be sought for in the political and social condition of Rome.

From an examination of the second class of my sources of information alone, we find that there was a period when South India was under great rulers, who gave the country peace and thus provided the indispensable security for commerce. This period can be shown to correspond to that of the Roman empire from Augustus to Caracalla. After this period we find the country in a condition of political flux. So then we may still find one, at least, of the most potent causes of this commercial decline in the internal condition of India itself. Pliny and Ptolemy do not mention the Roman cohorts at Muziris which the *Peutingerian Tables* do. The first exploit of the Red-Chera's father is the destruction of the Kaḍambu[1] tree of the sea. Another compliment that the poets never miss an opportunity of bestowing upon this Red-Chēra himself is that the Chēra fleet sailed on the waters of that littoral with a

[1] Padiṟṟappattu II, 11, ll. 12-13 11. 12,-13 11, 17, ll. 5-6.

sense of dominion and security.[1] The Kaḍambu mentioned above is explained as a tree of extraordinary magic powers which could not be cut down by ordinary man. I rather think from the context that it has reference to a piratical rendezvous of the tribe of people who were known as the Kaḍambas. This view seems to be directly countenanced by the extract 3 in the note before the last which says in effect that he crossed the sea, destroyed the Kaḍambu and brought his enemies to subjection.[2] If this view is correct, the advent of the said Chera brought along with it security. This would be in conformity with Ptolemy's reference to Āay, who was one of the seven chieftains known to literature as "the last seven patrons." From the body of works known to Tamil scholars as the Śangam works their contemporaneity could easily be established. I find the name Aay a distinctive name of two individuals, and not quite of a family. The

---

[1] Puram 128, Marokkattu Nappasalaiyār, on Malaymān Tirumudik-Kāri.

[2] It would be nothing surprising if the Kaḍambu tree, the country-date or some tree like it had been the tree-totem of this tribe. One tree in particular might have been regarded as peculiarly sacred by the tribe like the famous Oak at Dodono of the Ancient Greeks, or the slightly less famous oak trunk of the Saxons of the days of Charlemagne. Su h trees with the Tamils were called guard trees and cutting them down was an invitation to a war to the death; *cf.* the margossa tree of Paḻaiyan.

Āay must harve been the contemporary of, or a little older than Ptolemy, and the age of Ptolemy would practically be the age of the Red Chēra, and the Chēra ascendancy. This conclusion only confirms what has been arrived at independently of this class of evidence. The Gajabāhu of Ceylon who visited the Red-Chēra almost at the end of his reign, ruled according to the Ceylonese chronicle from A.D.113 to 135. Even allowing for the difference between the Ceyloncse date of the Nirvana of the Buddha, and that arrived at by modern scholars as Dr. Fleet, namely 60 years, that date for Gajabahu would be A. D. 173 to 193. The Chera ascendancy then would cover the middle fifty years of the second century A.D. Here has to be brought in the Paisāchi work Bṛhat-Kathā. Śātavāhana or Śālivāhana was the ruler in whose court flourished the minister Guṇāḍhya, who was the author of this stupendous work which stands at the root of all romantic literature in India, Sanskrit or Vernacular, and may be of the rest of the world as well. It was this work that set the fashion for the composition of the romantic epics. The age of the original is still matter under investigation. The latest authority on the question is the Dutch scholar Speyer who would place it in the third century A.D. at the earliest—a date clearly impossible according to our line of inquiry.[1] I shall not say more about it here; but only remark that one of the works clearly based upon this, has to be referred to a period anterior to the astronomer Varāhamihira, A.D. 533. This work Maṇimēkhalai refers to the asterism under which the Buddha was born as the fourteenth which according to modern computation following Varāhamihira ought to be the sixteenth.[2] The Ceylon chronicle also deserves to be given more credit than heretofore. So far investigations from different points of view only appear to confirm its chronology.

The date of the death of the Roman Emperor Caracalla corresponds closely to the disappearance of the Śātavāhanas of the Dakhan. According to the latest opinion the power of the Kushanas also vanished about the same period. In South India likewise the Pāṇḍya ascendancy passes into darkness.

This prosperous and flourishing Roman trade with India lasted over a little more than two centuries, as we saw, beginning almost from the reign of Augustus and coming to an end practically with the death of Caracalla. In India

[1] The Maṇimēkhalai knew the story as the Kasmirian Somadeva knew it, referring to the imprisonment of Udayana, the Vatsaraja, in Ujjain, and the stratagem by which Yaugandharāyaṇa brought about his escape.

[2] This can be otherwise explained as due to copying the older northern tradition irrespective of the date of the work containing the reference.

also the Kushana Empire in the north and that of the Andhras in the Dakhan and the rule of the Tamil kings in the South come to an eclipse almost about the same time, as the rise of Sassanid power in Persia. What may be the exact connection between the rise of the Sassanian power on the one hand and of the extinction of the Indian powers on the other has to be unveiled by future research. It is however clear that Roman commerce suffered practically, because of the rise of this power which interposed itself along the route of Roman commerce overland and perhaps to a smaller extent across the long over-sea route. The Persian Gulf route passed effectively under the control of the Sassanids, who seem early to have exerted themselves to capture the trade of the Arabs and whose efforts had succeeded so far in it that they could extend their voyages of commerce across the whole width of the Indian ocean and venture as far as the Shantung Peninsula in China. While the rise of this power seems to have diminished the maritime enterprise of the Tamils in the Arabian Sea region, it did not actually extinguish it. It left the Tamil enterprise across the Bay of Bengal unaffected although not altogether alone.

From what has already been said above, it is clear that the Tamils of South India had commenced their colonial enterprise across the Bay of Bengal earlier than we know anything of. The familiarity with which Śāvakam and the voyages thereto are spoken of, and the description of the imports into the port of Tonḍi in the Ramnad District and Kaveripatam at the mouth of the river Kaveri, which answer detail after detail to what we learn from the Periplus and Ptolemy, warrant the inference that the Tamils had an established system of over-seas trade on this side of the coast of the peninsula. Taken as a whole then, the knowledge we gain of the over-seas enterprise of the Tamils reaches back to times perhaps centuries before the age of the classical literature from which these details are gained. The ship coins of the Andhras whose provenance according to Sir Walter Elliot is the coast region between the two Pennārs, north and south, the region pre-eminently of a class of people known by the name Tiraiyar, goes only to confirm what we learn from Tamil literature. What is more we hear of a class of merchants described in Tamil as mā-śāttu-vāṇigam (Sans. mahā-sārtha-vaṇik) as great sea-going merchants, indicates the existence of a class of people whose profession it was to trade over-seas. When actually this communication began we are not in a position to state, but that there was something like a settled communication and regular voyage of commerce cannot be doubted. This prevalence of communication between

South India on the one side and the Malaya peninsula and the islands on the other, is confirmed in a very unlooked-for fashion by the recently discovered Koetei inscription to which we have already referred. That Brahmans emigrated to the distant east, as far east as the east coast of Borneo, and the character of the emigrant colony, make it indubitable that this was an emigration from South India, probably from the region of the early Pallavas.

Among the ruins of monuments discovered all over this region, both in Further India and the islands, the general position seems to be that the earliest monuments have reference to the worship of Vishṇu, according to recognised authorities. Śaivism followed, these two being followed later by Buddhism. This order of succession not necessarily exclusively so, seems to be the case in regard to further India as far as exploration work has gone on there. A similar conclusion seems warranted from all that we know of monumental Java as the position is explained by the explicit statement of Fa-hien in regard to his own Java which must be the same as Ptolemy's Sabadiu and the Tamil Śāvakam. That this Java is Sumatra and not the island Java, as we know at present, may now be stated with confidence for the following reasons, summarised by Colonel Gerini as a result of an elaborate investigation in his researches on Ptolemy's Geography, pp. 462.

"As to the name Jāva being applied to the whole or part of Sumatra, we have the evidence, (1) of the Kēdāh Annals (Ch. 13, Low's translation in Journal of Indian Archipelago, Vol. III) that Achin or Acheh, was called the country of Jawi (Javi) ; (2) of Ibn Batuta, who records Sumatra in 1345-46 under the name of "Island of Jāwah (or Java)" (See "Defremrey and Sanguinetti," Ed. and Trans., Vol., IV, p. 228) and (3) the still more decisive and far older testimony of the Pāgar-ruyāng inscription in the central part of the island (Menang-Kabau district), dating from A.D. 656, where King Aditya-dharma is called the ruler of the "First (or Primeval) land of Java," *Prathama-Yava-Bhū*, meaning, apparently, the first kingdom founded by the Yava or Java race in Sumatra, or, still better, in the Archipelago (see J. Bom. R.A.S., June 1861, Appendix, p. lxvii). It should moreover be noted that the natives of Nias speak of the Malays of Sumatra as *Dawa*, a term which evidently is but a corruption of Jawa or Java, especially as the Battak apply to the same people on their borders the slightly different denomination of Jau."

This Śāvakam was known to the Tamils as a kingdom ruled over by a king by a name Bhūmi -chandra. The name of his queen was Amara Sundari and both of them brought up a child, an avatār of Buddha, somewhat miraculously born of a cow. But the geographical detail in connection with this story is that it had for its capital a town known as Nāgapuram (see Maṇimekhalai). Colonel Gerini in his Researches labours hard to explain what Ptolemy's Argyre,[1] the capital of his Iabadiu or Savadiu actually was, and identifies it with Achin or Acheh on the north-west coast of Java. If Nāgapuram was the capital of Śāvagam, the capital of Sabadiu must be the equivalent of Nāgapuram. Ptolemy's Argyre does not come any way near it at first sight, but this Nāgapuram passes by the alternative designation Bhogavatīpura, and has yet another alternative Uragapura which comes nearest to Argyre. It is well known that Kāḷidāsa speaks of the capital of the Pāṇḍyas as Uragapura,[2] meaning thereby that the capital of the Pāṇḍyas was in his time known Uragapura. To the classical Tamils, although Madura is by far the most familiar, the term Ālavāy or Hālāsya (abr. of Hāla-hālāsya) was not unfamiliar. If the Tamil name Śāvakam was due to Tamil, the capital may well be ascribed to the same source, and if the capital city had been founded under the auspices of Madura, it might well take the name Uragapura giving Ptolemy his equivalent Argyre. Whether Uragapura in its alternative form

---

[1] *Opus, cit.*, pp. 656. ff.

[2] Raghuvaṁśa, Canto VI, Śloka 59.

Bhogavatīpura is actually responsible for the term Śrī-Bhoja for the later capital of Sumatra is more than we can assert at present. Hence it would be more reasonable from every point of view to regard Sumatra as the "Prathama Yava," the other island Java being so called by the immigrants from this original Jāva. As we pass from Fa-hien to the other Chinese traveller to whom we are indebted for a considerable volume of information regarding Java, we find a different state of things from the point of view of religion. This traveller I-tsing left the Shantung peninsula in a Persian ship and came down to Srī-Bhoja; proceeded from there to Tamra-lipti and travelled therefrom in India learning Sanskrit and collecting manuscripts bearing on Buddhism. Having lived a number of years in India, he returned to Śrī-Bhoja with hundreds of manuscripts. After taking a holiday home, he returned with several collaborators to Śrī-Bhoja. He stayed some years there and completed the translations of several of the manuscripts he had collected and sent home 500 volumes of translations. He settled down in Śrī-Bhoja for the obvious reason that he commanded the convenience for carrying on his literary labours. The period of his travels cover the last quarter of the seventh century. He then found the kingdom of Śrī-Bhoja which exercised authority not only over its own territory, but over the islands and principalities across the straits in the Malaya peninsula, so that we might say that the period of expansion of the kingdom of Śrī-Bhoja had already begun. He was hospitably treated and was provided with a state ship by the Maharajah of Śrī-Bhoja, who apparently supplied him with all requirements for conducting his literary labours after his return from India. The country was then essentially Buddhist. The change from just the beginnings of Buddhistic influence in the age of Fa-hien, to the dominance of Buddhism during I-tsing's stay in the island, gives us clearly to understand that the intervening centuries, the fifth, sixth and the seventh centuries of the Christian era, constitute the period of Buddhistic outspread in this region. It may be due to the influence of Buddhistic scholars like Buddha ghosha, who is said to have travelled from Ceylon to Burma on a religious mission. Either he himself or others like him, before and after, were responsible for this expansion of Buddhism. This does not seem unlikely as we know that the sixth century South India contributed three successive principals to the Nālanda University of whom perhaps the most distinguished was Dharmapāla of Kānchī. When Hiuen-tsang was in Kānchī, he had to cancel the project of going to Ceylon, where he wanted to learn certain parts of the Buddhist Vinaya. During his stay in Kānchī there arrived a number of Buddhist divines from Ceylon to Kānchī and they told him that the island was so disturbed by internecine war that it would not be worth his while going there then. When he told them what exactly his mission was, they undertook to instruct him themselves as they were by far the most learned in that particular section. This disturbed state of the country relates to the middle of the seventh century. Some of the Buddhists from Ceylon might have found asylum in Śrī-Bhoja, and that perhaps was the reason why in I-tsing's days Śrī-Bhoja had become a great Buddhist centre. Whatever the cause, Śrī-Bhoja in which I-tsing stayed was an important Buddhist centre where he could carry on his literary labours quite as well as in Nālanda itself, the climate of which was unsuitable to the Chinese scholar. Hence we see the outspread of religion from South India into the islands of the Archipelago probably was in the same order chronologically as in the case of Further India, namely, Vaishṇavism, Śaivism, and Buddhism, and that is what we discovered is the exact order in respect of the archæological monuments in Java. The most remarkable ones such as the Boro-Boudur are entirely Buddhist and this Java monument is described by competent authority (such as Prof. Foucher) to belong to the eighth or the ninth century A.D. In the central province of Java however on the heights of the mountains could be discovered ruins of temples dedicated to Śiva considered to belong to a period not later than the seventh or the eighth century. In the western part of Sumatra island however, Sanskrit inscriptions of a Vaishṇava character have been found. And these are ascribed to the period about A.D. 450 to 600. This according to Colonel Gerini indicates the order of religious overflow from Sumatra into Java. This, so far from the point of view of India, is essentially a question of wherefrom the emigrants started and to what particular region of South India they belonged. Vaishṇavism and Śaivism flourished side by side at the dawn of the Christian era and they could both of them have gone eastwards at any time since that period. If it should have been that the first colony went from the region of the Pallavas that is from the country extending from the mouth of the Krishna to that of the S. Peṇṇār, naturally Vaishṇavism would have been established first. Whatever was the origin of this chronological order, there is no question about the order itself. The Koetei inscription is evidence of the spread of Vedic Brahmans from South India. The Takopa inscription on a stone found near the mouth of the river Takopa in the Malaya Peninsula is again in Pallava characters of the seventh or the early eighth century, and relates to a Vishṇu temple of Nārāyaṇa Vēṇugopāla on the top of a hill called Nārāyaṇa higher up the river. The actual purport of this inscription is the construction of a tank near the temple, and the placing of it under the protection of certain communities of people described as Sēna-mukham, Maṇigrāmam, and Chāpattār (?). The first seems to refer to a military force, Sēna-mukham being explained as "the Royal Guards"; Maṇigrāmam is a well-known mercantile community of the west coast and "Chāpattār," the last, if the reading of the first part is quite correct (it is rather doubtful), would mean "body of archers." Maṇigrāmam is certain indication of a colony from the west coast. The origin of the colony would explain the Vaishṇava character of the settlement. So far then we see the influence of South India to have continued intact, and the period ranging from before the days of Ptolemy right on to the beginning of the tenth century almost may be regarded as the period of the greatest South Indian influence in this part of Asia.

During the period extending from the first quarter of the seventh century onwards, a new influence began to be felt in the rise and expansion of Islam in Arabia. The fall of Persia as a result of the successful war conducted by Khalif Omar introduced a new political element in mid-Western Asia which was likely to exercise a considerable influence upon Indian Ocean navigation. We hear of descents of Arab Muhammadan fleets on the coasts of the northern Konkan and the region of Sindh in the reign of Omar himself. But the Persians under the Sassanids seem to have established themselves so well on the Indian Ocean, that even this conquest did not displace Persian nautical enterprise in the eastern arm of the Indian Ocean. Late in the seventh century, the Persians so far maintained themselves as to carry on a regular trade, as far east as the Shantung Peninsula. That I-tsing travelled in a Persian ship from the Shantung Peninsula to Śrī-Bhoja in the island of Sumatra is the clearest possible evidence of it. At the same time the fact that I-tsing performed the rest of his journey to Tāmralipti in a ship provided by the Mahārāja of Śrī-Bhoja is equally a clear indication of the rising sea-power of this enterprising state of Sumatra. While therefore the Arab and Persian had to carry on eastern trade in a friendly rivalry, this new element of a native power in Sumatra was somewhat disconcerting to the rivals themselves. It cannot be stated that during this period the Hindus of South India and Bengal, and the inhabitants of Ceylon necessarily ceased their maritime activities. The Takopa inscription already adverted to, is evidence of some enterprise, as it happens, on the part of the colonists from the region of the Malabar coast; but more than that, this was the age of Buddhistic outspread from South India, and all this expansion, it would be difficult to assert, took place by means of available foreign shipping. The fact that an invasion set out from the coasts of the Pallava country against Ceylon consisting of a fleet of 300 ships is certain indication that nautical efforts on the Tamil coasts had not come to an end. A Tamil poet could still speak in the eighth century of ships bringing elephants and gold and lying in harbour at Mahabalipuram (the Seven-Pagodas of Anglo-India). There are records of several invasions of Ceylon and the West-Coast by the Cholas; what is more, of a greater invasion fitted out and sent against Rāmañña, the ruler of Pegu by the great Ceylon Buddhist King Parākramabāhu. The sounder conclusion from the available evidence therefore is that these had all traded together in peaceful rivalry during this period.

The rise of the kingdom of Śrī-Bhoja and the prominent position that it occupied when I-tsing was on his travels in India, that is, in the latter half of the seventh century A. D., was the beginning of a career of expansion for this kingdom. The number of references that we get to missions sent from this kingdom to China and the early references in Muhammadan Arab travellers, gives us clearly to understand that the kingdom of Śrī-Bhoja beginning as a small state was fast advancing to what might be described as a sort of imperial position in the Eastern Seas. Sulaiman (A. D. 851) speaking of Zabej says "that the entire region obeys a single king." Both Ibn-Khurda-dbih (A. D. 864) and Abu-Zaid of the later ninth century have much the same thing to say of the Mahārāja of Zabej. He is said to rule over a large number of islands stretching for a distance of a thousand parasangas (2,400 miles). Among his possessions are counted (1) Sarbaza or Serboza both of them alike standing for Śrī-Bhoja (modern Palembang), (2) Rami producing camphor (this Rami is the same as Lambri or Lameri including in it Fansur or Barus (camphor forests) and (3) Kālah on the Malay Peninsula. According to Ibn Khurda-dbih, it was ruled over by the Jaba prince of India (ruler of Pegu). But Abu-zaid includes it in the territory of the Mahārāja of Śrī-Bhoja. This position given to it in the ninth century is confirmed by later writers, those that obtained their information from previous writers, as well as those who wrote from first-hand information of their own. What we learn therefore from Arab writers would justify the inference that in the centuries of Chola ascendancy in South India, Śrī-Bhoja was the dominant power in the Archipelago. It is apparently of one of these rulers that Renaudot records a somewhat legendary story of invasion of what seems the Pāṇḍya country for the purpose of punishing the contemporary Pāṇḍya ruler for having spoken ill of the great Mahārāja.

To the Tamilian rulers however, across the Bay of Bengal, the Mahārājas of Śrī-Bhoja were rulers of Kaḍāram; as such they are brought to our notice in a few records relating to them. In regard to the identification of the rulers of Kaḍāram with the Mahārāja of Śri-Bhoja, the evidence has been discussed elsewhere.[1]

A ruler of Kaḍāram by name Chuḍāmaṇi Varman applied for permission and obtained a license from the great Chola Rāja raja for the building of a *vihāra* in Negapatam which is called in the record Chuḍāmaṇi Vihāra. About the same time an embassy went from him to China, asked for the blessings of "His Celestial Majesty" for a new vihāra that he built and obtained from him approval of the name and the presentation of bells. The vihāra perhaps was not completed in the time of Chuḍāmaṇi Varma. His son Māra Vijayottunga Varma purchased and made over to this vihāra two villages, the record conveying which is known to epigraphists by the name, "the large Leyden Grant." This is a Chola charter on copper-plates licensing or ratifying this transaction. This relationship apparently continued for about twenty years, when for

[1] Rājēndra, the Gangaigoṇḍa Chola in the Sir Asutosh Commemoration Volumes: Vol. III, Calcutta University.

some reason or other a cause of war had arisen. An expedition was fitted out against this Rāja of Kaḍāram, known this time Sangrāma Vijaya-uttunga Varma, probably the son and successor of Māra Vijaya-uttunga Varma. As is explained in the article quoted above, Rājēndra had, as a necessary preliminary to conquer Orissa, as the royal families of Orissa and Śrī-Bhoja appear to have been related to each other, both of them belonging to Śrī Śailēndra Vaṁśa. The war which Rājēndra carried on as far as the banks of the Ganges, and the thorough-going way that he carried it to bring the Kalinga rulers to submission to him were both necessitated for the safety of his own flank. One possible cause of this invasion oversea seems to be that the Tamil states in the east were being absorbed by the ruler of Śrī-Bhoja in his imperial expansion. The several embassies referred to in the record of the Chinese trade superintendent Chau-Ju-Kua,[1] and the one in particular of date A. D. 1033 from a Lo-Cha-Into-Lo Chulo is from Śrī-Rājēndra Dēva Chola, that is, Rājēndra the Gangaigonḍa had probably the same object in view. This distant embassy was apparently sent by Rājēndra with a view to putting matters on a permanent footing in

---

[1] Translated by Dr. Hirth in J. R. A. S., 1896, p. 489. Republished in book form in 1912 by F. Hirth and W. W. R. rockhill. See also Gerini *opus cit*, p. 609, Note 2.

respect of his eastern territory across the seas. The last mission we hear of, is of date A.D. 1077 from the Chola country belonging to the reign of the great Chola ruler Kulottunga, A.D. 1070 to 1118. The Sung history relating to this mission states that Chu-lien (the Chola country) had become tributary to San-fo-ch'i (Śrī Vijaya of the time) which seems to be the name that Śrī-Bhoja assumed at that time. The Sung reference cannot therefore be to the Chola country on the peninsula of India. It is apparently to the Chola possessions on the East coast and the islands of the Bay of Bengal. We do not hear of any relation between the Chola country and the east after this period, and therefore the inference seems safe that the Chola overseas dominance was thenceforward as good as given up. The century following is a century of the decline of the Chola power and a revival of that of the Pāṇḍyas. The great Pāṇḍya king who ruled from A.D. 1268 to 1310-11 had considerable maritime trade both with the west, as far as, at any rate, the Persian Gulf, if not Arabia, and as far east as China. But this vast trade which was the cause of the prosperity of the vast Pāṇḍya kingdom seems to have been in the hands of a chief of Arab Muhammadans whose head-quarters were in the Persian Gulf in the island of Kis or Kais. He was known by the title Malik-ul-Islam Jamalu-d-din and had not only the monopoly of the horse trade of the Pāṇḍya kingdom, but seemed also to have enjoyed the control of the eastern trade. His first agent Abdur-Rahiman-ut-Thaibi had his head-quarters at Kāyal, the chief port in the south-east of the Pāṇḍya country, and had control of the whole coasting trade. It was a cousin of this agent, a Jamalu-d-din (Chamalatang), who went on a mission to China on behalf of the great Pandya king Kulaśēkhara. This transformation, the trade passing from the hands of the natives of South India into the hands of the Arab agents of the local monarchs, seems to have come about in the course of the decline of the Chola power. The inference then is that the Cholas were the chief maritime power of the Coromandal coast, and that their decline meant the decline of the maritime activity of the Tamils.

The Arab Muhammadans must have for some considerable time settled down along this coast for purposes of trade. We have already stated that there were small settlements of these even in a town like Kaveripatam. That state of things must have continued, and it was probably the passing of the bulk of the eastern trade under their control, and of the Coromandal coast proving the exchange mart between the goods from the west and goods from the east, that explains the Arab name Ma'bir (landing-place) which the Arabs gave to the South Indian coast extending from Quilon to Nellore according to Wassaf. It is just about this time of the rising of the Arab agencies on the Indian coast that were founded a number of settlements of these Arabs along the Ceylon coast as well. It is to this age that is again ascribed the gaining of sufficient influence by the Arabs on the north coast of Java, wherefrom by a few important conversions to Mahammadanism they began to exercise that influence that ultimately led to Java, and the islands adjoining, adopting the Mahammadan faith. It is this conversion to Mahammadanism of the East Indian Archipelago that is responsible for the cessation of the Hindu maritime enterprise in the east. It does not appear however to have ceased entirely. The famous charter to oversea traders granted by the Kākatīya king, Gaṇapati, and which is found recorded on the pillar at Moṭupalli near the mouth of the river Krishna, seems to have revived a little of the Hindu enterprise in this particular. The Telugu poet Śrīnātha in the dedication of his poem Harvilāsam to one Avachi Tippaiya Śetti of Nellore says, that Tippaiya Śetti had the monopoly of supplying all valuable articles to the great Dēvarāya II of Vijaynagar, to the Sultan Mahammad of the Bahmani kingdom and the Reḍḍi chief, Kumāragiri Reḍḍi of Konḍavīḍu. He is said to have "imported camphor-plants from the Punjab, gold from Jalanogi, elephants from Ceylon, good horses from Hurimanji (Ormuz), musk from Goa, pearls from Apaga, Musk from Choṭangi (Chautang or Drishadvati) and fine silks from China."

Whether we should take it that he got them all through the agency of the Mahammadan overseas merchants may be doubted. There is however the patent fact that, in the two and a half centuries of the ascendency of the Vijayanagar Empire in Southern India, something like 300 ports were open to trade along its coast. There is no reference to any effort on the part of this Empire to build up or maintain a navy. It is the want of a navy on the part of Vijayanagar and its failure to provide one that opened the way for the enterprise of foreigners, European foreigners, in this period in India.

This somewhat cursory survey of the maritme enterprise of the Hindus of South India makes it clear that the South Indian Hindus exhibited commendable enterprise oversea, and carried their civilisation and religion across the Bay of Bengal to the East Indian Archipelago in the centuries, perhaps anterior to the Christian era. With the dawn of the Christian era, this enterprise takes form and shape and we begin to see therefore communities of South Indian inhabitants along the eastern shores of the Bay of

Bengal. These communities began to grow and flourish to such an extent that they cease to be merely temporary trade settlements becoming permanent colonies of Hindus necessitating even a considerable amount of Brahman emigration essential to the life of the Hindu community as a whole. The whole turn that was given to the civilisation of the East Indian Archipelago is the form that religious and cultural development exhibited in South India. Vaishṇavism and Śaivism, or subsequently Southern or Hīnayānist Buddhism spread over from South India and Ceylon to the east, and gave rise to those magnificent monuments, some of which even excel those of the mother country. The character of these monuments as far as they could be studied from their ruinous condition, and the few inscriptions that have been discovered indicate unmistakably that the inspiration came from South India. The culture was South Indian undoubtedly. The cause of prosperity of these might be regarded as due to South India, as it is South Indian enterprise that built up the trade of the Archipelago and the Malay Peninsula with which it maintained a continuous trade in commodities of rare value, and gained from her the practical monopoly for several of them. In the development of a commerce from their exuberance of nature, South Indian Hindus played a prominent part. At one time it looked as though it had succeeded in establishing a Greater India; but the want of sustained enterprise in this particular, combined with efficient rivalries, stopped them short as soon as it was well on the way to its full development. This failure proved a vital defect in the imperial career of Vijayanagar, and made a permanent Hindu Empire in India impossible.

CHAPTER XIX.

ADMINISTRATIVE EVOLUTION IN SOUTH INDIA.

As a result of recent research work, chiefly epigraphical, it is now generally agreed that South India, particularly the Tamil country, had developed a good and thorough-going system of local administration under the Cholas. This period extends from the end of the ninth century to well-past the middle of the thirteenth century. The same system continued during the Pāṇḍya revival with hardly any difference. Even the Vijayanagar rulers did not interfere with the system as it then obtained, but much rather confirmed and continued it. As in this particular region, Mahammadan rule was of a very temporary character, the system continued down to the British times, that is, down to the commencement of the nineteenth century when the East India Company took over the administration of various parts of South India. It can therefore be safely stated that the system continued more or less unchanged except under the British. Under the Cholas, the system stands revealed to us Minerva-like in full working order. When it actually did come into existence, who had the credit of originating it would be interesting speculation, but with the material accessible to us, it could be nothing more than speculation.

The first certain historical glimpse we get of this part of India is in a somewhat specific statement of Megasthenes preserved to us through one of his many successors who have, each in his own way, handed down to us such of the details recorded by Megasthenes as interested him. He says that Herakles begot a daughter in India, whom he called Pandaia. He is said to have assigned to her the part of India lying to the southward and extending to the sea. Herakles divided this territory into 365 villages and so arranged matters that each village brought into the royal treasury its revenue on a particular day so that the 365 villages brought in the revenues in the 365 days, obviously of the year. This arrangement is said to have been made with a view to giving the queen the assistance of the guard that brought in the tribute, so as to enable her to compel defaulters to pay up with their assistance if need be. He states that this queen had an army of 500 elephants, 4,000 cavalry and 130,000 infantry. She is said to have possessed great treasure in the fishery for pearls which according to Arrian were greatly prized by the Greeks and the Romans. This is the first clear statement that we get in regard to a governmental organisation in South India. The introduction of Herakles and the doubt among scholars as to the exact Indian deity for whom the Greek Herakles is made to stand would vitiate the correctness of the details given by Megasthenes. While differences of opinion may be possible in regard to the particulars, there could be no reasonable difference of opinion in regard to the part of the country under reference. This is the part of the country extending southward to the sea, obviously the peninsular part of India corresponding to the Strī-rājya of the Purāṇas, and what is more the specific mention of the pearl-fishery leaves no doubt that it is the Pāndya country, that is under reference in this passage from Megasthenes. Tamil tradition knows of a queen, daughter of the first king, Sundara, who is no less than God Śiva worshipped in the great temple at Madura. Being the only daughter she was heiress of the kingdom in her own right and probably it is this story that Megasthenes had heard of, thereby indicating that the tradition goes back, to an age anterior to Megasthenes. In this case Megasthenes' Herakles would be the equivalent of Śiva. The division of the territory into 365 villages or revenue units is an indication of early civil division of the Pāṇḍya territory. Some such division seems to have obtained in the age of the classical literature where we hear of divisions like Nāḍu and Vaḷanāḍu, explicitly and of fortresses dominating adjoining country. But anything like a clear and specific division of the country into various parts, and the actual organisation under which these parts were governed we are not enabled to see in this body of literature.

But we do gain a glimpse from the somewhat longstanding tradition regarding the country called the Toṇḍamanḍalam, that is the region extending between the two Peṇṇārs and surrounding Madras, the headquarters of the Presidency in modern times. This was originally forest country inhabited by people who were in the semi-nomadic stage of civilisation of cattle-rearers and cattle-lifters.

Civilisation was introduced into this country by the great Chola ruler, Karikāla, and his successor, through the agency of an illegitimate son, as tradition has it, who goes by the name Ādonḍai. This Ādonḍai was the valiant son of the Chola ruler through one of the women attendants of the palace and had been brought up secretly like a prince. He showed himself to be a young man full of spirit and fit to be entrusted with commissions worthy of royal princes. When the king discovered the young man, he entrusted to him the task of the conquest of the uncivilised region of Toṇḍamanḍalam. After several unsuccessful attempts against the fortress of Puḻal, which was the principal stronghold of these forest-folk, he ultimately captured the fortress through the miraculous intervention of Śiva himself.[1] Having brought the country under the authority of the Chola, the conquering prince was entrusted with the commission, under the authority of the said Chola himself, to reclaim the country to civilisation, and introduce the necessary means for its development. The very cultivators had to be introduced from the surrounding territory and as they could not be found in sufficient number for this vast region in the Chola country, they were imported from all over the surrounding region, quite a large number coming from Tuḷu. Hence down to the present times, the inhabitants of this region are composed of Veḷḷāḷas (land-holders and cultivators), who fall into several divisions, of whom the Ċhōlīya Veḷḷāḷa and Tuḷuva Veḷḷāḷa form the two principal sections. Before the introduction of these cultivators the country had to be secured and kept free of robbery by the predatory folk, who constituted its original population. This was done by clearing the better parts of the country and erecting in suitable localities 24 forts all over the region, each fort to dominate the country around it and be the citadel thereof. The country dependant on each fort

[1] This tradition finds reference in the Tēvāram of Sundara, early ninth century A.D. Tiruvada-Mullaivāyil 10.

was constituted into a division, to which the name of the dominating fort was given. Hence down to quite modern times, the region of the Toṇḍamaṇḍalam was divided into *Kōṭṭams*, the name of each one of which is derived from a fortified townlet or city. The larger divisions in this part of the country are therefore known by the term *koṭṭam* (Sansk. goshṭaka), answering to the *maṇḍalam* and *mahāmaṇḍalam* of the neighbouring regions. The survival of this division from a time long anterior to the great Cholas of South India confirms the tradition that this particular organisation had existed in early times. If a newly conquered territory had been thus organised, the presumption that the country already under a well organised government must have had a similar division would seem warranted. If the conquest and organisation was through the agency of the Cholas, it is perfectly natural that this organisation took on the form of the actual organisation then obtaining in the Chola country. The great Chola Karikāla, as is said in the poem Paṭṭinappālai, destroyed the forests where they existed, dug tanks where water facilities did not exist, and thus spread fertility over the region which for the far greater part of it, was remarkable for its unrivalled profusion. Whether this does not indirectly indicate his achievement in the conquest and civilisation of the Toṇḍamaṇḍalam does not seem to need discussion. It may be mentioned however that another old verse, relating to this Karikāla and his kingdom, states in so many words that the crops produced in other countries which watered by tanks and water-lifts would not equal the paddy gathered by gleaners after a harvest in the ancestral territory of the great Chola. This contains the clear indication that the efforts of the Chola to reclaim forest land and bring it under cultivation cannot be held to refer to the Chola country of his forefathers. Not very long after this age must have come in the rule of the Pallavas in the northern half of this region. One of the very earliest of the Pallava charters, the Mayidavolu grant, is a copper-plate charter which was issued from Conjeevaram by the then heir-apparent to the governor of this part of the country. The prince's name was Sivaskandavarman; but the father's name is not given; the latter is referred to however under the style "Bappadeva" which might mean, the revered father, as was pointed out already. What is of interest in this particular connection is that the prince issued the charter from the royal headquarters of Conjeevaram to what obviously was the provincial headquarters at Amarāvati in the Guntur district. The village granted is given the name Viripara [1] and is described as being

[1] There is a village of the name Vipparla about 12 miles west of Amarāvati.

situated in the Āndhra-pathā, the Vaḍugavaḷi of the Tamils, meaning the Andhra country of course. The royal charter granting this village was addressed by the prince to a hierarchy of officials which gives us an insight into the character of the political organisation of the country. As translated in the Epigraphia Indica it reads, "to the Lords of provinces, royal princes, agents, rulers of districts, customs officers, prefects of countries, etc."; but the original is capable of being rendered, "in all of this region, the royal prince, the general, the governors of districts, the customs officers and rulers of sub-divisions, those in the enjoyment of villages, the chiefs of cattle-herds and of cow-herds, ministers, officers of forests, commanders, peons, orderlies and others of our officers deputed by us on commissions, to tour the country."

This gives us the complete system of organisation that obtained in the government of this region. What is more it gives us clearly to understand that it is the kind of organisation we gain knowledge of in the Arthaśāstra. It shows further that this Mauryan organisation had been introduced in this remote part of the Dakhan, in all probability in the Mauryan age. The interesting question then would be whether the organisation, such as we are enabled to gain glimpses of in the Tamil country, is a copy of this. It would be reasonable to answer the question in the negative, so far as an actual copying of it is concerned, though one would notice a considerable similarity in the general character of these two organisations. It is impossible that some kind of an organisation should not have existed in the Tamil country before the forest region that intervened between the Krishna and the Kaveri had been brought into civilisation. The general lines of organisation however were not so different as between these two to make a ready assimilation impossible. As we shall see in the course of the later history of this territory, the unit of administration must have been the village or a group of villages. A certain geographical area containing a number of these units constituted a small division which in the Toṇḍamaṇḍalam was dominated by a fort, while in the Chola country an important town or city dominated it. A number of these bigger units taken together constituted a district; a number of these going to form a division giving us the regular gradation indicated both in the Chola division of administration and what we have already noticed in the Mayidavolu grant. That such divisions were not the inventions of the great Cholas is amply proved as these divisions are found recited in documents of the age of Pallava rule, certainly of the great Pallavas, extending from the commencement of the seventh century A.D. In all of these, and through all the periods of existence of this organisation, there is a well marked division of the sphere of the local and central governments recognised. All the officers mentioned in the Mayidavolu grant refer to a series composed of a certain number of royal officers; but these by themselves could not have been enough to carry on the administration. Even this small hierarchy could have exercised enough control and oversight, while the actual administration was carried on by local assistance. That is the feature that we find in full working order as we come to the age of the great Cholas for the very simple reason that we have access to a large number of official documents relative to Chola rule. The fact that such documents have not come down to us from an earlier period does not necessarily imply the absence of that kind of an organisation of the governing power. The one Mayidavolu grant is evidence of the existence of a similar organisation in the region of the Krishna river. Evidence in regard to the Tamil country is not however so direct for that early period.

Coming to the period of the great Pallavas we have a number of copper-plate charters issued by them, although they did not bear quite so largely and quite so directly upon matters of administration. Being the charters that they are, they give us a few glimpses of the organisation by means of which the administration was actually carried on. These generally show the same character of organisation that we find fully developed under the Cholas. The divisions of territory and the details of revenue and fiscal administration, as far as these charters give them, show the existence of an organisation quite similar to that which prevailed in the age of the Cholas. There is nothing in the now accessible documents to indicate that they were innovations by the Pallavas. At the very best the influence of the Pallavas might have gone to the extent of assimilating such organisations as existed in the Tamil country to that which obtained in the outermost southern frontier of the Mauryan empire of Asoka. We find no warrant for going farther in the direction of affiliating the one to the other.

The Tamil classic *Kuṛaḷ* to which reference had already been made, devotes the largest part of the work to Poruḷ (*Sans. Artha*, wealth) and deals with what might perhaps be indicated by the term political economy, a combined treatise on politics and economics. Like Sanskrit works bearing on the Arthaśāstra and Nītiśāstra, this section of the Kuṛaḷ has to do with the king and kingdom, even the abstract noun " state " being derived from a word standing for king. It would seem strange that there should have been no other organisation known than that of the kingly. It would be a mistake however to draw that inference. As in the Arthaśāstra so in this work the subject dealt with happens to be merely what would in modern language be called the central administration.

A central administration had to be superimposed upon such tribal and communal organisations as existed already when the state came to be recognised as such. This fundamental fact has to be clearly borne in mind in discussing the administrative organisation of the South of India. A similar caution seems necessary in respect even of other parts of India. What the text books teach us therefore is the character of the central organisation, which welded the local organisations for local purposes into one unity which might be the state of those times. The local organisations were certainly of a democratic character, and rested for certain purposes on the communal basis. The devolution of power was complete. The central organisation had merely the control of local administration, the maintenance of peace and order in the country, and providing for defence against external enemies. That being understood it is clear these begin with describing the king and defining the qualifications that go to make a good king. It was already pointed out in a previous section that this work exhibits considerable indebtedness to the Arthaśāstra ; the one chapter bearing on *upada*, makes escape from this conclusion impossible. Like the Arthaśāstra, the king is described as possessing the six *angas* such as the *army*, *people*, *wealth*, *counsel*, *friendship and fortresses*, or defences ; together with the king himself, it makes the total seven *angas* of royalty. He is to be easily accessible and one that speaks softly and pleasantly. If he deal out justice and protect the people from injustice, he comes to be regarded as a god on earth for his subjects. A king educated in the functions of royalty would find happiness only in the happiness of his subjects, a statement that reminds one of an important sentence in the proclamation of Queen Victoria. These are some of the personal qualities of the king according to this work, parallels to which one could find repeated in the course of the Sanskrit Rāmāyaṇa. The work goes on to describe the objects of rule as the maintenance of *Dharma* ; and this can be best obtained by the choice of suitable persons, well-born, and well-educated to assist him. He is to make the choice of his ministers on the lines laid down by Chāṇakya by subjecting them to temptations with the four objects of desire, and accept those who show themselves to be beyond temptation. He has to see to the spreading of fertility over the land and the removal of obstacles that may come in the way of prosperity. His rule of righteousness is at the root even of the Vedas of the Brahmans who, if his rule were otherwise, would forget the Veda. Each one of the six *angas* then comes in for description in turn.

The minister must be a man fully informed in the knowledge of the duties of a king, equipped with learning by means of which to enforce those duties upon all about, and possessed of the skill and judgment to adopt the proper means for carrying out his object. In this manner each of the angas gets described and the whole of this political science occupies about 70 chapters, out of the 133 chapters of the work ; that is, just a little more than half of it. But the point to be noticed here, as in the Nīti Śāstras of Sanskrit Literature, is that all this applies to the central government.

Such as it is described here the government seems at first sight to be an autocratic power dependant entirely upon the will of the individual man who occupies the throne for the time being. So it appears at first sight ; on a careful analysis however it will be found that it is hedged in by so many restrictions, all of them enforceable by the will of the community so long as that community had an organisation to express that will. Such an organisation was provided by the assembly of ministers, who constituted five groups. These were the priest, the great accountant, the Brahman judges, the tax-collectors and the secretarial establishment; that is how the old classic 'Śilappadhikāram' defines it. Of these groups two were composed of individuals. The other three constituted boards, apparently with establishments of their own. When a king died, it was the charge of this "group of five" to consider what had next to be done, the choice of a successor, even where the succession was hereditary and the making of the arrangements for the carrying on the administration. It is in a connection like that, that this group of people are brought in in the work under reference. In another connection, regarding the consecration of a temple only the first three of these figure along with the sculptors and architects. Thus then this council had a recognised standing, and they were susceptible to public opinion. What the force of that public opinion was, and how far it expressed itself effectively we have no means of ascertaining definitely. But as we shall see the documents that issued under the Chola administration do require the counter-signature of two at least of the ministers for their validity, an indication of their responsibility in regard to the matter. These ministers are referred to as men of unchanging word and appeared like the four divisions of the foreign Kośar, omitting the accounts officers in that particular, by the author of the poem *Maduraik-Kāñji.* That would mean that these ministers were expected to speak their minds fearlessly and did do so oftentimes.

The central administration thus constituted had first of all to provide for the defences of the country by occupying the frontier fortresses provided with adequate defences both in material and men. They had to see to the prevalence of peace and goodwill within the country by interceding in disputes between communities and corporations. They had to be constantly on the look-out for means of increasing the prosperity and fertility of the country, thereby increasing their own revenues and warding off such evils as may befall the people or their property and interfere with the prosperity of the community as a whole. There their duties ended.

Local administration was carried on entirely by popular assemblies constituted under a form of election and lot combined so that these administrative bodies may be regarded as aristocratic in character with a democratic responsibility. Elaborate regulations were laid down for their constitution. Serious misdemeanour disabled not only the individual, but all of his relations of the first degree from the exercise of political franchise. Judgment in regard to the misdemeanour was the judgment of the community, and that was perhaps the most effective way possible then of making representatives responsible to the community as a whole. The property qualification was the possession of about an acre and a half of land. The alternative educational qualification laid down consisted in the capacity to recite a Veda in the orthodox fashion or the capacity to expound one of the Brahmanas, which required perhaps a more or less equal degree of intelligence and effort. A town or a community was divided into wards, according to size and the worthy men in the wards were registered. From out of this group of the worthy men, the men that actually constituted the administrative bodies, were chosen by lot. The village accountant was the umpire in all matters of dispute and had to hold himself unconcerned in matters of material interest with the various communities constituting the township. A large committee thus chosen was broken up into sub-committees, generally into 5 or 6, each with its duty defined. There were committees for the supervision of tanks, committees for looking after temples, and a number of other committees like that. One committee however seems to stand out distinct from all these. It is called by the compound name *panchavāravāriyam.* The last word '*vāriyam*' seems to mean control, training or discipline, such as in the expression *vāśi-vāriyan* or horse-trainer. These were probably men who had to control the affairs of the community generally from day to day, and the previous word *pancha* seems to indicate that that body was composed of five members. That was the supreme *panchāyat*, under whose control, the various committees carried on the details of the administration. Where general matters were concerned, they were brought before the assembly as a whole and discussed, and resolutions were arrived at. It was the duty of the village accountant to keep a faithful record of all these and that is why he was expected to keep himself uncontaminated by the party politics of that locality.

These local bodies practically controlled all revenue matters included in the revenue administration of modern times. They had charge of the communal lands; they controlled the division of land among the members of the community under their charge. They arranged for the reclamation of uncultivated wastes by giving them to enterprising cultivators on favourable terms beginning with free cultivation gradually rising through a series of years to the normal revenue roll of the district according to the quality of the land. If individuals or communities or even royalty wished to purchase lands to make gifts to temples, the Brahmans or to some other party or body, the village assembly had to make the necessary preliminary enquiries, assessed the value of the land, arranged for its purchase and completed the transaction. It is on a satisfactory report from them that the final order for the conveyance of the property was made from the head-quarters. The community received the compensation in the case of communal lands and administrated it at their discretion. It was they that estimated the outturn of particular holdings and assessed the revenue thereon, which sometimes was less than the dues according to the revenue register, sometimes even exceeding it. The state seems however to have carried out general surveys and classification of lands, and we have references to three such surveys in the records that have come to us. The first of these was undertaken in the reign of Rāja Rāja A. D. 985-1016. The next one was apparently a local revision settlement for some reason or other, which is not clearly explained to us, under his son Rājēndra A. D. 1011-1044. The next one which seems to be more or less a general survey under Kulottunga A. D. 1070-1118. The last operation was undertaken in the year A. D. 1086, the year of the Doomsday-survey in England. Holdings were carefully registered and they were correctly measured, or calculated correct to $\frac{1}{52000}$th of a square inch.

Disputes about holdings, or about incidences of revenue, etc., were settled by the assembly, and if it was a question of graver matter in regard to these, assemblies from the neighbourhood were made to join together and make their award, which the controlling officer of the region accepted and issued as a general order.

Transfer of land from party to party had to be done with the final approval and sanction of the headquarters authority with the direct sanction of the monarch, where a complete register of holdings was maintained and that constituted in all probability the authoritative record of holdings of land. One such instance under Rāja Rāja III is that the lands had to be transferred from the royal register to the register of temple-lands (dēva-dāna).

One good instance of the division of responsibility between the officers of Government and the local bodies has recently been made accessible to us in an inscription of the time of Dēvarāya II. The inhabitants of Vaḻudilambaṭṭu in the Tanjore District had suffered successively from the irruptions of the Hoysalas, and consequently a considerable amount of confusion was introduced in the revenue administration of the division. The inhabitants were oppressed by the uncertainty of the demands, and therefore began to leave the locality in small bodies, so much so that at the time the cultivable lands were lying waste and uncultivated. In this condition the matter was brought to the notice of the king, who immediately ordered an inquiry as to the circumstances that brought about the state of things. It was found on enquiry that since the days of the Hoysala irruption, the local authority had become weak or non-existent; that the demands upon the lands became uncertain and there came to prevail some kind of local anarchy. The inhabitants found it intolerable to go on in the division in these special circumstances. An order was issued at once that the assemblies of the surrounding unions together with such of the inhabitants of the suffering unit itself as were present might assemble together, conduct an enquiry and make a register of revenue incidences as they prevailed in the days previous to the irruption of the Hoysalas. The inquiry was conducted and the document called for was set forth in full. This document was incorporated in a royal circular and issued to the locality calling upon the original inhabitants to return under the assurance that they could go on as before under the authority of the document thus issued. This record illustrates that the authorities of the Central Government did not directly interfere in these matters, and even in a serious case like this, they had to work through local agencies and see to it that there was nothing arbitrary in their proceedings.

In regard to the functions of the village assemblies which would come under the department of public works, it was the duty of the assembly to see that the tanks and the irrigation channels were kept in good condition, that the roads of which there are references to some as wide as 64 spans and 100 spans, were kept in repair. Large irrigation projects were not carried out by the village assemblies. Such projects were undertaken either by the Government itself in which case Government became proprietor and let out the land, or these were undertaken by wealthy and enterprising individuals. In such a case, they were given certain privileges by way of special allotments of revenue or by the assignment of a fraction thereof. In either case, the completed works were made over to the possession of assemblies ; it was the charge of the assemblies themselves to see to their being in an efficient condition and to put them through repairs when called for. The assemblies also regulated the local taxes and dues, which seem in the first instance to have been levied by themselves under a recognised royal schedule. It was the duty of one of their committees that the villagers rendered free labour. They were bound to see that no undue advantage was taken of it. We have instances of vexatious taxes or dues being removed. One such act apparently gave the great Chola Kulottunga, the title "the

Chola that abolished the tolls." Tolls were specially set apart as royal revenue and is regarded even in the Kuraḷ as one of the legitimate sources of royal revenue. We do not know under what circumstances exactly Kulottunga abolished the tolls. We have instances on record of the great Vijayanagar ruler Krishna Dēvarāya abolishing marriage taxes, and taxes upon barbers so that the abolition of taxes which proved to be oppressive or irksome, certainly was not unknown under Hindu rulers.

The village assemblies had the responsibility of tracking crime. They had their own village officers whose special duty it was; when criminals were traced, they were brought before the assembly for punishment. The guilt was brought home to the culprit before the assembly, and the punishment was accorded according to law by the special body of judges, who had knowledge of it, or by royal officers when once the guilt was proved to the satisfaction of the assembly. These assemblies went about administering justice, generally tempered with mercy. We have numbers of instances of death brought on by neglect, or under circumstances of peculiar provocation. Allowances were made in extenuation of the crime of murder in these cases. In circumstances of peculiar enormity, or where desperate gangs of robbers sometimes defied the village authorities, Government assistance was invoked and was readily provided. We have one instance in point. A certain number of Brahmans and others set up as dacoits, and carried on their depredations in defiance of the village authorities. The village appealed to the local governor, who provided a section of the guards to arrest the criminals. They arrested the culprits once, who even went so far as to overpower the guards and escaped. A second successful arrest was made, and among those arrested happened to be a couple of Brahmans, who were ring-leaders. Then a question arose whether as Brahmans, they could be punished as robbers. A reference was made to headquarters and the ruling was obtained, that since they set up as robbers, they were guilty of an act unworthy of a Brahman and ceased to be such. They were liable to be punished according to the law like other robbers. The punishment was accordingly carried out.

The Cholas dating from the time of the ancient Karikāla were remarkable for their works of irrigation. The Hindus of South India are credited with the discovery of the device of controlling the water of a river at the head of the delta and taking off irrigation channels to regions which could not be irrigated under gravitation ordinarily. The delta of the Kaveri is a supreme instance of the achievements of the Cholas in this particular. The very last irrigation channel known, branching off from the south main arm of the river Kaveri within 25 miles of the sea, and the artificial canal taking off from the Coleroon, were alike made in the days of the great Cholas. The great Gangaikoṇḍa Chola was responsible for what must have been an enormous irrigation tank near his capital, the feeder channel for it coming from the Coleroon river, higher up.

The waste water of this tank must have gone to fill the now famous Vaṭṭāṇam tank. This is now known as one of the best irrigation tanks of the South Arcot district. Another great tank in a more arid tract of the Tanjore District was made by another Chola, whether he was a ruler or prince we do not know. This is the great irrigation tank in the village Vaḍuvur about 10 miles from Mannārguḍi. This is fed by a canal branching from Veṇṇār and passing close under the fortress walls of Tanjore to this particular tank. This canal was known Vīraśoḷa-Vaḍavāru.

They were builders of temples as well. The Tanjore temple itself is one instance. There are numbers of other instances which could be cited ; for example, the temples at Gangaikoṇḍa Cholapuram, Tirbhuvanaṁ and Dārāsuram near Kumbhakoṇam. Some of these are typical in regard both to magnitude and majesty. It was already pointed out that the age of the Cholas was an age of great literary output chiefly in Tamil literature although they extended their patronage to a certain extent to Sanskrit also. In point of religion, it was a period of organisation as in other fields of human activity; the religious organisation in this age took on the form of the organisation of the sects as was already pointed out. In these matters, the succeeding dynasties carried on the tradition of the Cholas undiminished and in some respects improved upon in art, architecture, literature and administration, in fact in everything that constitutes a successful human organisation of society. The Empire of Vijayanagar is but a development and extension of what this organisation was under the Cholas. Some of the magnificent buildings that stand in South India, temples in particular, some few civil buildings also, show the development to which they are indebted to Vijayanagar; the magnificent colonnaded halls, each composite column or portion of which is covered with sculptural representations, form the work of the age of Vijayanagar.

We have instances of their irrigation activity in Vijayanagar, in some of the tanks in the peculiarly arid locality of the ceded districts, as for instance those at Anantapur, Anantasagara, Kambam, etc. We have reference to an anicut work on the Tungabadra above Vijayanagar itself.

Learning flourished under Vijayanagar and the rulers extended their patronage according to locality to the various languages and to Sanskrit. Several of the great governors and officers of Vijayanagar were scholars themselves and patronised scholars. Vidyāraṇya, Vēdānta Dēśika and Appayya Dīkṣita, to mention only the preeminent, born in any age or country would have shone as luminaries of the first magnitude in literature. The usurper Sāluva Narasimha is recorded as a Sanskrit scholar and one Sanskrit work is ascribed to him. The great Krishnadēvarāya was a Sanskrit and Telugu scholar, and two works of his have come down to us. Jāmbavatī Kalyāṇam is a Sanskrit work and Āmuktamālyadā, a high class Telugu work, are ascribed to him. Tirumalarāya, the king who occupied the throne after the battle of Talikotta is considered as a scholar, and one learned commentary at any rate, is ascribed to him. The example of royalty was imitated by provincial governors, who several of them set up as scholars and have more systematically encouraged scholars. The full efflorescence of the spirit of encouraging literature is seen in the Tanjore ruler Raghunātha Nāyaka. He was ruler, scholar, musician, patron and warrior, all rolled into one. He could himself compose both in Sanskrit and Telugu, and a version of the Rāmāyaṇa that he wrote in Telugu was considered so excellent that a lady of his court rendered it into Sanskrit and earned the title Madhuravāṇi (lady of sweet speech) for the service. Another lady of his court wrote an epic in Sanskrit, Raghunāthābhyudayam, and was such a great expert in the various kinds of composition in eight languages including Sanskrit, that she was elevated to the dignity of *Sāhitya Sāmrājya*, and other instances could be quoted.[1]

This is enough to indicate the patronage extended to literature by the rulers of Vijayanagar.

Before closing, it would be well to draw attention to a certain number of political maxims, for which King Krishnadēva Rāya of Vijayanagar is given credit. He scatters through the fourth canto of his Telugu work Āmuktamālyadā,[2] a number of these, which in substance agree more or less with what we find laid down in professed works on the Nītiśāstra and could be traced in the Dharma Śāstras as well as in the Tamil work Kuṛaḷ. The peculiar importance of these maxims coming from Krishṇadēva Rāya is this. We have the means of proving that this monarch did make successful efforts at putting his precept into practice.

This monarch apparently found Brahman officials of great service to him, and he speaks in

[1] See Sources of Vijayanagar History, Publication by the Madras University.

[2] To Mr. A. Rangaswami Sarasvati, University Research Student, now Assistant Epigraphist belongs the credit of collecting and translating these extracts.

glowing terms of Brahmans "as administrative officers both civil and military." He would entrust fortresses, well-equipped, to Brahmans. He would have his Brahman officers, mature men between 50 and 70, who "are scholars, who are afraid of *adharma* and who are well-versed in *rāja nīti*, and offer to rule according to *rāja nīti*." He gives his reasons also, "because a Brahman would stand to his post even in times of danger and would continue in service though reduced to becoming a subordinate to a Kshatṛya or Śūdra. It is always advisable for a king to make Brahmans as officers." This high opinion that he had for the Brahman, he carried into practice. His chief minister and adviser was the Brahman Sāḷuva Timma whose brother Sāluva Govinda was the first Governor of the recently conquered province of Ummattūr in Mysore and was subsequently promoted to be killedar of (governor of) Vijayanagar itself.

The new provinces conquered from Kalinga or Orissa were entrusted to the Government of two nephews of the minister Timma. When Udaygiri in the Nellore district was taken from Orissa the organisation and administration, and the holding of the new conquests against attack fell to Rayasam Konḍamarasayya, another Brahman. It is not exactly that other officers were not appointed or that the Brahman officers were all of them unerring. He had a number of officers who were not Brahmans but the most trusted ones among them seem to have been Brahmans. One Brahman proved false, as did one Sudra. The Brahman Vīra Narasimha Rāya revolted in the last year of Krishnadēva Rāya ; so did Nāgama Nāyaka of Madura. Krishna wanted that the temple management should be kept separate from the other departments of administration, for the good reason that the temple revenues were not to be mixed with the others in the administration as these were specially liable to peculation. He wanted horses and elephants kept in royal stables and superintended by royal officers, and not to be entrusted to governors which was the practice of mediæval administration. He adopted this device as the best remedy against rebellion. According to him a king should improve the properties of his country and encourage commerce ; this he tried to put into practice as did some of his predecessors and some of his successors by the treatment that they accorded to the Portuguese and to the other foreign ambassadors that came into the country for commercial purposes. When Udayagiri fell, some of the ladies of the household of the Orissa Governor, who was uncle of the king of Orissa, fell into his hands. The Portuguese Chroniclers have it on record that he treated these royal ladies in quite a kingly fashion. There is one verse of Krishna which prescribes exactly this kind of treatment. He has another reference to treatment of princes, who may become prisoners. He followed that precept into practice by what he did to the son of the Kalinga Ruler Pratāpa Rudra. Prince Vīrabhadra was taken prisoner at Koṇḍavīḍu. According to the Portuguese chronicler, Nuniz, he was made a prisoner and was insultingly asked to exhibit his swordsmanship against the professional fencer of the Court. The prince, according to this chronicler is said to have committed suicide as a result of this insult. We have records however that show that prince Vīrabhadra was governor of Maligabennūr Śīme in the Mysore state, and made a grant for the spiritual benefit of his own father and his royal master himself, there again showing that Krishna was as good as his word in regard to his precept in this particular instance as well. These few instances go to show that even the maxims of polity had considerable weight in shaping the administration of monarchs who made their mark and left their impress upon the government of the realm that came into their charge.

Thus then in matters of administration in all its branches, South India established for itself a distinct line of development which, as in other branches, have continued quite down to modern times and have been in several particulars carried down into the present day administration of the locality itself. It would require far more space to trace these in detail, but this must suffice to indicate the distinct character of South Indian administration.

INDEX.

N.B.—The numbers refer to the pages.

The following abbreviations are used:

C. P. C. = Copper plate charters.

Chal. = Chālukyas.

Dy. = Dynasty.

F.N. = Foot-Note.

Insc. = Inscription.

K. = King.

Pall. = Pallava.

Tam. Lit. = Tamil Literature.

Vaish. = Vaishnava.

INDEX

A

B

C

N

O

P

R

S

T

U

FINIS

ERRATA.

Page	45	For	Vidavengadam	read Nadavēngadam.
,,	136	,,	Darmida	,, Dramida
,,	188	,,	Vayalur plates	,, Vayalur pillar inscription.
,,	210	,,	Tirnmangai	,, Tirumangai.
,,	219	,,	to the Siyāḷi	,, to be Siyāḷi.
,,	275	,,	Nandivarman I	,, Nandivarman Pallavamalla.
,,	295	,,	Kulasiktara	,, Kulasēkhara.
,,	300	,,	Haribare I	,, Harihara I.
,,	327	,,	Situatio	,, Situation.
,,	362	,,	Workship	,, Workmanship.